The Latino Student's Guide to STEM Careers

The Latino Student's Guide to STEM Careers

Laura I. Rendón and Vijay Kanagala, Editors

Foreword by Mildred Garcia

An Imprint of ABC-CLIO, LLC
Santa Barbara, California • Denver, Colorado

Copyright © 2017 by ABC-CLIO, LLC

All rights reserved. No part of this publication may be reproduced, stored in a retrieval system, or transmitted, in any form or by any means, electronic, mechanical, photocopying, recording, or otherwise, except for the inclusion of brief quotations in a review, without prior permission in writing from the publisher.

Library of Congress Cataloging in Publication Control Number: 2017025631

ISBN: 978-1-61069-791-0
EISBN: 978-1-61069-792-7

21 20 19 18 17   1 2 3 4 5

This book is also available as an eBook.

Greenwood
An Imprint of ABC-CLIO, LLC

ABC-CLIO, LLC
130 Cremona Drive, P.O. Box 1911
Santa Barbara, California 93116-1911
www.abc-clio.com

This book is printed on acid-free paper. ∞

Manufactured in the United States of America

*To every Latinx student who is exploring, seeking, fighting for
the countless possibilities that a
STEM college education and career can offer*

*~ may you and your efforts be fierce and fruitful;
may the powers of our ancestors, our teachers, and our familias
gently watch over you on your journey. ~*

Contents

Foreword

"Leadership tomorrow depends on how we educate our students—especially in science, technology, engineering, and math."

—President Barack Obama, September 16, 2010
(U.S. Department of Education, 2014)

As a first-generation college student, a woman of color, and the daughter of two factory workers who had no more than eighth-grade educations (not from lack of intelligence but from lack of opportunity), I faced a myriad of obstacles throughout my academic journey, including a lack of educators with whom I could discuss possible career options.

My parents always said, "The only inheritance a poor family can leave their children is a good education," and they wielded the power of that profound truth, which almost sounds poetic in Spanish, to light a fire under all seven of their children. When my father died when I was 12, my mother courageously carried the torch, using her job working in the Brooklyn factories to not only provide for us, but also ensure we understood the power of education could propel us to careers outside those factories and, in turn, manifest better lives for ourselves and our future families.

My teachers in elementary school, while providing me a very solid educational foundation, never discussed the possibilities of a career in science, technology, engineering, or math (STEM). As I marveled on the accomplishments of science, such as the first person walking on the moon, it was clear to me that those careers weren't for people who looked like me or came from extreme poverty. So, as I read this book, it took me back to those early days of my life, prompting me to wonder what a difference this book could have possibly made in my own career choices.

The Latino Student's Guide to STEM Careers is a must-read compendium and resource book for K-16 educators. It provides the tools necessary to educate the Latinx population, underscoring the need to inform parents and students about the wonders of engaging in STEM, available STEM careers, and the colleges and universities that best align with a student's skills and aspirations.

It is also a wonderful resource for students and parents hoping to fully understand what it means to major in STEM and how to reach their academic goals and life dreams. Parents can learn about the multitude of important careers available to students who major in STEM along with the potential economic advantages of such careers. Finally, all readers of this book will come away with a deep understanding and appreciation of the importance of STEM, not only for students and families, but also our country and the world.

Rendón and Kanagala, the editors of the book, set an excellent foundation as to why the changing demographics in this country warrant the need for all educators to adapt and evolve to better serve Latinx students. In less than 25 years, by the year 2060, the Latinx population in the United States is projected to reach 119 million, constituting 28.6 percent of the nation's population and making up the largest ethnic group (National Population Projections, 2014). Let's imagine, for a moment, how much the United States would progress if this "new majority" had both equitable access to a quality education in STEM and equal opportunities to contribute to the scientific discoveries of the nation and world.

Careers in engineering, medicine, space, aeronautics, cyber, mathematics, and beyond would grow exponentially, and the next generation of leaders in these industries would mirror the incredible diversity of both our nation and the global society in which we hope to lead and succeed. This will benefit not just the Latinx community in STEM but all students and professionals in STEM, and the discoveries in this ever-expanding field would become the nation's most important asset.

Each of the 10 chapters continues to educate the reader on STEM careers and what it takes to achieve one—from preschool to PhD and beyond. Many of the book's authors are successful STEM scholars, individuals who share the facts along with their own particular journey. They pour out their hearts, explaining the joys, and yes, the challenges in getting to where they are, firmly acknowledging that it is all well worth it—for themselves, their families, their colleagues, and the nation.

Vielma in Chapter 1 addresses what it will take to prepare for these careers, utilizing lessons learned throughout her educational journey, which culminated with her graduating from Massachusetts Institute of Technology. In Chapter 2, Cuellar and Garibay provide detailed information on how to choose the right college and STEM program. This is particularly important because, for far too long, many Latinx students chose colleges based on reputation and/or where their friends may be attending, yet the research shows that choosing a college that fits the student's particular needs, style, and interests is essential for success. Size, geography, student body and faculty demographics, types of academic programs, and support services all play a huge part in student success. This chapter provides those areas to think about before actually applying.

Further, for many Latinx students, paying for college can become a barrier. Several studies point to the fact that Latinx students in particular shy away from loans. Thus, knowing about financial aid and scholarships becomes crucial, and Chapter 3 authors Carales, Bledsoe, and Nora provide detailed information about paying for college as well as valuable web resources for further information relevant to obtaining the necessary resources for the university of choice.

A plethora of higher education research exists to demonstrate that the first-year experience is critical for students of color. With the enrollment of first-generation, low-income Latinx college students on the rise, Kanagala, Gonzalez, and Leon, in Chapter 4, provide key resources and practical strategies for the students to not just survive but to thrive in their first year of college. Like most students, Latinx students, alongside their parents, ponder on how to choose a STEM major and what career options will be possible upon graduation. When we question why more Latinx students are not entering STEM fields, the possible answer may lie in the fact that they simply don't know about all the possibilities. Chapters 5 (Smith and Laanan) and Chapter 7 (Banda and Flowers) delineate the steps necessary to ensure students enter higher education fully prepared to succeed in their chosen field. Moreover, the chapters provide career options, job titles, and midcareer salaries, educating the reader about the vast possibilities. They too provide additional online resources.

Coward, Koledoye, and Smith inform us in Chapter 6 that "occupations in STEM are among the highest paying, fastest growing, and most influential jobs driving economic growth and innovation." Yet for many of these STEM careers, it is essential that students pursue their education by obtaining a master's and/or doctorate degree. These authors discuss the road to graduate work, once again providing detailed and important information that will assist students pursue an advanced degree.

In Chapter 8, the narratives and personal stories of the authors pursuing their STEM educations and careers are very profound. The readers may think that because of where they are from, their large families and responsibilities, the struggles of being poor and/or being a first-generation college student means that STEM careers are not a viable option for them, yet these narratives provide powerful accounts about how it is possible. Further, the students can see that there are others out there to whom they can look up and reach out. Indeed, these students are not alone, and these amazing authors are truly role models who provide guidance and mentorship for all those who seek it.

Chapters 9 (Gogue and Childs) and Chapter 10 (Villarreal and Price) continue to provide further information in order for students to make informed decisions. In Chapter 9, you find the best STEM colleges for Latinx students, and Chapter 10 gathers resources for making informed decisions and possible additional readings.

Indeed, this book is a much-needed guide for all K-16 educators, as well as Latinx students and their families, and should be read as early as possible in a student's educational journey; there is an urgency to ensure that students from all backgrounds are introduced to the wonders of STEM education early and often.

Students and their families need to be informed, learn about STEM majors, examine possible careers, know the stories of others who have already taken the STEM pathway, and understand that there are role models and programs along the way to assist them through every step.

According to the President's Council of Advisors on Science and Technology, about 1 million more STEM professionals must be produced over the next decade for the United States to remain globally competitive. "Given Hispanics are projected to account for 75 percent of the growth in the nation's labor force between 2010 and 2020, Latinos completing certificates and degrees in STEM fields will be vital to meeting the national STEM college completion goal," the report says.

Indeed, the future of our nation and our collective drive to be globally competitive hinges on our ability to educate all students, especially Latinx students, in ways that empower them to lift our communities and country. The endeavor begins with an educated populace that is knowledgeable and engaged in STEM.

This book begins the progress.

Mildred García, President
California State University, Fullerton

REFERENCES

National Population Projections. (2014). Table 10. Retrieved from www.census.gov/population/projections/data/national/2014/summarytables.html

U.S. Department of Education. (2014). *Hispanics and STEM education: White House initiative on education excellence for Hispanics*. Retrieved from http://sites.ed.gov/hispanic-initiative/files/2014/04/WHIEEH-STEM-Fact sheet.pdf

Acknowledgments

When Kim Kennedy-White, senior acquisitions editor, ABC-CLIO/Greenwood contacted us in early 2014 to write *The Latino Student's Guide for STEM Careers*, we were both expecting and experiencing significant career changes. Knowing how important and valuable this book could be for Latinx students and families, especially from first-generation and low-income backgrounds, who were exploring college and STEM disciplines, we were unsure if we would be able to dedicate the necessary time and caring effort needed to bring this idea to life and hesitated to commit to writing this book. Kim was relentless and persuasive. In the midst of Laura's impending retirement from the University of Texas at San Antonio's faculty, and Vijay's exciting new beginnings as an assistant professor at the University of Vermont, we accepted the invitation to write this book. We immediately commenced the work of putting together this important resource for Latinx high school and college students. As the book project progressed, we experienced unexpected twists and turns. However, one thing remained constant: Kim's unwavering and unconditional support to us. She emailed us weekly and made periodic phone calls to check in with us about the progress we were making on the book. She supported us with designing the book cover, managing author contracts, coordinated production schedule, and sent gentle reminders when we missed deadlines. Throughout this process, our common belief that this book was invaluable and a much-needed resource for Latinx students aspiring to enter STEM careers guided our dedication to complete this book. We appreciate you and your commitment to our work and this book, Kim!

Our own life experiences guided us in writing this book. A first-generation Latina from a low-income background, Laura has championed issues of access and success for first-generation students from low-income background, especially Latinx students. A generation 1.5 immigrant, Vijay is passionate about the educational opportunities and collegiate experiences of underrepresented, underserved, and understudied students of color in American higher education. Reflecting on our own educational journeys and the many barriers we overcame allowed us to quickly recognize how a guide book like this one could have introduced us to the world of college. We understood the value and power a resource such as this guide book could be for students and families. Rather than just the two of us write this book, we decided that we ought to tap into the wealth of knowledge and wisdom our friends and colleagues who were doctoral students, practitioners, college administrators, and professors could offer. Many of these authors share characteristics such as being first-generation and low-income, having innumerable years of experience working with Latinx students and underrepresented and underserved communities, and in some instances, have graduated with STEM degrees themselves. We are grateful to each of the chapter contributors for accepting our invitation to lend their expertise to carefully and thoughtfully craft each chapter. Our deepest gratitude goes to Rosa M. Banda, Ripsimé Bledsoe, Vincent D. Carales, Sarah Maria Childs, Leslie A. Coward, Marcela Cuellar, Alonzo M. Flowers III, Juan Carlos Garibay, Demeturie Toso-Lafaele Gogue, Josephine J. Gonzalez, Dimitra Jackson Smith, Kimberly A. Koledoye, Frankie Santos Laanan, Jose Adrian Leon, Amaury Nora, Sarah Price, Stella L. Smith, Karina I. Vielma, and Cynthia Diana Villarreal. The information and resources they share are what makes this guide book an important resource for Latinx students interested in pursuing STEM majors and careers.

If there was a singular goal that we championed as we wrote and co-edited this book, it was accessibility of language. What was the point of a guide book that was full of academic and higher education jargon that students could not understand, we reasoned? We wanted to ensure that this book was going to be accessible to every Latinx high school and college student, especially first-generation students who are trying their best against many odds to understand the complex pathways to and through college. We also wanted to make sure this book was also a valuable resource for family members, school counselors, career coaches, mentors, and peers who have an interest in ensuring Latinx student success overall and most importantly in STEM disciplines.

With accessibility of language as a cornerstone of this book, we invited 14 Latinx individuals who are doctoral students, scientists, college professors, administrators, and managers to share their personal stories. These individuals successfully pursued STEM degrees and careers using many of the strategies that are outlined in the book. Making use of *testimonios*, Stephany Alvarez-Ventura, Alejandro Araiza, Diana Del Angel, Julissa Del Bosque, Xiomara Elias Argote, Dana M. García, Karla Gutierrez, Rodolfo Jimenez, Ricardo Martinez, Olivia Moreno, Elvia Elisa Niebla, Semarhy Quinones-Soto, Marina B. Suarez, and Simon Trevino narrate in their own words and with immense pride their compelling life stories and transformative college experiences that tell the truth of the myriad ways in which these Latinxs navigated the complex pathways to college and careers in STEM. We are deeply indebted to all these trailblazers for allowing us to offer to the world their powerful, authentic, and vulnerable stories. Our hope is that these inspiring stories role model and resonate with any Latinx student, who is wondering if they can pursue a STEM degree in college.

We were very fortunate that President Mildred García of California State University, Fullerton, agreed to pen the foreword for this important resource. As a preeminent scholar and one of few Latina presidents of four-year institutions in the United States, her nuanced insights and understanding of the issues impacting higher education and Latinx students is much appreciated.

Special thanks are due to Demeturie Toso-Lafaele Gogue and Ripsimé Bledsoe, graduate research assistants for Vijay Kanagala and Laura I. Rendón, respectively. We want to recognize their efforts with technical aspects of the book and feedback on several sections as the book was being written.

Vijay would like to personally acknowledge the support of the University of Vermont's Higher Education and Student Affairs Administration (UVM HESA) 2016 student cohort, especially Alexander T. Boesch, Daniel W. Fairley II, Josephine J. Gonzalez, Joey A. Leon, Andrew W. Mayer, and Atiya McGhee. These individuals made it a point to check in and inquire about the progress of the book every week during class over these past two years!

A Note to the Reader

Note: The editors and authors of this book use the word *Latinx* as a gender-inclusive and a gender-neutral alternative to the more common Latino, Latina, or Latin@. In doing so, the editors and authors wish to move beyond gender binaries and be mindful of the intersectionality of social identities such as race and gender. In addition to cis-men and cis-women from all racial backgrounds, Latinx is inclusive of individuals who identify as trans, queer, questioning, agender, nonbinary, gender nonconforming, intersex, and/or gender fluid. Also, the words Latino, Latina, Latin@, Latinx, and Hispanic are used interchangeably in this book.

INTRODUCTION

What Is STEM and Why Is It Important for Latinx Students?

Laura I. Rendón and Vijay Kanagala

Congratulations on considering a STEM career! Your participation in STEM will help to assure the future of American advances in science and technology. Because Latinxs constitute a fast-growing, major segment of the population in the United States, they are destined to become the next generation of creative innovators who will produce technological advances such as better cell phones, televisions, computers, robots, space ships, cameras, and safer cars. Latinx STEM graduates can also make advances in the areas of agriculture and soil science, climate change, sustainable energy, human genetics, stem cell research, digital media, cybersecurity, and computer programming. Further, Latinxs will likely play a key role in finding the cure for diseases and conditions such as antibiotic-resistant bacteria; HIV/AIDS; cancer; Ebola; and Alzheimer's, heart, liver, and Parkinson's disease. These are just a few examples of the many different ways that Latinxs can contribute to new breakthroughs in STEM fields of study: Science, Technology, Engineering and Mathematics.

The opportunities for Latinxs in STEM are exciting and seemingly endless. Many "firsts" for Latinxs are still for the taking, and there are many examples of Latinxs who despite significant life challenges (poverty, lack of guidance and resources, or experience of civil war in their home country) have succeeded in STEM fields of study. Consider the following:

- How about having a dinosaur named after you? In Part IV of this book, you can read the inspirational story of Dr. Marina Suarez, now an assistant professor of geology at the University of Texas-San Antonio, who always loved rocks and geology. As a graduate student at Temple University, Suarez, along with her twin sister, Celina, discovered evidence of a new species of dinosaur. *Geminiraptor suarezarum*, named for the Suarez paleontologists, lived during the Cretaceous period. This is the actual time period of many of the dinosaurs you might have seen in the movie *Jurassic Park* (McNeel, 2016).

- Want to be considered in the ranks of Einstein? Then read the story of Sabrina Gonzalez Pasterski, a Latina being dubbed "the next Einstein," who is exploring some of the most challenging and complex issues in physics (Fox News Latino, n.d.).

- Think that you have too many financial and social challenges in your life to really succeed in STEM? Two very inspiring films are worth watching that may help you believe in the power of strength, courage, and determination and that regardless of the challenges you have faced in your life, you have an opportunity to succeed in STEM. One of them is the documentary, *Underwater Dreams*—http://www.underwaterdreamsfilm.com. You might also watch the movie *Spare Parts*—https://www.youtube.com/watch?v=myjar5KoqZA. These two films feature the true story of how the sons of undocumented Mexican immigrants learned how to build an underwater robot from inexpensive parts bought from a Home Depot store. Their robot was so functional and well built that it defeated the Massachusetts Institute of Technology (MIT), one of the most prestigious universities in the nation. This story is also captured in the book written by Joshua Davis (2014), *Spare Parts: Four Undocumented Teenagers, One Ugly Robot, and the Battle for the American Dream.*

- Don't have any examples of individuals who succeeded in STEM in your life? Then take time to read the uplifting stories of Latinxs who have actually succeeded in STEM fields featured in Part IV of this book. Time and time again, despite obstacles and challenges, Latinxs have shown that they can indeed realize their dreams in STEM fields of study. Now it's your turn to succeed!

WHY THIS BOOK ON STEM?

This book is written specifically for Latinx students and their families who are interested in learning more about what it takes to prepare and succeed in science, technology, engineering, and mathematics fields of study. This book is an essential resource that Latinx students and families need to make the best decisions about entering and succeeding in a STEM career. It can also be a valuable tool to aid faculty, counselors, and advisers to assist students at every step of entering and completing a STEM career.

WHAT IS STEM?

STEM is an acronym that represents the holistic nature and close relationship among science, technology, engineering, and mathematics fields of study. In other words, STEM fields are considered to be interrelated. One specific STEM field can inform the other STEM areas. Students can participate in STEM in all grade levels in schools, as well as in colleges and universities (Gonzalez and Kuenzi, 2012).

According to a report of the Congressional Research Service (Gonzalez and Kuenzi, 2012), STEM has been both broadly and narrowly defined. Some federal agencies, such as the National Science Foundation, have used a broad definition. This broad definition of STEM includes psychology and the social sciences (e.g., political science and economics) as well as the physical sciences and engineering (e.g., physics, chemistry, and mathematics). A narrower definition of STEM has been used by other federal agencies, including the Department of Homeland Security (DHS) and U.S. Immigration and Customs Enforcement (ICE). These agencies use a narrower definition that generally excludes social sciences and focuses on mathematics, chemistry, physics, computer and information sciences, and engineering.

STEM can be used to address education policy, curriculum, and teaching and learning practices designed to improve competitiveness in science and technology. Students in STEM fields of study engage in understanding scientific and mathematical principles, acquire a working knowledge of computer hardware and software, and develop problem-solving skills.

Sometimes the term, STEAM is used instead of STEM, which can be confusing. Recently, there has been a push to ensure that a STEM curriculum also includes an emphasis in the liberal arts. STEAM adds the "A" for the arts, a means for adding creativity and skills such as critical thinking, cultural understanding, and the ability to apply and integrate knowledge in a complex world. Advocates of STEAM argue that adding the arts can also provide a broader range of educational and career-path opportunities and a more well-rounded academic experience that will help students in their life pursuits (Jolly, 2014; Jackson-Hayes, 2015).

WHY IS STEM IMPORTANT FOR LATINXS?

Perhaps more than any other academic concentration, STEM fields of study hold great promise and opportunities for Latinx students. Getting into a STEM profession is important for Latinxs given the facts listed below.

Fact I: The nation's Latinx population is experiencing dynamic growth.

The face of the United States is changing, and brown is becoming the new white. By 2044, it is expected that people of color (Latinxs, African Americans, Asian Americans, and American Indian/Alaska Natives) will be the majority population in the United States (see, http://nationalequityatlas.org/data-summaries).

It is a well-known fact that the U.S. Hispanic population has been growing by leaps and bounds. Given how fast the Latinx population is growing, it makes absolute sense that this group will constitute the future generation of scientists, engineers, mathematicians, and technology experts. Here is what we know about the growth of the Hispanic population in the United States:

- People of Hispanic origin are now the nation's largest ethnic minority, constituting roughly 17.3 percent (about 55 million) of the U.S. population (Stepler and Brown, 2016).
- In 1980, Hispanics constituted only 6 percent of the nation's population, but by 2050, Latinxs are expected to constitute roughly one-third of the nation—see Figure I.1.

Latinxs should not only grow in numbers, they should also excel in education and become the next generation of American leaders in STEM professions. The biggest roadblock faced by Latinxs is the unfortunate fact that this group remains behind in terms of academic achievement. As a group, Latinxs have suffered from a history of exclusion, discrimination, and racism. Many have suffered from poverty, undocumented status, and from attending poorly funded, segregated schools. All of these inequalities have worked against Latinx students and families (Rendón, Nora, and Kanagala, 2014; Valenzuela, 1999; Zambrana and Hurtado, 2015).

Fact II. Latinxs continue to be among the least educated groups in the nation.

Simply stated, it is critical that more Latinxs graduate from high school and from college. While it is true that the numbers of graduates have increased, it is also a

Figure I.1   Growth of Latinx Population

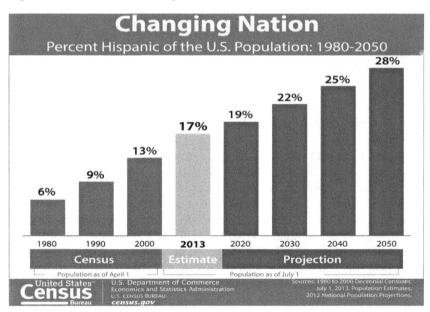

fact that Latinxs remain behind. It is critical that Latinx families and students understand the importance of graduating from high school and college.

High School Graduation. Noting that persons of Hispanic origin may be of any race, U.S. Census Bureau (2012) data indicate that Hispanic adults had lower rates of high school attainment than adults of other racial/ethnic groups. Consider the following facts:

- In 2010, about 63 percent of Hispanic adults over age 25 had completed at least high school or its equivalent.
- Conversely, 88 percent of whites, 89 percent of Asians/Pacific Islanders, and 84 percent of blacks had done so.
- Among persons of Hispanic origin, Mexican Americans were the least educated cohort with 57 percent graduating, compared to 75 percent for Puerto Ricans and 81 percent for Cubans.

College Graduation. College and university completion also needs improvement based on the following data (U.S. Census Bureau, 2012):

- In 2010, only 14 percent of Hispanic adults earned at least a bachelor's degree.
- This compared to about 52 percent of Asian/Pacific Islanders, 30 percent of whites, and 20 percent of blacks.
- At the college level, Mexican Americans remain the least educated cohort, with only 11 percent graduation, compared to 18 percent for Puerto Ricans and 26 percent for Cubans.

Fact III: Latinxs are underrepresented in STEM fields.

While Hispanics are growing in number, it is important to understand that they remain underrepresented in STEM fields of study. Latinxs make up less than 10 percent of the STEM workforce (Leonard, 2016, p. 1). According to a report from the American Institutes for Research (2012), "Women, racial and ethnic minorities, and persons with disabilities are underrepresented in the STEM disciplines. Collectively, these demographic groups represent the largest untapped STEM talent pool in the United States."

Latinxs are earning many of their degrees in STEM at Hispanic-serving institutions (HSIs). HSIs are colleges and universities where Hispanics make up 25 percent or more of their student body. According to a report from *Excelencia in Education* (Santiago, Taylor, and Calderon, 2015), while more STEM degrees have been earned, it is important to note that the degrees are more likely to be in lower-paying service occupations such as electromechanical assemblers and chemical technicians. Fewer degrees are being earned in high-paying STEM professional occupations such as electrical engineers, chemists, and software developers. Consequently, much more needs to be done to increase the numbers of

Latinxs enrolled in STEM fields of study, including the highest-paying professional careers.

Fact IV: Latinx students have important assets that they can use to succeed in college.

Many low-income students who are the first in their family to attend college or to enter a STEM field have overcome multiple obstacles such as poverty, poor schooling, and lack of guidance and resources. Yet, despite these obstacles, there are many examples of such students who have succeeded in college. New research and information tell us that many students from poverty backgrounds have strong assets that they use to make the transition to college, navigate the world of college, overcome obstacles to success, and finally get to the finish line of college completion (Rendón, Nora, and Kanagala, 2014; Yosso, 2005; Zambrana and Hurtado, 2015). In other words, the hopeful message is that Latinx students, regardless of socioeconomic background, can and do succeed.

Latinx students have remarkable assets that they use to their advantage (Rendón, Nora, and Kanagala, 2014; Yosso, 2005). Among these assets include the following:

1. Having high aspirations; hopes and dreams of succeeding in life.
2. Knowing and using more than one language (Spanish and English) and ways to express themselves in different situations.
3. Family support and *consejos/advice*, as well as family modeling of hard work and perseverance.
4. Peer validation, encouragement and support, for example, friends supporting and learning from each other through study groups and in student organizations.
5. Ability to navigate the transition to college and to move back and forth among their personal worlds (family, peers, work, spiritual, and native country) and the world of college.
6. Ability to resist microaggressions, including sexism, discrimination, marginalization, and stereotyping and ability to overcome hardships such as poverty.
7. *Ganas*/perseverance that leads to inner strength and determination to succeed.
8. Ethic of giving back, to want to help their families and communities.
9. Faith in God or higher power and a sense of meaning and purpose.
10. Ability to work through contradictions (i.e., being able to handle the dual experience of having a Mexican heritage yet identifying as American; being able to negotiate the dual experiences of being previously undocumented and now documented; being able to manage being both in the foreign world of college and in the familiar world of family and community).

The critical importance of using these assets to succeed cannot be overstated. In fact, the use of these strengths can be seen in the powerful, inspirational stories of Latinxs who entered and succeeded in STEM featured in Part IV of this book.

Fact V: STEM occupations are growing and pay well, but there is a lack of candidates to fill these jobs.

Simply stated, there are not enough college graduates in STEM to fill labor market demands in STEM. Latinxs can help fill this void if enough of them enter STEM fields, graduate, and assume high-paying jobs. The National Association of Colleges and Employers (2016, January 27) indicated that those who graduated with STEM degrees in 2016 can expect to have the highest salaries. Among the report's findings included that the top three projected salary earnings were for engineering, computer sciences, and math and science graduates, with business majors landing in fourth place.

The hopeful message of this book is that Latinxs can and must become a part of the new generation of STEM graduates. All Hispanic families should be aware that their children can be future scientists, innovators, inventors, engineers, and technology experts. There is no doubt that Latinxs are growing in numbers, and they must not be left out of America's STEM revolution. The need is urgent, and the time is now.

How Is This Book Organized?

This book is organized into six parts. Parts I through III are interconnected and consist of a series of seven steps that will guide Latinx students towards a career in STEM (see Figure I.2.). Each step is written as a book-chapter by experts, who are very knowledgeable about the specific focus of the chapter. Part IV features 14 uplifting stories of Latinx doctoral students, scientists, faculty, administrators, and managers who have actually succeeded in STEM fields. Part V and Part VI identify several key resources (colleges, universities, programs, scholarships, and books) that will aid Latinx students interested in STEM majors and careers.

Each part/step/chapter is described in more detail below.

Figure I.2   Pathway to a Career in STEM

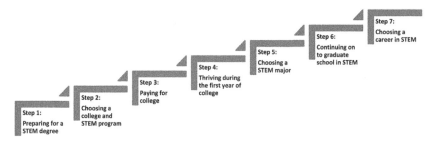

Part I: Planning for a Career in STEM

Step 1: Preparing for a career in STEM—This chapter provides information on coursework needed to prepare students for college majors in STEM.

Step 2: Choosing a college and STEM program—This chapter provides information and resources on the top colleges that best support and prepare Latinx students for STEM careers.

Step 3: Paying for college—This chapter provides information and resources on financial aid, scholarships, and other financial considerations relating to STEM and paying for college.

Part II: Succeeding in College

Step 4: Thriving during the first year of college—This chapter provides information on time management, campus services, and STEM-specific academic supports.

Step 5: Choosing a STEM major—This chapter provides information on choosing majors for specific careers and/or in preparation for graduate degree programs in each of the STEM areas.

Step 6: Continuing on to graduate school in STEM—This chapter offers information on master's and doctoral programs in STEM.

Part III: Choosing a Career in STEM

Step 7: STEM majors—This chapter outlines the plethora of careers available in each of the major STEM areas—for example, agriculture; computer and information sciences; engineering; biological and biomedical sciences; mathematics and statistics; and physical sciences and technologies.

Part IV: Sharing Stories

This section provides the personal narratives of 14 Latinxs who are success stories in STEM.

Part V: College and University Directories for STEM Programs

This section provides a listing of some of the best STEM U.S. colleges and universities for Latinx students.

Part VI: Resources

This section provides several helpful websites and books.

REFERENCES

American Institutes for Research. (2012). *Broadening participation in STEM: A call to action*. Retrieved from http://www.air.org/sites/default/files/downloads /report/Broadening_Participation_in_STEM_Feb_14_2013_0.pdf

Cohen, P. (2016, February 21). A rising call to promote STEM education and cut liberal arts funding. *The New York Times*. Retrieved from http://www.nytimes .com/2016/02/22/business/a-rising-call-to-promote-stem-education-and -cut-liberal-arts-funding.html?_r=2

Data summaries. (n.d.). *National Equity Atlas*. Retrieved from http://national equityatlas.org/data-summaries

Davis, J. (2014). *Spare parts: Four undocumented teenagers, one ugly robot, and the battle for the American Dream*. New York, NY: Farrar, Straus and Giroux Originals.

Fox News Latino. (n.d.). 22 year-old Latina has physics world abuzz, dubbed "the next Einstein". *LatinLife*. Retrieved from http://www.latinlife.com/article /1462/22-year-old-latina-has-physics-world-abuzz-dubbed-the-next -einstein

Gonzalez, H. B., & Kuenzi, J. J. (2012). Science, technology, engineering, and mathematics (STEM) education: A primer (CRS Report No. R42642). *Congressional Research Service*. Retrieved from http://digital.library.unt.edu /ark:/67531/metadc122233/m1/1/high_res_d/R42642_2012Aug01.pdf

Jackson-Hayes, L. (2015, February 18). We don't need more STEM majors. We need more STEM majors with liberal arts training. *The Washington Post*. Retrieved from https://www.washingtonpost.com/posteverything/wp/2015 /02/18/we-dont-need-more-stem-majors-we-need-more-stem-majors-with -liberal-arts-training/

Jolly, A. (2014, November 18). STEM vs. STEAM: Do the arts belong? *Education Week (Teacher)*. Retrieved from http://www.edweek.org/tm/articles/2014/11 /18/ctq-jolly-stem-vs-steam.html

Leonard, K. (2016, May 19). Building a Latino wave in STEM. *U.S. News & World Report*. Retrieved from https://www.usnews.com/news/articles/2016-05-19 /building-a-latino-wave-in-stem

Mazzio, M. (Director). (2014). *Underwater dreams*. [Motion picture]. United States: 50 Eggs Films.

McNeel, B. (2016, March 20). UTSA scientist gets dinosaur named after her, continues climate change research. *The Rivard Report*. Retrieved from http:// therivardreport.com/utsa-scientist-looks-to-rocks-for-clues-about-climate -change/

Movieclips Trailers. (2014, June 26). Spare parts office trailer #1 (2015)—George Lopez drama HD [Video file]. Retrieved from https://www.youtube.com /watch?v=myjar5KoqZA

National Association of Colleges and Employers (NACE) Staff. (2016, January 27). STEM grads projected to earn class of 2016's highest average starting salaries. *National Association of Colleges and Employers*. Retrieved from http://www.naceweb.org/job-market/compensation/stem-grads-projected -to-earn-class-of-2016s-highest-average-starting-salaries/

Rendón, L. I., Nora, A., & Kanagala, V. (2014). *Ventajas/Assets y conocimientos/ knowledge*: *Leveraging Latin@ strengths to foster student success*. San Antonio, TX: Center for Research and Policy in Education, The University of Texas at San Antonio.

Santiago, D. A., Taylor, M., & Galdeano, E. C. (2015, June). Finding your workforce: Latinos in science, technology, engineering, and math (STEM). *¡Excelencia in Education!* Retrieved from http://www.edexcelencia.org/research /workforce/stem?utm_source=Excelencia+Contacts&utm_campaign=f330 e3d60a-FYWF_STEM_release_05_20_2015&utm_medium=email&utm _term=0_717a0c9d98-f330e3d60a-126088161

Stepler, R., & Brown, A. (2016, April 19). Statistical portrait of Hispanics in the United States. *Pew Research Center (Hispanic Trends)*. Retrieved from http:// www.pewhispanic.org/2016/04/19/statistical-portrait-of-hispanics-in-the -united-states-key-charts/

U.S. Census Bureau. (2012). *Educational attainment by race and Hispanic origin: 1970 to 2010 (Table 229)*. Retrieved from http://www2.census.gov/library /publications/2011/compendia/statab/131ed/tables/12s0229.pdf

U. S. Census Bureau. (2014). *Changing nation: Percent Hispanic of the U.S. population: 1980–2050*. Retrieved from https://www.census.gov/content/dam /Census/newsroom/facts-for-features/2014/cb14-ff22_graphic.pdf

Valenzuela, A. (1999). *Subtractive schooling: U.S.-Mexican youth and the politics of caring*. Albany, NY: State University of New York Press.

Yosso, T. J. (2005). Whose culture has capital? A critical race theory discussion of community cultural wealth. *Race Ethnicity and Education, 8*(1), 69–91. doi:10.1080/1361332052000341006

Zambrana, R. E., & Hurtado, S. (Eds.). (2015). *The magic key: The educational journey of Mexican Americans from K-12 to college and beyond*. Austin, TX: University of Texas Press.

PART I

Planning for a Career in STEM

CHAPTER ONE

STEP 1: Preparing for a Career in STEM—*¡Preparate!*

Karina I. Vielma

I proudly identify as a first-generation, Latina mathematician. Growing up, my parents did not have the knowledge or the resources to help me prepare for a college degree. They did, however, model good work ethics, as well as support and motivate me to try my best in all that I did, especially in school. Although I did not know what I wanted to do in elementary school or high school, I discovered a love of math and science early on by playing outdoors, observing patterns in nature, and creating new design concepts with anything I could find. While taking courses, writing, solving problems, creating new ways of doing things, and playing sports, I discovered my career aspirations. I tried my best in all that I did, but I did not know that I was preparing my résumé to apply to some of the top universities in the country. Unaware of the science, technology, engineering, and mathematics (STEM) world, I prepared by taking the most advanced math and science courses offered at my high school.

As the applications rolled in, I applied and was admitted to programs in mathematics and engineering schools. After visiting several colleges, I decided to enroll at the Massachusetts Institute of Technology (MIT). Coursework and internship experiences prepared me for a rewarding career in the STEM fields. Graduating from MIT remains my highest and toughest academic achievement. Looking back, there are times that I wish someone had helped and guided me along my journey into the math and science fields. For this reason, I share tips that can help first-generation Latinx students enter a rewarding field in math, science, or engineering with greater success. My experience working indirectly with the admissions office at MIT to recruit and select strong college candidates also gives me a different perspective that I share with you. Finally, my research examines the experiences of successful students who earned degrees in STEM fields, particularly Latinas and underrepresented students.

Here are some tips to help make your journey into any of the many STEM majors a successful one.

Before High School

Before high school, you may or may not know your future career interests or whether you would like to enter a science, technology, engineering, or mathematics STEM field. Regardless of your situation, it is important to evaluate your interests. Think about the answers to the following questions: What do you like to do for fun? What school courses do you enjoy the most? What are you good at? In other words, what are your skills? What would you like to do in your future job? Do you see jobs in your community that interest you, that look both fun and rewarding? Have you met a person whose job interests you? Are there other jobs or opportunities that you would like to explore or learn more about? What are some questions that you have about your future interests? Reflecting often on these questions can help you begin to understand yourself and your personal and career interests. Write down the answers to these questions in a journal or a spot to which you can come back. Answer these questions every summer, and reevaluate your past and current interests.

If you have decided that a career in STEM is the best fit for you, welcome to the club! I knew early on that I loved math and science, finding patterns, designing things—anything—and I liked helping people. Counselors and teachers guided my decision to pursue a career in STEM. There are so many exciting opportunities ahead for you! These could include summer jobs and internships, science fairs, summer programs, or other activities to prepare you for a STEM career. As an aspiring scientist and engineer, you also have questions to consider regularly. What STEM career most interests you? Why is that career interesting? How does working in that career match your skills and abilities? What can you do to be prepared to enter into this field? Do you know anyone who has a job in this area? If so, have you talked to them about their experiences? What are some questions or concerns you have about the STEM career? Develop a great habit of reflecting in a personal journal to help you understand any changes you are making and to look back at the evolution of your decisions. You will learn a lot about yourself and your decisions this way.

It is never too early to develop strong academic practices as a student that will prepare you for high school, college, and a STEM career. Take challenging courses that give you the best opportunities to learn. Get to know your teachers and counselors, and, more importantly, let them know of your personal and academic interests. Look for enrichment programs, especially in the summers and after school, which introduce you to science, technology, math, and engineering careers. Get involved in volunteering opportunities and extracurricular activities that you enjoy where you can develop interpersonal, teamwork, and leadership skills. Learn about STEM careers by searching the Internet, reading, and talking to people. When you meet an engineer or a scientist, ask them questions about their experiences, especially their experiences in school. View every opportunity as a chance to learn about your interests. Do not let others tell you what you should do (or should not do); discover what the best fit is for you.

There are many, many opportunities in various STEM branches that you could pursue—environmental scientist, geographer, climate change analyst, astronomer, computer hardware or software engineer, computer programmer, aerospace engineer, architect, biochemical engineer, math teacher, economist, mathematician, statistician, and the list goes on (see Chapter 7). Even within a field, there are many different jobs that you can perform. Not all activities will be enjoyable as you explore the different STEM fields. For this reason, it is important to evaluate what you dislike and like about each experience and always try new things. When you come across an activity that you dislike, ask yourself: What did I dislike about this activity? Why did I dislike these things? What are the things that I liked about this activity? What would make this activity a great experience for me?

Sometimes we come across a class or a project that we dislike, but instead of ruling the entire activity out, ask yourself the questions posed earlier. Your answers will help you learn more about your interests. This practice can also help you come back to the activity and try it again with a different perspective. For example, in middle school, I took a very difficult math class. After the first days, I wanted to switch the class. My parents helped me think through what I disliked about the class and why I disliked it. I learned that the teacher intimidated me, I was scared of failing the class, and I liked knowing what I was doing and being successful at it. I also learned that I wanted the challenge to learn math well enough to prepare for college, and I liked that the teacher had high expectations for all students. In the end, I decided to stay. It was the best decision I made in middle school. I had the same teacher for the next three years in pre-algebra, algebra I, and algebra II. These classes were the foundation for my future career in mathematics. This might also happen to you. Do not give up! Reflect and learn from every experience.

High School Preparation

High school is a very exciting time in your life! You will meet new teachers and students with a variety of experiences and interests. This is the time to explore your academic interests more in-depth, prepare for college admissions, and hone in on a future career. It is an exciting time to try new activities, take different courses, learn from your trials (mistakes), and develop new strategies to prepare for college. The tips in this chapter can help you explore your interests in a STEM career and give you knowledge to make a stronger decision and become better prepared to apply to a STEM program and enter college. Knowing that you are interested in a STEM field is a huge step towards your preparation for college. It means you can now focus on gaining experiences that will make you a competitive college applicant and prepare you for a fulfilling profession that you can enjoy. Preparing for a career in STEM begins early with the habits you develop, the courses you take, and the persistence you cultivate.

Here are a few tips to help you as you navigate your high school years toward a STEM career.

During your high school years, there are courses and study habits that you should strive to acquire to help you be successful. Colleges will be looking at the coursework and the grades on your high school transcript along with the activities you participate in and the leadership roles you take on at school and in your community. Your high school years are the time for you to shine!

Courses

First of all, you can prepare for your academic transcript by taking math and science courses that challenge you to learn and think in new ways. Do not settle for taking the classes where you are guaranteed an A grade. Challenge yourself to take advanced courses that will teach you new concepts and give you different experiences. Since you are preparing for a career in a STEM field, strive to take as many math and science courses as possible such as calculus, trigonometry, biology, physics, and chemistry. Remember that each mathematics course prepares you for the next one, so try your best at each level. Learning about different sciences also helps you become an informed scientist and engineer in the future.

What about grades? I cannot deny that grades are an important component of your college application. High school grades show a trend of success in your schoolwork, so it is important to try to make the best grade possible. However, you should never sacrifice your learning for a guaranteed grade. In your college applications, you will have an opportunity to discuss your grades or talk about any challenges you confronted. This is your chance to describe why you chose to take more difficult classes and challenge yourself to learn more difficult material in your high school classes, so even though grades are important when you are applying to college, they should not be your motivation to add or drop a class. Challenge yourself and aim for the best grade you can.

College admissions programs have access to the coursework that your high school offers. Competitive admissions programs look to see that you attempted to take the most advanced coursework offered at your school. They will determine if you took pre-calculus because it was the highest mathematics course offered at your high school or if more advanced courses were offered and you chose not to take them. Take advantage of the advanced courses that your high school has to offer, and pay close attention to any Advanced Placement (AP) courses offered. The tests offered at the end of these courses give you the opportunity to earn college credit. Some high schools allow students who successfully complete an AP course to take the exam for free or at a reduced cost at the end of the year. Ask your school counselor about the advanced courses and Advanced Placement courses offered at your school, especially courses in mathematics and science.

During your senior year, you may have the choice to work, graduate early, or take advanced courses. If possible, try to take advanced courses that will prepare you for your STEM major. Make learning a priority. Some high schools also offer the opportunity to enroll in college coursework while you are still a high school student. You can choose to take college classes that might help you be a more rounded college applicant or might help you explore your STEM career interests. This is also a good opportunity to understand the college culture. Most classes do not meet every day or every other day like they do in high school. The college professors usually do not remind you of every reading assignment you need to complete, so taking a college course in high school will acclimate you to the college experience. Be aware that not all college courses transfer to other universities. For this reason, before you enroll in a college course, make sure you have all the information that you need. Call the universities you are interested in attending, and ask them if the college credit will transfer to their university. If you are opting to work, choose a job that will give you experience in the field or fields that you are interested in pursuing during college and after college. Do not choose to work only because you want income/money. Remember, your focus is learning. What will you learn from the job? How will it help you in the future? If you find a company or a job that you are interested in learning more about, ask for opportunities to work or volunteer there. It is a great idea to observe these jobs while you are a high school student to learn what interests you about the jobs. Many companies welcome student volunteers and will gladly mentor you.

Additionally, there are other courses you might want to take depending on your desired field or fields of interest. Some high schools offer engineering, computer programming, statistics, or lab courses. Depending on your interests, these courses may serve as good learning opportunities before you apply to college. Again, meet with your guidance counselor, and ask questions about the opportunities to be better prepared for a STEM career.

Try to develop good working relationships with your teachers and counselors in high school. These individuals will be the ones who you will ask to write letters of recommendation for your college admissions applications, and they will need to know you better to write a great recommendation. They need to observe how you learn and how you challenge yourself academically. Teachers and counselors should also know more about your background and activities, such as any hardships that you and your family have faced and how you have overcome these hardships, what you like to do for fun, and any leadership positions you may hold. Let them know what your goals and interests are and how you are preparing for college and your future. Tell them more about your life experiences growing up, and ask if they know of any opportunities that might help you acquire skills to attend college and major in a STEM degree. These mentoring relationships are very important for you to be successful in high school and to also pursue a college education.

Extracurricular Activities

Extracurricular activities are a large part of the college admissions application process. Yes, your academic record is important, *and* college recruiters and admissions officers look for students who are involved in activities outside of the classroom and are well rounded. They want to see how you have developed not only as a student but also as a unique individual and future leader, so it is important for you to explore your interests through the activities you pursue and participate in outside of the school day.

Definitely do the things you enjoy. Whether you participate in band, sports, dancing, clubs, church, or other programs, find something that you love to do and do it! Colleges seek students who have a record of participating in long periods of time (years) in activities they enjoy. Competitive colleges also look for your development as a leader, and this can be seen through the years you were involved in extracurricular activities or in the leadership positions you held throughout your participation in these activities. If you have the opportunity to develop leadership skills through extracurricular activities, these skills will also help you when you enter a STEM major in college and a STEM career after college. STEM careers, along with other careers, require teamwork in projects with peers and colleagues as well as communication skills that can be developed early. Many companies have supervisory positions that require you to understand others' needs and help them do the best job possible. Being involved in extracurricular activities and being a leader in these activities will help you develop skills necessary for your future.

As a student preparing for the STEM fields, it is also very important that you seek opportunities to learn skills such as computer programming, design, mathematics, and physics. You will become more comfortable with these skills as you do academic work and also fun hobbies. Look for extracurricular activities that help you expand this knowledge. Participating in a local or state science fair can be a good way to present your STEM skills as well as learn what others are doing. After school do-it-yourself (DIY) programs, computer programming camps, or summer STEM preparatory camps also help you develop indispensable, diverse thinking skills needed for your future. At most of these programs, you will also find passionate teachers and mentors with whom you can connect. Ask them questions about their experiences. Find a mentor in one of these activities or simply find friends who have similar interests as yours. This is how you build your network of peers and mentors.

Try New Things

High school is a great time to learn what you like and do not like, and it's a great time to learn and try new things. Trying new things may mean that you extend yourself into situations that are different, and doing so can help you see what you like and do not like about other activities. When you decide an activity or a course is not for you, take the time to reflect and ask yourself why it did not work out for you. Was the environment, the people, or the activity something that you did not enjoy? What did you like about it? What made it difficult to stay in the activity? Answering these questions will give you good information that helps you get to know your interests and as you make important decisions for your future. For example, when you get to college, you might be given a choice to work alone or work in a group, come to class early or take a class later in the day. Knowing what you like in different situations and how you work best will help you make better choices. There are times when you may not have a choice, and in these cases, try to learn the most you can, but reflect and think about what you enjoy and do not enjoy about different situations. Most importantly, stretch yourself to try new activities that you are interested in. Volunteer if you can. Ask to shadow someone at a job you find interesting. Ask questions. Learn as much as you can with every new experience!

Do Your Research

At times, students decide to go to a particular school because their friends are also going to attend that institution, it is the school they can afford, or it is where the family tells them to go. Then they end up having to choose a major that is offered at that school even if it is not the best match for the student. For this reason, it is extremely important to first look at what you want to do as a career and research which universities offer programs to prepare you for that specific career.

During high school, you can begin looking more in-depth at the majors that most interest you. For example, if you are interested in engineering, try to narrow down what kind of engineering field or fields interest you—biological engineering, chemical engineering, electrical engineering, mechanical engineering, biomedical engineering, aerospace engineering, and the list goes on. Ask yourself why you may be interested in a specific field. When you get ready to apply to college, you will be asked to write an essay that targets your reasons for selecting your major. It is a good idea to reflect early about your choice of major and why you are interested in that major. Do not be afraid to change your mind or have several options. Think about the choice as trying it on, identifying what you like and do not like about the choice, and having the option to change. It is better to know early, because once you start college, you will be taking courses that fulfill requirements for your specific major. After you narrow down your options, explore all the jobs that you could do with those degrees, and think about your interests and abilities. These jobs will be options after your college graduation, and you should be looking forward to applying to one of these jobs.

After you have narrowed down the field or fields that you are interested in studying, look for universities that provide training in these fields. Make a list of the schools, where they are located, the average cost of attending, the application deadline, the admissions requirements, and other relevant information that will help you apply. Even if you begin creating this list during your first year in high school, you will be aware of the requirements, and you can go back and edit it as you change your mind or find out about new programs. This list will also give you an idea of the academic preparation needed to apply such as the minimum SAT or ACT score, the courses needed for admissions to the college of engineering (or school of engineering), honors program requirements, or other special financial aid opportunities. You will discover that state universities have a cheaper price tag than out-of-state state universities or private colleges. All this information will help you make a better, well-informed decision when you prepare to apply. More importantly, you will be searching for schools based on your interests. Not all universities have extensive STEM degrees. There are some universities that have very specialized STEM programs, and if you are interested in a career in one of those fields, you will need to apply to a select group of colleges.

Once you know the universities' admissions requirements, you can prepare for and take the SAT or ACT tests, AP tests, and other requirements needed if you meet their criteria for attending. I once heard a counselor say you should have a list that is made up of one-third safe schools, one-third match schools, and one-third dream schools. This guarantees that you are applying to schools you know you can get into as well as schools that are more challenging to receive acceptance but you have dreamed of attending. You know what they say—you never know until you try! You might be one of those students who applies and gets accepted to a top university (or many top universities), and if you had not tried, you would not have known.

Visit College Campuses

Each college has a different campus environment and learning culture. You can find out if a university fits your style of learning and your student needs by visiting and experiencing the campus. Many high schools offer students opportunities to visit university campuses at a reduced price or completely free of charge. These are great experiences to take advantage of and are an opportunity to ask questions that will help as you prepare to apply and eventually attend a university. If you have a list of schools that offer majors you are interested in, I recommend you try your best to visit these schools. When you visit the campus, make sure you are asking questions to learn about their admissions process as well as the student experience. Ask specific questions about STEM majors. What kind of academic support does the college offer for tutoring in STEM fields? How long does it take to graduate with a STEM degree? What is the graduation rate of STEM majors? What are the average salaries and placements of STEM graduates? Does the university or department host career fairs and post internship and job openings for STEM students? You should take advantage of your campus visit and speak to current college students majoring in a STEM field, especially in the STEM major that you are most interested in. You can also request to talk to other Latinx students to understand their experiences attending that college.

Talk to Current College Students

You may be fortunate to connect with a college student majoring in your interested STEM major while you visit the campus, but do not be afraid to ask for students' contact information to contact them after your visit. You also do not need to physically visit the college campus to talk to current college students. Take the time to befriend others who are in their first year of college and others who are majoring in STEM degrees that you are interested in. Learn from their experiences, and accept advice they might give you to help while you are in high school or going through the college admissions application process. Ask them questions about their perceptions of the college and their current major along with questions about their goals and aspirations. Begin to create pros and cons for yourself for each of the universities you attend or are interested in, and be sure to include information about the STEM programs to which you are applying. Try not to completely rely of one perspective. Everyone has a different experience. Talk to as many people as you can so that you get a well-rounded perspective of the college and programs.

Ask Questions

As a lifelong learner, you can be sure that asking questions will guarantee you will learn something new often. One thing I learned in college was that it was not about how "smart" I was, but how smart I worked. Asking questions is an important component of working smart. By asking questions, you can clarify expectations from parents, teachers, counselors, and coaches. You can also learn new things you may not have known before you asked the question. Many times, you will also find that other people were also wondering the same thing you were but were too afraid to ask. More importantly, practicing the art of asking questions helps prepare you to confidently navigate college and the STEM fields. There will be many times where you will need to ask for help and clarify things or just get more information. In math and science classes especially, it is important to learn how to ask questions. Be clear about what you do not understand. Try to explain what you do understand and how you understand it. Then ask if your understanding is correct, or ask a specific question about what you did not understand. But whatever you do, do not be afraid to ask!

Seek Financial Assistance

Similar to seeking out colleges that offer STEM majors of your choice, you should also seek financial assistance for your college education early on. Make a list of available scholarships, grants, and other awards or competitions that you qualify for based on who you are, what your background is, or what you are interested in studying. Find out the deadlines and their requirements. Note the deadlines on a calendar, and set a reminder at least a month before the due date to get letters of recommendations and essays in on time. You will find there are many financial opportunities for students interested in STEM fields, especially for first-generation students, Latinx, and underrepresented minority groups. You can update this list of financial aid opportunities on a regular basis. Then you will know the deadlines and requirements for each application. If you need letters of recommendation, make sure to request them ahead of time. Your recommenders may not be available or have time to write if you ask them last minute. Remember that financial awards are not guaranteed, but it is well worth the time to apply to all that you qualify for. This is extra money that can only help fund your future education.

There is also the Free Application for Federal Student Aid (FAFSA), which most colleges accept to grant you federal student aid. This application can be filled out as early as January of the year you wish to begin coursework. As soon as your parents file their income tax return, it is a good idea to fill out your FAFSA form. The FAFSA requires that you enter information from your parents' income tax return, so be sure to ask your parents for a copy of that return for your financial aid application. Your state may also have a state application for financial aid.

Study Habits

When I was in high school, academic success came easy to me, and I hardly studied for exams and quizzes. This might also be the case for you, and you may be missing out on some useful time management and study skills development opportunities. I did not need to study much or manage my time since I always managed to find time to do all that I needed to do for school, co-curricular activities, and even a job. However, I wish I had worked on these habits early, before attending college. In college, I had a lot of what I assumed was free time, and I started getting involved in many activities. However, my grades suffered drastically during my first semester. I learned my lesson, minimized my participation in co-curricular activities, and focused on my studies. It is a great idea to begin good academic habits early. Start by getting a planner and write in it dates when your assignments are due, the activities that you participate in, and any other commitments that you might have. Make sure you include family commitments as well. If you own a computer or a smartphone, an electronic calendar will also work. You can sync this calendar on your phone as well as on your computer. Regardless of which method you choose to use, remember to consult your calendar before scheduling a new event. This helps you see what you have coming up in the near future and not over commit yourself. Schedule times when you will work on your homework, practice for band or sports, or attend church.

Once you know when things are due, try your best to study a little every day for each class that you are taking, especially your core classes such as English/reading/writing, math, science, and social studies. Set aside a set time for each course. Know that even though you are preparing to enter college as a STEM major, you still need to know and excel in other required courses such as writing, history, literature, or philosophy. Most people first work on assignments they enjoy or that are easy for them. However, it is a good idea to begin tackling your hardest classes first when you have the most energy. Later, when you are tired, you can work on assignments that are easier or more enjoyable. This is a good habit to adopt during high school. Consider yourself in preparation to be successful in college while you are in high school.

Whether it is for your classes, for entertainment, or to learn about current events or your future STEM job, set aside time to read and write every day (and not on social media). This is important to prepare for any college career and for your future as a professional. A habit of reading every day grants you the skills to explore new ways of thinking and learning. Keep a journal where you can write every day. It can be a spiral notebook or an electronic file. It is important to keep track of your thoughts and ideas. Reflect often on your goals through reading and writing. In college, you may be asked to keep journals when you take chemistry or biology lab courses. Lab and field notes will become an important part of your STEM coursework and later in your job. When you become a scientist or an engineer, it is important to keep track of your thoughts and ideas using a researcher's journal.

Persistence

Many people who are interested in STEM fields might hit a point during their careers when they feel like it is too much to handle, and they might consider giving it up. It is important to understand that hardships will be a part of the experiences you will face in any field. In STEM fields, there might be a class that challenges you so much that you may feel like quitting forever! Or there might be an instructor whose expectations are so high that you feel like you are being pushed out of the entire field. Much research about students pursuing STEM degrees tells us that the climate can be very competitive and academically rigorous. For this reason, it is important to practice persistence. Here are some tips to help you practice this important habit.

Compare your successes to your own successes. What did you learn that you did not know before? What can you do now that you could not do before? Do not compare yourself or your performance to others' achievements. When you compare yourself to others, it can negatively impact your performance in classes and activities that you perform. Instead, try to focus on growing at your own pace and challenge yourself to do new things regardless of what others are doing. Compare your learning, growth, and successes with your own experiences. Oftentimes you will be surprised to learn that you can achieve much more than you ever imagined if you focus on your own skills and talents. Remember, we all come from different backgrounds, have different experiences, and contribute to STEM fields in different ways.

Asking for help is sometimes seen as a "dumb" thing to do, but from my experience, the one who seeks answers is the smart one. Seek help whenever possible by asking questions. Try to work out your assignments on your own, with a group, or do both. Then consult with your teacher. Even when you feel you have the correct thinking strategy, it is always good to seek clarification. Then, to make sure you have learned the information properly, explain your thinking process to another person. Teaching others a difficult concept will help you understand it even better and persevere during the most difficult content. (Trust me, I am a teacher!)

Also, many STEM courses usually have a competitive aspect to them through a project or an experiment. Competition is meant to challenge the best in us and create better products and designs. Do not fear competition. Instead, be confident about your contributions. You have a different outlook than anyone else. Be proud of your unique outlook and share that knowledge with others. Doing so lets others know more about you and also helps you persevere through challenging competitions or projects. Your peers will know you for your contributions, and you might become an expert at a new talent or skill.

For a long time, I went through MIT as a confused student. I thought there was something wrong with me until I learned that being confused was a good thing. Did you know if you are confused, then you are doing a good job of learning? Did you know that when you are comfortable with the knowledge presented then you would not be confused? When you are receiving new information, your mind tries to make sense of it and causes you to be confused for a period of time. This is how learning happens because your mind is being challenged in new and different ways. Become comfortable with confusion, and learn new ways to ask questions, practice problem-solving skills, and change your strategies to help you get out of a confused period. These strategies will help you learn. This is important because in college you will be presented with new information all the time. Being confused will be an common occurrence, but this only means that you are learning lots of new information. Don't give up through those confusing periods. Adopt strategies that will help you learn through these times.

Finally, learn to de-stress. Part of persevering through the difficult times, especially in the STEM competitive world, is learning to relieve stress in productive ways that will fuel you up to continue doing good work. What healthy activities currently help you relieve stress? Maybe running, meditating, writing, napping or swimming help you relax a bit. Think about what helps you to de-stress, and make a list of those things that you enjoy. When you are confronted with a difficult period or heavy workloads, lots of assignments or projects, or just a tough time with teammates, teachers, or parents, you can go to this list and engage yourself in an activity or two that will help you relieve some stress. Make sure to take periodic breaks.

Stay Connected

When stressful times occur, many people withdraw from their loved ones and isolate themselves, thinking they need to work extra hard and work alone. Unfortunately, working harder and isolating yourself from others usually creates more stress. Therefore, it is important to keep close ties with your loved ones—family, friends, church members, and other groups—your support network. They will help you when times get difficult. Sometimes just a conversation with a loved one can motivate you to continue with your studies. This is a good habit to develop early on and connect with those you love.

Additionally, if you do not have a role model in the STEM fields, try to find someone you can talk to and who can motivate you to endure during your time in high school and in college. There might be a student who is an advanced STEM major, an employee pursuing a STEM career, or a math/science teacher or professor whom you consider a mentor. Connect with them often in person or through text messages, social media, or with a phone call. Tell them you value their advice and experience. Ask them if you could contact them outside of their role and if they are willing to serve as a mentor to you. Tell them your goals, and stay connected with this person or persons, especially when times become difficult.

Know Yourself

We are all different. We bring different ideas and experiences when we work together. For this reason, it is important to know yourself, your interests, and your motivations (why you do things). Do not be afraid to share with others who you are and what you stand for. Be proud of your background and how you grew up. Know that it will all contribute to your experience for the rest of your life. It will make you a better scientist and engineer. You may have motivations that others do not. For me, I was motivated to help others who were growing up in poverty through educational opportunities.

It is also good to know other things about yourself. What is the best time of day for you to work? I went to a university where students worked all night long on their assignments, but I worked best very early in the morning. Do you need exercise or special nutrition in your life to maintain a healthy routine? What are your religious beliefs? Knowing all these aspects of yourself and staying proud of who you are will allow you to search for opportunities and contribute in unique ways. Do not stop doing the things that make you who you are to try and fit a mold that will impress colleges or employers. Be you!

Understand the STEM Landscape

Finally, I want to present a topic that may be difficult to communicate to young, aspiring scientists and engineers. The STEM culture is very exciting, providing enriching educational and career opportunities for your diverse ideas to flourish. You will meet new and interesting people who will help you along the way and validate your experiences both personally and professionally. Currently, there is a shortage of American-trained engineers and scientists, and the United States is raising standards for educational preparation from elementary through the college level in an attempt to develop new talent in the STEM fields.

However, the STEM culture can also present a cold, competitive atmosphere, selective of specific individuals. Some people may want to exclude others from their research because of preconceived notions or simply because they have different ideas. Historically, women and underrepresented racial and ethnic minorities have been excluded from pursuing STEM fields and careers.

For this reason, it is important to note that in the United States there is a lack of representation of women, Latinx Americans, African Americans, and Native Americans in the STEM fields. White males fill the majority of STEM jobs (51 percent).

You may walk into a classroom to find that you are the only female or the only Latinx student in the room. Do not be intimidated. Know that you are an important component of the future for your STEM field. It is important to understand that each of your talents, skills, and backgrounds are needed in these important fields. Your contribution is essential. For these reasons, it is important to be well-informed, persist through difficult times, find mentors and others who will support you along the way, and understand the values that you bring to the field. *¡Preparate!*

CHAPTER TWO

STEP 2: Choosing a College and STEM Program

Marcela Cuellar and Juan Carlos Garibay

In this chapter, we focus on helping you to choose the college that is best suited for you and the right science, technology, engineering, and mathematics (STEM) program of study. There are many different colleges and universities where you can pursue a degree in STEM. In other words, you have many options as you decide on which college and STEM program may be the best for your education. Colleges and STEM programs share some common characteristics, but each are unique in their own ways.

Choosing a college and STEM program involves a series of steps. These steps include exploring the various options, applying to colleges and programs that interest you, and then deciding which college or program in which you will enroll. We will describe some of the factors you should consider as you explore which college and STEM program will be the best fit for you.

CHOOSING THE RIGHT COLLEGE FOR YOU

You may have heard of some institutions being referred to as *colleges*, while others may be referred to as *universities*. While we generally refer to education beyond high school as college, there are significant differences between *colleges* and *universities*. Colleges usually offer undergraduate degrees, most likely associate's or bachelor's degrees. By contrast, universities usually offer bachelor's degrees as well as more advanced degrees, such as master's, doctoral, or professional (medicine and law) degrees. Colleges are generally smaller than universities. In fact, universities are often made up of several colleges that are organized according to particular areas of study. For example, many universities will have a college of engineering, a college of biological sciences, and a college of letters of sciences. Sometimes these colleges within a university are referred to as schools. STEM programs will often be spread out through the various colleges or schools within a university that best match the general area of study to which that program belongs. For the remainder of the chapter, we will simply refer to colleges and universities as *college*, but we wanted to be sure to give you a general sense of the major difference between these terms.

Types of Colleges

There are many different types of colleges and universities. Finding the right college for you is very important because you want to be sure the college is the right fit for your interests.

Two-Year or Four-Year College?

A major distinction between types of colleges is whether it is a two-year or four-year institution, since this will determine what type of degree you can earn there. Two-year colleges, also commonly referred to as community colleges, offer associate's degrees in STEM. These degrees are intended for students who are planning to then transfer from the community college to a four-year institution. Four-year institutions offer bachelor's degrees in STEM. While the names "two-year" and "four-year colleges" suggest that this is the amount of time it will take to earn your degree at that institution, it is important to understand that at some institutions it may take longer to complete your degree. Also, it may take a little longer than four years to complete a bachelor's degree in some majors.

After obtaining a bachelor's degree in STEM, you can choose to enter the workforce or continue your education in a graduate program to earn a master's degree or a doctoral degree. You can also choose to enroll in a graduate program after working as well. Depending on your ultimate career goal, you may need a graduate degree. For example, students who want to conduct research in STEM should pursue a doctor of philosophy (PhD), while those who want to practice medicine should obtain a doctor of medicine (MD). If you want to pursue graduate school, you will want to do a similar search in exploring the various colleges and programs available in your interests. You should become familiar with the degree you will need to reach your career goals, the average time it takes to complete the degree, and explore the resources available that can help you create an academic plan that will help you reach your goal of earning your degree.

Public or Private College?

Another important distinction to consider is whether an institution is public or private, which may partly influence the cost of attendance. Public institutions receive some funding from the state in which they are located and are generally less expensive than private institutions. However, it is important to know that the cost of attending a particular college will be influenced by a variety of factors, so do not simply look at whether a college is public or private in deciding where to consider applying. There are many different types of private colleges as well. Some may have been around a long time and have a strong reputation, while others may be newer and less known. In addition, some may be more expensive than others. A critical piece of information to know is if a private institution is accredited, meaning the courses and the degrees you complete there will be accepted at other colleges if you want to transfer or continue into graduate school and that potential employers will value a degree from that college as well.

Minority-Serving Institutions and Gender-Specific Colleges

A growing number of colleges are called minority-serving institutions (MSIs). These colleges have unique histories and missions in the education of particular racial groups, such as African Americans, Latina/Latinos, Asian Americans, and Native Americans. Historically black colleges and universities (HBCUs) are the oldest MSIs and emerged as the primary college option for African Americans when racial segregation was the law in the United States. While HBCUs continue to educate a significant proportion of African Americans, many Latinx students are now enrolling at these institutions. Hispanic-serving institutions (HSIs) are colleges that enroll many Latinx undergraduates (at least 25 percent enrollment or more in each college). Many of these colleges receive additional support from the federal government to develop programs and services to enhance the education of Latinx and all students at that college. Some HSIs have used these funds to support STEM programs.

In addition, there are women's colleges that may be a good option for Latinas, and some may also enroll males. Understanding there are these different types of colleges is important as you explore your options, since this will influence your undergraduate experience. Your high school guidance counselor can be helpful in pointing you to the names of MSIs and gender-specific colleges and universities.

College Characteristics: Location, Size, and Residential Status

A major consideration as you explore colleges will be where they are located. There are several colleges in each state. You may want to attend a college in the state where you live now or in another state. While there are many differences between states and locations, the weather in different regions may be one of the most visible differences. For instance, winters in some regions of the United States include snowfall and cold temperatures, whereas in other regions, the weather may be very similar throughout the whole year. If weather matters to you, this is something to keep in mind as you consider the location of colleges.

In addition, college locations vary by the size of the surrounding community. For example, colleges can be located in large urban cities, suburban areas, or rural communities. These locations will provide you with very different college experiences. Colleges located in large cities, such as New York University and the University of

Illinois, Chicago, usually have access to many resources, such as public transportation and many entertainment options. Colleges in suburban areas may have similar options but will be some distance from a larger city. Colleges in rural areas, such as the University of Iowa and the University of Virginia, are usually located in towns where most of the social and job opportunities revolve around the college itself. These are usually referred to as college towns. For all of these reasons, the location of a college will shape the type of experiences you may have there. A college's location may differ from where you currently live, but it may be a great time for you to explore and experience something different.

Beyond the size of the surrounding city or town, it is also important to consider the size of the college itself. Some colleges are small, enrolling less than 2,000 students, while others are much larger with as many as 35,000 students or more. The size of the college is not necessarily related to the size of the surrounding area. There are small colleges located in large cities, such as Loyola Marymount University in Los Angeles, just as much as there are large colleges located in smaller college towns, such as the University of Michigan and the University of California, Davis. The size of the college may influence many aspects of your college experience. For example, smaller colleges will usually have smaller class sizes and may provide more opportunities for interacting closely with your professors and classmates. In contrast, larger colleges may have large classes, mainly lectures, where there can be hundreds of students in one class. Interactions with professors in these environments may require you to visit your professor's office hours where you can ask questions about the course and get additional guidance from your professor.

Another physical characteristic that is important to consider is whether a college is primarily a residential or commuter campus. At residential campuses, most of the students will live on campus in residence halls, and students' academic and social life takes place largely on the campus. A commuter campus is one where students mostly live off campus and primarily come to campus for classes, such as California State University, Los Angeles and Florida International University. Students may drive to campus or take public transportation to classes and other college events but live at home with parents or in other living arrangements in the surrounding community. Some campuses may enroll a mix of residential and commuter students. These differences may influence how much you interact with some of your peers outside of the class. As you can see, these various physical characteristics can influence your college experience inside and outside of the classroom, so these are important to consider depending on the type of college experience you are hoping to have.

College Academic and Social Climate: What Does the College "Feel" Like?

Colleges can also be described in terms of its general vibe and feeling. Some of these characteristics may be less visible than the physical characteristics. However, these environmental differences may influence your college experiences in different ways and are, therefore, important to consider in your exploration and decision of which college will be best for you.

Academic Climate

The academic environment of a college may differ according to the type of college and the range of physical characteristics we discussed. One element of the academic environment may be connected to the college's mission. For example, some colleges are focused on a research-oriented education, which means students will be expected to write many papers using research as evidence, whereas this may happen less at other colleges. The academic expectations of different colleges may also feel more rigorous and demanding than others. The college's academic environment may be shaped by its reputation and how hard it is to get into. Students at some campuses may be more collaborative and often work together to support each other, while in other institutions students may be more competitive with each other. It is important to know that even in campuses that might feel more competitive overall, there are opportunities in other spaces where students can find or create the type of environment that will help them succeed regardless of the broader campus environment. Another factor that can influence the academic climate is whether a college follows a semester or quarter calendar. Colleges on semester offer most courses in two terms (fall and spring—approximately 16 weeks each), and those on quarter offer them in three terms (fall, winter, and spring—approximately 10 weeks each). The pace of courses is thus different. All of these factors can make some colleges feel more welcoming, while some may feel intimidating depending on what you prefer.

Social Climate

The diversity of the students attending a particular college can also vary and affect how a campus feels. For example, some colleges may enroll a racially diverse student population. In some of these campuses, Latinx students may represent a significant proportion of student body. In other campuses, Latinx students may be a numerical minority. This may be an important factor as you consider the type of college experience you may want. For example, you may want to attend a college where you will be able to meet and interact with students from very different racial backgrounds from your own.

Colleges will also vary in terms of the representation of males and females. Overall, females tend to outnumber males on most campuses these days, and as we discussed earlier, some colleges are women's colleges, which means that the overwhelming majority if not all of the students will be females. However, the representation of men and women may differ within specific STEM programs. Colleges may also enroll students who come from very different socioeconomic backgrounds, sexual orientations, age groups, religious backgrounds, and political perspectives. Further, many colleges are enrolling large numbers of international students from all over the world, which adds more diversity to the student population.

Depending on where you live or have grown up, you may or may not have interacted with people who come from very different backgrounds from your own. Your choice of a college can thus provide you with an incredible opportunity to expose yourself to people who may have different views of the world. These experiences can provide you with a rich educational experience and can prepare you for working with very diverse people.

Resources and Educational Opportunities

Colleges also offer various resources and educational opportunities that can enhance your personal and professional development.

Financial Aid

One of the most important resources that colleges provide is access to financial aid, which can come from many sources. The federal government, for example, provides grants (money that does not have to be repaid), loans (money borrowed that must be repaid after you are no longer enrolled in college), and work-study (money paid through a job at the college). Your Free Application for Federal Student Aid (FAFSA) will help determine which types of financial aid to which you may have access. The FAFSA takes into account your parents' income, if you are a dependent, or only your income if you are an independent student along with the cost of different colleges. In addition, most states offer grants to students who meet certain eligibility criteria, and colleges themselves often offer grants and scholarships to help students pay for college expenses. These institutional grants and scholarships often require additional applications, so be sure to ask if colleges that interest you offer these other types of financial aid. Each college has a financial aid office that will help administer your financial aid for your tuition and fees.

Academic Support

Most colleges offer additional academic support to help you in your academic and career planning. Advising will look different at every college, so it is important to become familiar with how this works at the colleges that interest you. For example, at some colleges, there are advising centers where students can go meet with academic advisers/counselors who can help students explore major options, understand requirements for a major, or plan out course schedules. Community colleges also have transfer centers where advisers can help students develop plans to transfer to four-year institutions.

Some colleges may also have advisers within particular STEM programs to provide more detailed information to students in those programs. Further, some campuses offer academic support programs to help first-generation, low-income students transition into college such as the Educational Opportunity Program (EOP), TRiO Student Support Services, and the Puente Project in California and Texas. In some campuses, advising may be easy to find, while in others it may be harder, so be sure to consider this additional support as you explore your college options.

Most colleges also provide career advising through career centers. In these centers, students usually have access to information that can help them navigate the job search, create a resume, and get tips for interviews. These centers often have counselors ready to help students explore their career options and also find internship opportunities for the summers during college. Moreover, many colleges also provide additional support services for students with disabilities and those who were in the foster care system as minors. Lastly, colleges also offer health and mental services for students. It is important to be familiar with the additional resources a college offers to see how much support is available to help you succeed academically and personally.

Cultural Programming and Services

Many colleges have ethnic or multicultural centers to provide additional support to students from different cultural backgrounds. Many of these centers have a long history at the individual campuses and were created to help Latinx students succeed in college in a manner that acknowledges and celebrates the students' culture. For example, Stanford University has El Centro Chicano y Latino, which was created in 1977 to support Chicana/Chicano and Latina/Latino students academically, personally, and socially. These centers may offer additional advising and mentoring to help students navigate the college environment and also opportunities to become engaged with student organizations or community service in the surrounding community. Also, many colleges have centers for lesbian, gay, bisexual, and transgender (LGBT) students and centers for women and men. More recently, many colleges have developed centers that provide support to undocumented students (often called AB-540 centers in California) who may need support to access financial and legal resources. As you consider your college options, be sure to know if there are centers available that will support your academic, personal, and social needs.

Many students who attend college are also interested in international learning experiences such as studying abroad at some point during their undergraduate education. If you are one of these students, it is important to consider if there are already established study abroad programs at the colleges you are considering. If you are interested in studying abroad in a particular country or continent, you can ask if the college has resources in place to help make this a reality. Studying abroad is very appealing because the cost for study abroad is generally the same as a term at the college. You will also get credits for the courses you take abroad. Additional expenses may include travel. Some campuses, however, offer additional scholarships to help cover costs for study abroad.

Undergraduate Research Opportunities

A key high-impact STEM learning experience is doing undergraduate research where you can work directly with professors on a research project. Be sure to take advantage of undergraduate research opportunities. These programs are very important because they will significantly build and enhance your STEM skills. Research opportunities will help you learn about a new area of research, develop your research and writing skills and build connections with faculty. These research opportunities can also provide invaluable experiences and also prepare you for graduate school.

There may be many different types of programs that support undergraduate research, but a common one at many colleges is the McNair Scholars program, which provides first-generation, low-income students (usually in their third year of college) an opportunity to work closely with a faculty mentor for a year and receive additional support to plan and prepare for advanced graduate study. In some colleges, there may also be opportunities to write an honors thesis or participate in an honors program. These academic opportunities allow you to interact closely with either a professor or a small group of students on research, which may result in a writing project. If any of these special educational opportunities interest you, it is important to consider if they exist at the colleges where you are interested in applying.

Student Organizations

Student organizations within different colleges also provide additional resources and opportunities to become involved in a range of social and educational purposes. Student organizations are usually created by and run by students. There is usually a difference between colleges in the extent to which students are involved in various student organizations. Some colleges are known for having students who are highly active in these organizations, while others may have fewer students who engage in these organizations. Student organizations may be very active, which can contribute to the general atmosphere of that college. It is important to be aware as well that some student organizations may exist in some colleges, but they may not exist in others. Knowing some of the student organizations in which you may want to be involved in during college may then inform which colleges you may want to consider exploring more.

Student Government and Political Clubs

One of the most common student organizations that exists at almost every college is student government, representatives elected by the general student body to address issues that are important to students. The structure of student government and its responsibilities may look different at every college. In addition, there are also often political clubs for students who want to become more involved in national politics or interact with students who hold similar political views.

Sports Organizations

Often, intramural sports are available at many colleges that are different from the official sports teams that may exist in some colleges. These intramural sports provide students an opportunity to play sports with students within the college.

Fraternities and Sororities

Another common student organization that exists on many colleges are fraternities and sororities. Some are described as Greek organizations because of the Greek letters that are used to name the different fraternities and sororities and have been around for almost 200 years. Some of these fraternities and sororities were originally created to provide opportunities for students to socialize with each other. Some fraternities and sororities exist nationally at many different colleges and are referred to as chapters of a particular Greek organization. There are many different Greek organizations, and each has a different purpose and a unique set of events and activities to be part of the fraternity or sorority. There are also many that were created as Latinx fraternities and sororities to foster Latinx culture and identity on college campuses. These organizations often also include community service as a central part of their mission as an organization. Further, there are other fraternities and sororities that may appeal to students that focus on academics, professional networking, or community service. While fraternities and sororities are fairly common in colleges, some may not exist in certain colleges.

Latinx Student Organizations

On many college campuses, there are also many student organizations that focus specifically on issues that may matter to Latinx students. These Latinx student organizations may promote awareness on issues affecting Latinx communities, create a space for celebrating Latinx' cultural heritage, or provide community service. Many colleges, just as in many high schools, have a Movimiento Estudiantil Chicano de Aztlán (MEChA) chapter. In addition, many colleges may also have performance groups that celebrate Latinx culture, such as Ballet Folklorico or Mariachi. Latinx student organizations may also exist that provide additional support and a supportive environment for the identity development of students. For example, many colleges also have a La Familia student organization that supports LGBT Latinx students. Also, many colleges have student organizations that focus on Latina or Latino issues specifically. Many of these Latinx student organizations may be associated with the ethnic or multicultural centers on a campus.

Participation in these student organizations often help students make many important connections and learn many valuable skills outside of the classroom. Through these organizations, students interact with other students who are interested in similar issues, build connections to staff and faculty on a college, and develop networks that can last a lifetime. In addition, through your involvement in these types of organizations, you can make an impact within the college and surrounding community and develop important leadership skills that can help you succeed after college. Indeed, for many Latinx college students, their participation in these student organizations will play a critical role in helping them succeed in college and beyond.

As you explore your college options, it is important to understand there are various types of colleges that differ in their physical characteristics, academic and social climate, resources and educational opportunities, and in the range of student organizations. Altogether, these various differences may shape your college experience at a particular institution. Thus, it is important to become familiar with these distinctions among colleges as you explore the choice that makes the most sense for you. As you are exploring colleges broadly, it is critical to consider these same factors for the particular STEM majors and programs that you are interested in because not every college will necessarily offer the same academic programs, and the differences between these programs at different colleges may also impact the college experience you will have.

CHOOSING A STEM PROGRAM

When choosing a STEM major, a student is not only choosing a set of particular courses that make up a degree but also a college environment, which includes the classrooms and the program, the department, and perhaps even the field if one is trying to pursue a career that is directly related to your academic major. Thus, it is important to have a strong understanding of these environmental factors when making your decision to choose a particular STEM major. You will find that this choice can have lifelong career implications. In this section, you will find information on the various types of STEM majors as well as additional factors to consider when choosing a major in STEM.

Types of STEM Majors and Programs

The total number of STEM majors varies depending on which list you look at. There are 415 majors that belong to STEM disciplines according to the 2012 STEM-Designated Degree Program List from the Department of Homeland Security (DHS, 2012). However, the National Science Foundation's (NSF) STEM Classification of Instructional Programs lists only 136 (Louis Stokes Alliances for Minority Participation, n.d.).

While these lists are long and demonstrate the complexity of STEM majors, most of those majors can be listed under umbrella disciplines such as agricultural sciences, chemistry, computer science, engineering, environmental science, geosciences, life/biological sciences, mathematics, and physics/astronomy, among others. Each of these areas has several specializations. For example, some engineering majors include aerospace/aeronautical and astronautical engineering, civil engineering, chemical engineering, electrical engineering, mechanical engineering, and industrial engineering. Some majors listed under environmental sciences include environmental studies and environmental science. Majors listed under physics/astronomy include astronomy/astrophysics, physics, optics/optical sciences, and acoustics, while some majors listed under chemistry include chemistry, theoretical chemistry, inorganic chemistry, organic chemistry, materials chemistry, and polymer chemistry.

At some institutions, students can choose from more general or theoretical majors, which often include the words "general" or "theoretical" or are simply listed as the discipline (i.e., mathematics, chemistry, and physics) to those that are more applied, including applied mathematics, applied physics, and many others. More general or theoretical programs tend to focus more of their coursework on the theoretical underpinnings and development of disciplinary concepts, whereas more applied majors have more classes that apply concepts to real-life issues. Additionally, STEM majors continue to evolve as new fields emerge or become more interdisciplinary, drawing from two or more branches of knowledge, including neuroscience, biotechnology, nanotechnology, sustainability, mathematical biology, biochemical engineering, and biostatistics, among many others. If you are pursuing a specific major, not only is it necessary that the institution(s) you are considering offer the major, but there are other factors to consider when selecting the degree program as well.

Program Characteristics

Similar to the college level, physical or structural characteristics of STEM programs can shape your learning experience. One of the most important is the size of the program. Some programs are very large with several hundred perhaps even over 1,000 students currently enrolled, while others may be fairly small. In programs that have higher numbers of enrolled students, it is likely the majority of your classes in your major will be large or have high student-to-faculty ratios, whereas in smaller programs, most of your major classes are likely to be small. However, large courses also often have smaller discussion sections that meet each week and provide a lower student-to-instructor ratio. There are many benefits to being in smaller classes as you will be able to interact more with your instructors and get more individualized attention, though many larger programs also structure smaller learning environments into their program to meet student needs.

Program Climate

As a Latinx student pursuing a STEM degree, you may be one of a few in your degree program given that Latinx is an underrepresented group in the STEM fields. However, the specific numbers of Latinx students vary from program to program and institution to institution. For example, there may be fewer Latinx students in the environmental science program than the biology program at an institution, or vice versa. Additionally, the environmental science programs at other institutions may contain greater numbers of Latinx students than the environmental science program you may be considering. When you are only one of a few or the only Latinx student in a given program, there may be an unreasonable amount of pressure specifically placed on you to continuously perform at a very high level, resulting from others questioning your skills and whether you belong. This can cause you to feel isolated from others in the program, and you may even begin to question your own abilities and whether you belong despite possessing the talent, credentials, and skills. While this additional stress may not occur for everyone, it is important to understand that these contexts are often difficult to navigate, especially when students do not have departmental and institutional support and may lead some to leave STEM majors.

Certainly, being the only Latinx student in your program should not be a deterrent from enrolling in or continuing in the program. Breaking barriers is an important feat, especially for the generations behind you. However, it is important for students and parents to think about the climate of inclusiveness and ask those currently enrolled or alumni of the particular programs about their experiences and how they navigated their program. If you do find yourself entering a challenging or unsupportive climate, an important thing you can do to cope is to try to find supportive peers and mentors to get through the difficult times. Some ways to do this are to utilize the resources available within your program and participate in student and professional organizations.

Resources and Educational Opportunities

A strong and well-established program will have important resources available to you that are integral to your academic success, including academic/career and peer advising, internship opportunities, and opportunities to conduct research. Some or all of these resources may be at the department or institutional level, but the closer they are to your specific program, the better the resources are likely to be more tailored to your interests and needs. For example, if you are a biology major, having academic and peer advisors who work primarily with biology majors can be more useful and effective. Biology-specific advisers are likely to be much more familiar with the needs of biology students and know other resources and opportunities that are designed specifically for biology majors. The same can be said for math advisers, chemistry advisers, engineering advisers, and so on. The message here is to choose an adviser who represents the specific major you are pursuing.

Peer Advisers

These advisers may be available in some colleges, and they can also help you during your undergraduate career. Some peer adviser programs pair students and advisers based on similar academic and extracurricular interests. Peer advising is designed to provide students with a caring, supportive environment and to promote academic excellence. Peer advisers can help in ways that other mentors may not be able to because your peer adviser has taken many of the classes you will be taking, knows which faculty members are encouraging and perhaps which ones to avoid, and is aware of other important intangibles that are necessary for succeeding in the major. They also provide students with information on services and resources available at the institution, encourage involvement in institutional organizations and activities, and help increase student success.

Internship Opportunities

Providing students with internship opportunities is another way departments and institutions can help you with your long-term success in STEM. Internships give students a chance to apply classroom learning to real-world problems, provide the chance to explore a particular field, and help students gain valuable experiences in work settings. Many institutions have centers or offices that help students with the internship process. Additionally, some states have programs that facilitate the placement of students and recent graduates in certain fields. For example, the Massachusetts Life Sciences Center's Internship Program helps connect students and recent graduates who are considering career opportunities in the life sciences with the life sciences industry and helps place individuals in paid internships across the state.

Research Opportunities

Many institutions also provide opportunities to conduct research in STEM. Research opportunities are vital to success in STEM. Take advantage of them! These opportunities often materialize through established programs such as the Maximizing Access to Research Careers (MARC) and Minority Biomedical Research Support- Research Initiative for Scientific Enhancement (MBRS RISE) programs, which are structured biomedical research and training programs for undergraduate students who are underrepresented in the sciences and desire to pursue biomedical research careers. Another important program that is sponsored by the National Science Foundation is Research Experiences for Undergraduates (REUs), which allows students to spend a summer conducting research in a variety of STEM-related areas at a host institution. However, one can also participate in research in more informal ways, as some STEM faculty members will develop research projects with students who are interested in research careers.

There are many benefits for STEM undergraduates who are exposed to and conduct research, including better understanding published research studies, hands-on experience with the research process, and promoting one's aspirations to pursue and enroll in graduate studies. By participating in research, students are able to gain a deeper understanding of classroom learning, understand some of the nuances of research designs and formulating research questions and hypotheses, and gain firsthand experience in what it means to be a researcher and scholar. Other benefits of conducting research are that students are able to collaborate with others and gain on-the-job experience, possibly gain an ongoing source of one-on-one mentorship from a faculty member, and explore whether research is a potential career path. For students considering graduate and professional studies, not only does exposure to research guide some students to discover their passion for research, but many graduate and professional programs highly value research experience for admissions. In other words, if you at some point want to consider going beyond earning a bachelor's degree and moving on to earn a doctoral or professional degree, then having completed research projects is going to be a definite plus factor to get you admitted to advanced studies in STEM.

The opportunities and resources available to you in a given STEM department and college are important to consider when choosing a STEM major. Taking advantage of them will not only help you succeed in the major but also can lead to success beyond the bachelor's degree. Before choosing a particular major and college, you should seek out more information on whether these resources and opportunities are available. While this requires you to conduct additional investigation about STEM programs and resources on your own, you may discover additional resources on the college websites that are unique to your program or institution. Ultimately, the additional research you conduct on your own may help you choose the right program for you.

Professional Organizations

Whatever major you choose, there are often STEM-related student organizations and professional associations that provide critical opportunities and resources that can help you succeed. In fact, most fields have professional associations often with national, state, and regional chapters that students can join. Some examples include: the American Physical Society (physics), the American Chemical Society (chemistry), American Mathematical Society, American Institute of Biological Sciences, American Society for Biochemistry and Molecular Biology, National Society of Professional Engineers, American Society of Civil Engineers, National Association of Environmental Professionals, Association for Environmental Studies and Sciences, and the Institute of Electrical and Electronics Engineers, among many others. There are also organizations that are specifically focused on supporting the education and advancement of women in STEM, such as the Society of Women Engineers, Association for Women in Computing, Association for Women in Mathematics, and the Association for Women in Science.

While this may or may not factor into your decision to choose a particular STEM major, professional and student organizations are certainly important as they can broaden your knowledge about your field, provide career-related resources, and enhance your network. By joining an organization or association, students gain access to an enormous amount of information about different fields through access to journals, newsletters, magazines, and other publications. Additionally, professional associations provide career resources for its members, including job listings, tips on effective resumes or cover letters, negotiating strategies, seminars and training, and information about scholarships and other opportunities for furthering your career.

Furthermore, these associations often have national or local conferences and sponsor events where you have the opportunity to learn about current research, new ideas or best practices, and breaking news in your field. At conferences and events, one can also volunteer, meet and develop friendships with people in your field as well as find mentors or even become a mentor. While membership in these associations and organizations provide important resources, it is also important to note that listing on your resume that you are a member of a STEM-related association or organization is highly regarded by many employers and graduate schools as it shows that you are dedicated to your profession.

STEM-Related Latina/Latino Professional Organizations

In addition to the general STEM-focused student organizations and professional associations, there are a variety of STEM professional organizations and associations that have been established to support Latinx students pursuing STEM careers. Some of these groups include the Society of Hispanic Professional Engineers (SHPE), National Society of Hispanic Physicists (NSHP), Society for the Advancement Chicanos and Native Americans in Science (SACNAS), and Latino Medical Student Association (LMSA). Additionally, there may be student organizations that are campus-specific such as Chicanos/Latinos for Community Medicine at the University of California, Los Angeles. Similar to organizations for Black/African American and American Indian STEM students, many of these organizations were created to challenge stereotypes of Latinx students in STEM and provide important networks and resources for career development.

Similar to the general STEM-focused professional associations, STEM professional organizations and associations that support Latinx students pursuing STEM careers sponsor events and conferences, have student and professional chapters, provide information about scholarships and jobs, and allow one to access to a variety of publications. Many of these organizations describe in their mission statements goals of academic success for Latinx STEM students, celebrating cultural heritage, developing agents of change, and empowering Latinx communities. For example, the Rensselaer Polytechnic Institute SHPE's statement of values (SHPE-Rensselaer, n.d.) states, *"We are brought together by heritage, social responsibility and desire to improve the equality of all people through the use of science and technology. We value excellence in education, professional pursuits and leadership. We obtain excellence through integrity, empowerment, achievement, diversity and continuous improvement."*

Making an Impact with Your STEM Degree

If you are wondering whether you can make a significant impact with a STEM degree, the answer is YES! With your STEM degree, you will be able to make a positive impact on your community or society at large. You may sometimes hear other students asking, "What am I going to do with this in the future or in my life?"

Also, you may hear from some STEM professors that if you "want to make a difference in society, you should pursue a social science degree." The truth is that both a STEM degree and a social science degree can lead individuals to make a significant impact on society.

One of the most significant ways to use your STEM degree to make a difference is pursuing a health-related career. Latinx communities face growing inequalities in access to health care, and research has shown that health and dental professionals who are Latinx (as well as American Indian and Black/African American) are more likely to serve racial/ethnic minority and medically underserved communities. Doctors Without Borders is an international medical humanitarian organization that provides opportunities for health professionals to serve communities in need throughout the world.

Similarly, Latinx communities and other communities of color in the United States face a disproportionate burden of pollution and other environmental health hazards, which lead to many problems for our communities. Thus, by pursuing degrees focused on environmental science, environmental studies, environmental engineering, and sustainability, one can certainly address these very critical issues faced by Latinx communities. There are many environmental justice organizations in communities across the country as well as other nonprofit organizations and agencies that address these important issues.

Given the structural and health issues many Latinx communities experience, individuals can make a significant impact through engineering. Biomedical and biological engineers work on many medical, health, and environmental issues. Civil engineers design, construct, and maintain the physical and naturally built environment. As a result, civil engineers influence what our communities look like, including whether large sources of pollution are built near schools or people's homes. Engineers Without Borders is an international organization that serves the needs of disadvantaged communities through engineering projects.

Students can also make a positive impact on Latinx communities and society by pursuing careers in research. Degrees in mathematics and statistics, for example, can provide a strong foundation of the quantitative skills one needs to conduct research. Well-designed research studies can have a meaningful impact on underserved communities, and computer and mathematical modeling can be used to examine an array of societal problems. Indeed, one can transfer these skills and utilize them in many different fields, whether that is in STEM or non-STEM areas of research. Finally, you can use your STEM degrees to make a difference for Latinx communities and low-income communities by becoming a STEM teacher in underserved elementary, middle, and high schools, as well as by working in nonprofit organizations or in the policy arena.

CHOOSING THE BEST COLLEGE AND STEM PROGRAM

From this chapter, you can see that there are many types of colleges and STEM programs. Every student is different and may be seeking different experiences while attending college. To find the best fit for you, it will be important to consider the many factors that appeal to what you are wanting from your college experience and future career in STEM. This will require you to do your own research and find answers that can give you a sense of what each college and its STEM programs offer.

You can find much of this college information online. There are popular websites such as U.S. News & World Report (https://www.usnews.com/best-colleges) and Peterson's Guide (https://www.petersons.com) that compare and rank colleges on different characteristics. The U.S. Department of Education also has two websites, College Navigator (http://nces.ed.gov/collegenavigator) and The College Scorecard (https://collegescorecard.ed.gov) that provide information on colleges where you can compare colleges on various factors. Although these resources are a great place to start learning about different colleges, it is important to focus on the characteristics that matter most to you. Once you gather a list of possible colleges that interest you, you can go directly to those colleges' websites where often there will also be more detailed information on the STEM programs. You can also speak with your teachers and counselors at your school. If your school has a college/career center, be sure to stop by there, and attend information sessions for colleges that interest you if they are available. Often, if these are not offered at your high school, cities or communities host college nights where many colleges come to share information. Be sure to attend these if possible to gather information and ask questions.

You can also find information in books or magazines that will highlight some colleges and programs, and then look further into those by reviewing their information online or speaking with an admission officer from that college. It is also important to visit some of these colleges in person so that you can get a feel for that college's academic and social climate. If you do not have a chance to visit a college before applying, you can still visit after you are admitted to ensure that it is a good fit. If finances are of concern, some colleges often provide you with travel scholarship/financial support to make a campus visit possible once you are accepted.

You will want to start your research on colleges and STEM programs as early as possible so that you become aware of the various options that may be a good fit for you. Be sure that you are aware of the admissions requirements for each college and STEM program that interest you. Take the necessary classes to meet entrance requirements, including Advanced Placement (AP) or honors courses if these are offered at your school, and do well in all of your classes, especially in math and science. Be sure to take the college entrance exams (SAT or ACT) if a college requires these and do your best.

Apply to several colleges that seem like a good fit. Aim high and apply to several colleges, even if they seem more difficult to be accepted. This is especially true if it is a college that seems to provide the various things that you are seeking for in your college experience. Again, try not to let finances affect your decision on whether to apply, since many colleges do offer fee waivers to help students who qualify to apply without having to pay the application fee. Each college will have its own process for these fee waivers. Ask your guidance counselor or a college admissions representative if you have specific questions about your application material.

Try to have someone review your college essays if they are required, or have someone review your applications so that you make sure they are complete and ready for submission. Submit your applications on time, and also be sure to respond to any follow-up emails that colleges may send you as they are reviewing your application. Many colleges now use online portals where all this information is updated as your application is being reviewed. If this is the case, you want to be sure to visit the portal frequently to make sure that you remain informed along the way. Also, be sure to submit your FAFSA on time, send your college test scores to the colleges where you apply, and apply to any additional scholarships for which you may qualify.

Throughout this process, it is also important to discuss your college aspirations and plans with your family or any other individuals, such as teachers, advisers and counselors, or other community members who are interested in your success. These individuals can provide instrumental support whether they attended college or not. In fact, for many Latinx students, families serve as a primary source of motivation for pursuing college. In addition, some of these individuals may be able to provide additional guidance in the research and application process. If you are financially dependent on your parents' income, keeping them informed is especially important, since financial aid documents will rely on their income. If your parents have any concerns about the colleges you are interested in attending, it will be critical to connect them to extended family members, other parents who have children who have gone to college, or to college representatives who can provide information that will address any questions your parents may have.

Once you hear back from colleges about your admission's decision, you will have to decide which college is the best for you. Consult with your parents, teachers, counselors, and any other trusted individuals who are committed to your success. Take into consideration all of the factors that matter the most to you, and select the college and STEM program that provides you with an academically and personally rewarding experience and a strong foundation for your future success.

REFERENCES

Department of Homeland Security (DHS). (2012). *STEM-Designated degree program list*. Retrieved from https://www.ice.gov/sites/default/files/documents/Document/2014/stem-list.pdf

NSF STEM Classification of Instructional Programs Crosswalk. (n.d.). *Louis Stokes alliances for minority participation*. Retrieved from https://www.lsamp.org/help/help_stem_cip_2010.cfm

SHPE-Rensselaer. (n.d.). About Us: Welcome to SHPE-Rensselaer! Retrieved from http://shpe.rpi.edu/about-us.html

CHAPTER THREE

STEP 3: Paying for College

Vincent D. Carales, Ripsimé Bledsoe, and Amaury Nora

One of the most important decisions in a young person's life is deciding to go to college. Once that decision has been made, the student is left with the question—how do I pay for that college education? For many families, financial aid is the only way to help pay for the costs associated with a college education. Without financial aid, some students cannot afford to go to college. In this chapter, we will go over the different types of federal and nonfederal financial aid available to science, technology, engineering, and mathematics (STEM) and non-STEM students. We will begin by reviewing the purpose of student financial aid, see who can receive financial aid, and go over the application process. We will tackle such questions as—What happens once you complete your Free Application for Federal Student Aid (FAFSA)? What is an award letter? What is the process for receiving financial aid awards from a college? In addition, we will discuss what grades are necessary to keep your financial aid eligibility, commonly called maintaining *satisfactory academic progress*. We conclude the chapter by providing tips on paying for college, offer guidance on financial literacy and provide a list of important resources related to financial aid and planning for college.

FEDERAL AND STATE FINANCIAL AID

What Is Financial Aid?

The U.S. Department of Education gives federal financial aid to college students in the form of grants, work study, and student loans. Financial aid helps cover college expenses such as:

- tuition and fees
- room and board

- books and supplies
- transportation

It is also intended to help pay for personal or miscellaneous expenses including:

- costs associated with taking care of a dependent child
- having to purchase classroom lab equipment
- buying a necessary computer
- studying abroad

If you believe that you have any unusual expenses that might affect your cost of attendance (i.e., medical or disability), you should contact your college's financial aid office. There are many types of financial assistance available, including institutional, state, and federal aid. While the intent of this chapter is to provide a general overview of federal financial aid programs that are available to STEM students, a brief discussion will also be provided on institutional and nonfederal aid programs.

How Do I Qualify for Financial Aid?

To qualify for federal financial aid, there are five basic eligibility requirements that you must meet:

- earned a high school diploma or GED,
- enrolled in a degree-seeking or certificate program,
- maintain satisfactory academic progress,
- have U.S. citizenship or eligibility as a noncitizen,
- registered with the Selective Service (for males only).

The most useful pieces of information needed in applying for federal financial aid are: (1) the student's and parent's Social Security numbers, (2) appropriate tax returns, (3) W-2s, and (4) records of untaxed income or individual financial statements. Although many of these items are not necessarily needed or required, having them available at the time you are completing the FAFSA application will be useful in helping to accurately answer questions on the application. For more specific information on eligibility requirements, you can visit www.studentaid.ed.gov.

What Is the FAFSA?

The *Free Application for Federal Student Aid* (FAFSA) is the application that is required of all students to start the process of applying for financial aid. The application can be accessed through the website www.FAFSA.ed.gov and is available in both English and Spanish. Detailed step-by-step instructions for completing the

FAFSA can be found at https://studentaid.ed.gov/sa/fafsa/filling-out. The website offers a toll-free number that you may use to help in completing the application. Most high schools and colleges also offer *free FAFSA nights or college fair programs* to help students complete their FAFSA applications. It is highly recommended that families attend these informational sessions. These programs are offered in early January and extend through April. It is not required that the application be completed by a professional individual, and you are *not required to pay anyone* to complete the FAFSA application. You and your family should be very cautious of agencies, companies, or online entities that offer to submit the FAFSA application for you, especially online advertisements offering to "find you free money."

What Is the First Step to Apply for Financial Aid?

The first step in applying for financial aid is a request for a federal student aid (FSA) ID, a username and password combination that allows you to sign your FAFSA electronically. FSA IDs can also be used to access other financial aid information online. Although you typically request a FSA ID at the same time you complete the FAFSA form, it is also possible to acquire a FSA ID ahead of time to help speed the application process. Receiving a FSA ID may take some time. Both you and at least one of your parents can obtain a FSA ID at https://fsaid.ed.gov. Finally, make sure you and/or your parents have completed and submitted your income tax returns to the IRS. Filling your taxes allows you to transfer all tax information into your FAFSA through the IRS link, the fastest way to get tax information into your FAFSA.

When Do I Apply for Financial Aid?

Most students apply at the beginning of their final semester of high school. In the past, January was the earliest students and their families could begin filling out their FAFSA using the income earned in a prior year. However, recent rule changes now allow you to apply for financial aid as early as October of your senior year, using your family income from two prior years. Completing the FAFSA earlier will provide you with the opportunity to find out sooner rather than later what types of financial aid packages you can expect. This new rule serves as a huge advantage for you and your family if you would like to save time and get a clearer financial picture as early as possible.

Additionally, in order to be eligible for financial aid, you must *re-apply every year*, even if you have previously received financial aid. While different colleges set different priority deadlines, a good rule of thumb is to submit the FAFSA application by February 14th (Valentine's Day) of every year that you are enrolled in college. It is best to check with your college about any specific priority deadlines, especially when applying for merit-based institutional or state aid. Oftentimes, missing a priority deadline means becoming ineligible for potential gift aid in the form of state or institutional grants and scholarships. *Applying online is the easiest and most efficient way to submit an application.* While you can submit paper applications, it is not recommended as it will delay the approval process and the disbursement of funds to your school. The most important reason for completing and turning in a FAFSA application early is that you will be able to carefully evaluate the different aid packages that colleges will offer.

Can I Apply for Financial Aid at Multiple Schools?

One last important aspect of FAFSA is that you can apply for financial aid and send FAFSA application data to 10 institutions all at the same time regardless of whether you have been admitted or not to any one of those 10 institutions. Using an online search option on the FAFSA application, you may select 10 institutions of your choice. The FAFSA application also gives you the ability to compare each college's tuition costs, their graduation rates, and other considerations. If you are admitted to multiple institutions, you will receive multiple award letters to consider. An award letter from an institution is an official financial aid notification, and it includes a detailed listing of the types of financial aid (i.e., grants, loans, and work study) that you will be able to accept or decline. Keep in mind that *you will still need to accept or decline your awards* at the institution you finally choose to attend. The award letter just tells you what you have been offered at that college. Follow the directions on the letter, or find out what you need to do to accept your award money.

How Do I Know If I Qualify as a Dependent or Independent Student?

The federal government determines a student's dependency status based on a variety of circumstances, but the most common criteria is a student's age. This important status establishes if you will be required to submit your parent's income information. Most students coming out of high school are *considered dependent until the age of 24.* However, a student may also be considered as having *independent status* if they are:

- married,
- working on a master's or doctoral degree,
- taking care of children who receive more than half of their support from the student,
- on active duty in the Armed Forces or a Veteran,
- in foster care or have been a ward of the court since the age of 13,
- an emancipated minor or have legal guardianship as determined by their state of residence,
- homeless or at risk of being homeless.

One of the most common misconceptions about how students qualify for independent status is the belief that if you do not live at home with your parents, you are automatically granted independent status and, therefore, should not include parental information on the FAFSA. Not living at home or having parents that refuse to contribute financially for an education is not a justifiable reason to change your status from dependent to independent. *Even when your parents no longer claim you as a dependent for tax purposes, that does not qualify you for independent status.* On the other hand, certain *special circumstances* do exist that allow an institution to consider you as an in independent student for financial aid purposes. Some of those circumstances include but are not limited to: (1) parental incarcerations; (2) history of abuse in the home; and (3) other mental or emotional extenuating circumstances. It is advisable to check with your college's financial aid office to understand the proper steps in establishing dependency status especially if you wish to be considered as independent. If that is the case, it will not be necessary to supply your parents' information on the FAFSA application. Acquiring independent status could change the type of financial aid available to the student but *it does not necessarily guarantee more money for financial aid.*

What Does Cost of Attendance Mean?

Cost of attendance (COA) is the average amount of money necessary to pay for tuition and fees, room and board, books and supplies, transportation, and other educational expenses, and it is determined by the institution you plan to attend. It is included in an official award letter. The amount necessary to attend college depends on the college you choose to attend. Most two-year and four-year colleges calculate the annual cost of attendance based on two long semesters, fall and spring. Colleges that follow a quarter-system calculate the annual cost of attendance over three quarters—fall, winter and spring. Whenever summer financial aid is awarded, it is based on the actual number of summer months attended.

What Does Expected Family Contribution Mean?

An *expected family contribution* (EFC) is the total that financial aid staff uses in determining how much and what types of financial aid you will receive. EFC is *not the amount of money that your family will have to pay* but it is *the amount indicating what your family should be able to pay* for you to attend college for that year. The EFC amount is provided right after the FAFSA application is submitted electronically. More importantly, it is not the amount of federal student aid you will receive. Colleges use the EFC to calculate the type and the amount of financial aid awarded to you.

Based on the information you reported on the FAFSA application, a formula is used to determine your EFC. Information such as the size of your family, the number of family members who will attend college during the academic year, family taxed and untaxed income, assets, and benefits (such as unemployment or Social

Figure 3.1   Calculating Financial Need

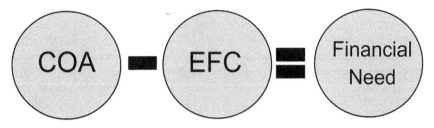

Security) are some of the components used in determining your EFC. This estimated family contribution, along with the cost of attending college, is used in determining your *financial need* and the types of aid that can be awarded by your college's financial aid office. See Figure 3.1 to calculate financial need using a simple formula.

What Types of Financial Aid Are Available?

There are two types of financial aid: *need* and *non-need* based financial aid. Need-based financial aid is based solely on your financial need and is determined through the FAFSA. This type of aid includes grants, work study, and subsidized loans. Non-need-based aid programs are unsubsidized student and parent loans. Also included in non-need-based aid programs are those financial aid programs based on merit, usually in the form of state grant programs or institutional scholarships. Merit-based aid programs are awarded based on academic performance (grades) or standardized test scores and are sometimes designated for students in specific areas such as athletics, music, etc.

What Are Grants?

The largest and most common federal financial aid program is the *Federal Pell Grant*. The amount of grant money you receive depends on your EFC. Moreover, maximum amounts vary each year. For example, the maximum amount of money that students could receive for the 2015–2016 award year (July 1, 2015, to June 30, 2016) was $5,775 based on *financial need*, cost of attendance (COA), enrollment status (full- or part-time), and whether the student was enrolled throughout the whole year.

Important Details About Pell Grant:

- Pell Grant available for no more than 12 semesters (about six years).
- Student notified when close to maximum number of semesters.

- Receive full Pell Grant if enrolled full-time.
- May not receive Pell Grants at multiple institutions at the same time.
- If enrolled at multiple institutions, accept Pell Grant at institution where pursuing degree/certificate.

Another type of federal grant assistance is the *Federal Supplemental Educational Opportunity Grant* (FSEOG) program. These grants are handled directly by your college's financial aid office, but not all colleges participate. Check with your financial aid office to determine if the campus offers the FSEOG.

Important Details About FSEOG:

- Awards range from $100 to $4,000 yearly.
- Dependent on financial need and other need-based aid awards.
- FSEOG grants are limited since they are campus-based, meaning not all colleges participate in program, and allocations may vary.
- Awards usually for students who meet priority deadlines for institution.
- Crucial to *apply early and meet deadlines* to ensure eligibility for FSEOG and other campus-based financial aid.

State-based aid grant programs are also awarded based on need and meeting priority deadlines. Priority deadlines are application deadline dates (the date that your application must be submitted to the school) usually set by the financial aid office as part of the eligibility criteria for certain types of financial aid program. These types of grant programs and deadlines are different in every state, and anyone interested in those grants must contact financial aid offices in those states to inquire about specific requirements related to their state-based grant aid programs.

What Is Federal Work Study?

The Federal Work Study (FWS) program is a need-based federal program that provides employment opportunities for students. The purpose of work study is to provide students with a work environment that is convenient and flexible. Most work study positions will work around your class schedule. As a source of employment, the work study program offers colleges the ability to provide part-time jobs for full-time and part-time undergraduate and graduate students to help pay for the cost of their education. Depending on the amount of the award, you can work up to 20 hours a week while classes are in session. Similar to a regular job, the college will provide you with an actual pay check, usually bi-weekly, that you can then cash and use for college expenses.

Important Details About Work Study:

- Part-time jobs usually offered on or off-campus depending on institution/department offering job.
- Apply for work study positions that closely align with academic or career goals.
- Indicate interest in work study on FAFSA application.
- Always decline work study award if you decide not to work.
- Work study positions typically pay based on amount awarded in FWS, hours worked per week, period of employment, anticipated wage rate, and amount of other need-based financial aid awarded to you.
- Average pay for most FWS jobs is federal minimum wage (some college departments will offer higher hourly wage depending on job duties).
- Some work study positions can be extended to regular part-time positions after federal work study funds run out.
- Major benefit of a work study job is access to more opportunities for work experience and professional development.

What Type of Loans Are Available to Students?

When you submit a FAFSA application for financial aid, you are automatically considered for a student loan as well. Regardless of whether or not you are interested in applying for a loan, many financial aid awards will include some type of loan. With student loans, you are considered the borrower and responsible for repayment. More likely than not, these loans will be direct *subsidized* or *unsubsidized loans*. Many colleges also offer state-based loans or other types of institutional or campus-based loans as part of the financial assistance provided to students. Interest rates on federal student loans vary by year; you are highly encouraged to check with your institution's financial aid office to obtain current rates as they can change each year.

What Are Federal Direct Subsidized Loans?

A *direct subsidized* student loan is also known as a need-based loan. The benefits associated with this type of loan are that you do not pay any interest on the loan while you are enrolled in college at least half-time, and, after graduation, there is a six-month grace period before you must begin to repay the loan. Furthermore, any interest accumulated will be paid by the government during the period you are enrolled in courses at least half-time. Annual award limits are based on the school year in which you are enrolled and range between $3,500 for first-year students and up to $5,500 for seniors.

What Are Federal Direct Unsubsidized Loans?

Direct unsubsidized student loans are non-need based awards. In other words, you do not need to show financial need. For these types of loans, you are responsible for repayment of the loan plus accruing interest from the moment you receive the loan. You have the option to pay *only the interest* (billed quarterly by the lender) during the time you are enrolled in school, or you can opt to have the interest be *capitalized* (added to the loan principal) and must pay it back when the loan enters repayment. Payments are required after you are no longer enrolled for a period of more than six months, or if you are enrolled less than half-time. In much the same way, as with direct subsidized loans, annual award limits for direct unsubsidized loans are based on your year in school and can vary anywhere between $5,500 to $12,500.

What Are Federal Perkins Loans?

Federal Perkins loans are a source of federal financial assistance awarded to undergraduate, graduate, or professional students with financial need. However, these types of loans are only available to you if you attend a college or university that actively participates in the program. You should check with the financial aid office in the college you are attending to see if your institution is participating. These loans are made available to students from a college's revolving account that consists of repayments made from previous student borrowers. Because some colleges have high default rates on the part of their students, funds are not available at all colleges for these federal Perkins loans.

Interest rates for both undergraduate and graduate Perkins loans are 5 percent, slightly above the current rates for undergraduate subsidized and unsubsidized loans. However, the interest rate is fixed and does not change over the life of the loan. Perkins student loans must be paid back to the college that awarded the loan. Undergraduate students may qualify for an annual award of $5,500 (and a maximum of $27,500 as an undergraduate). Graduate students may qualify for an annual award of $8,000 (and a maximum of $60,000, including previous undergraduate Perkins loans).

What Are Federal Direct PLUS Loans?

PLUS loans are federally funded loans that graduate students and parents of dependent undergraduate students can use to help pay for educational expenses. The main qualification for these types of loans is the borrower's creditworthiness. Typically, one of your parents must be creditworthy, or, in other words, they do not have bad credit history. The maximum loan amount can cover the full cost of attendance (determined by the college) minus any other forms of financial aid awarded. The parent borrowing the money may receive the funds directly or have the funds apply to your tuition bill or invoice. Repayment begins after the full loan amount is disbursed, but the parent who borrowed the loan has the option to defer payment if they are also enrolled in college.

Are There Other Types of Aid?

Although Title IV federal financial aid programs (grants, work study, and loans) funded by the federal government provide the largest means of financial aid to students to attend college, they are not the only source. Other sources of federal student aid include *tax credits* that can be used when filing taxes and aid that is specifically targeted for healthcare professions, teachers, and veterans. These forms of financial assistance available to students and their parents are often overlooked, and it is advised that students research these opportunities carefully.

Nonfederal sources of financial aid include public and private state grants and loans and *prepaid tuition or college savings plans*. A full description of these types of resources is beyond the scope of this chapter, and it is strongly encouraged that you contact your state educational agency regarding the availability of state financial aid programs. Oftentimes, information of these types of state programs is difficult to find. You are highly encouraged to contact your institution's financial aid office regarding these funding opportunities. In many instances, the eligibility criteria for these financial aid opportunities are specific to the individual student, making it necessary to inquire as to the nature of those criteria. *Financial aid administrators are keenly aware of their respective state's financial aid programs and are typically the best resource to contact.*

How and When Do I Receive My Financial Aid?

Figure 3.2 provides you with a college and FAFSA application timeline that begins during the junior year of high school and continues until you begin attending college. These are the overall steps to receiving your financial aid:

Step 1: Submit FAFSA application, and complete all financial aid requirements set by the college you are attending.

Step 2: If you are admitted to an institution, you will receive a financial aid award letter from the college for you to review the aid given to you.

Step 3: Your financial aid awards are credited to your account minus tuition, fees, and any other institutional expenses such as books and housing that are billed by the college.

Step 4: A refund of the remaining balance (after college bills are paid) will be issued via check or direct deposit to your bank. *Note: It is important to have direct deposit setup with your college's accounting office prior to disbursement of funds; otherwise a check will be mailed.*

Important Things to Keep in Mind:

• At some institutions, receiving your financial aid payment occurs after the enrollment census date (usually two weeks into the semester).

Figure 3.2   College and FAFSA Application Timeline

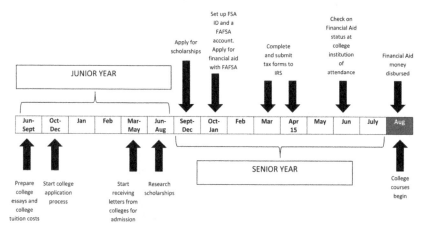

- Financial aid awards can be adjusted and reduced based on the number of hours that you enroll in or if you have dropped any courses.
- It is your responsibility to ensure that your financial aid monies are used specifically for housing off-campus and other educational expenses.
- The college will only give you the balance of your financial aid after institutional costs have been subtracted.

NONFEDERAL FINANCIAL AID

What Are Institutional (College or University-Specific) Scholarships?

One of the most important tasks for high school students to undertake at the end of their junior year and during the summer before their senior year is to begin searching for scholarships. You should visit individual college campuses and the department of your major to find out what types of scholarships are offered and their specific deadlines. For many colleges, their deadlines fall between December and February. Most colleges typically have one scholarship application form that they use in awarding institution and department scholarships. Keep in mind that to be eligible for these scholarships, most higher education institutions require that you be admitted to the college. Campus-wide scholarships, commonly known as *institutional scholarships*, are awards that are funded through private donors, alumni association, or endowment programs and have been set up for respective departments (e.g., science, technology, engineering, and math). In the case of department scholarships, these awards are specific to a major or program of study. For example, if you are majoring in biology, the institution's college of sciences might have scholarships specifically for biology majors. In most instances, these types of awards require *separate* scholarship application forms. If you are interested in this type of scholarship, it is important to check with the individual department that admitted you as a student. Currently, many departments list their scholarships on their departmental websites for each specific program or major. Make sure that you inquire about these opportunities with the appropriate departments.

What Is the College Scholarship Service Financial Aid PROFILE®?

The *College Scholarship Service (CSS) Financial Aid PROFILE®* is an application developed by the College Board and is used by many colleges to award scholarships and other types of aid. The CSS Financial Aid PROFILE® asks for more information than the FAFSA form and is designed to provide a better analysis of a student's finances. It is required (in addition to the FAFSA) by almost 400 colleges, universities, professional schools, and scholarship organizations to award nonfederal financial aid. However, there is a fee that you or your parents must pay to complete the CSS/Financial Aid PROFILE®. Fee waivers are available for low-income students. You must make certain that the CSS/Financial Aid PROFILE® is completed and submitted if you are admitted to a college that requires it, or if you are applying for a specific scholarship that also requires the form. Regardless of your situation, you should always confirm whether the college you plan on attending has any additional requirements other than the FAFSA application. For more information regarding the CSS Financial Aid PROFILE®, please visit http://css .collegeboard.org/.

What Are Student Research Grants?

Research grants or scholarships are usually awarded by departments at different universities and colleges in specific majors. The Louis Stokes Alliances for Minority Participation Program (LSAMP) and the Minority Biomedical Research Support—Research Initiative for Scientific Enhancement (MBRS RISE) are two examples of these types of funding opportunities. The intent of these scholarships is to encourage students to engage in research opportunities with faculty in different subject areas. If you are interested in pursuing research while enrolled in a program of study, you should speak to representatives from specific colleges, departments, and major programs regarding these opportunities to seek out these types of scholarships.

Tips for Writing the Scholarship Essay

Oftentimes, applications for scholarships require that you write an essay as part of the application process. A good strategy is to develop one very strong essay that can be used for all scholarship applications, making slight revisions depending on the scholarship. You should begin to write a draft of your essay by the end of your junior year. A good starting point for your essay is addressing your current goals and accomplishments. Include what steps or actions you took in achieving those goals. Writing about experiences in your community, participation in extracurricular school activities, involvement in church happenings, or helping with family expenses are good examples of personal journeys to use for your essay. Other topics for you to consider are: *What makes you, as an individual, unique? What experiences helped shape who you are?*

Important Things to Keep in Mind as You Search for Scholarships and Write Your Essay

- Treat the search process for scholarships like a part-time job.
- Be willing to go the extra mile during the search process.
- Extra effort and time will often lead to finding free money.
- Make sure you have a FAFSA on file regardless of whether a scholarship is merit or need-based.
- Have one of your teachers or counselors review your essay; it makes a difference.
- Keep in mind that changes to your essay will be necessary as you apply for admissions at different institutions or when you apply for a variety of scholarships.
- Begin to ask for letters of recommendation from teachers, counselors, or others leaders in your community at the end of your junior year or at the beginning of your senior year.
- Make copies of those recommendation letters, as they will be needed for admissions and scholarship applications.

Managing Your Money

Most colleges and universities have a financial aid department that can help you budget your money. It is no surprise that students who are smart in how they spend their money while in college are better off financially when they finish. *A very important piece of financial advice is not to use or rely on credit cards to meet college expenses.* The following tips are intended to help you manage your money:

- Borrow smart and do not borrow more than you need.
- Develop a spending plan to track college expenses and determine personal educational needs and wants.
- Keep track of expenses and always budget for needs (i.e., rent, car payment, tuition, books, clothing, and living expenses) *versus* wants (i.e., eating out and going to concerts).

• Visit Adventures in Education at www.aie.org for useful online tools on managing and reducing debt, understanding and managing credit cards, developing good spending habits, and learning how to manage student loan repayment.

Maintaining Eligibility and Satisfactory Academic Progress

To remain eligible for financial aid each year, you must meet and maintain *satisfactory academic progress* (SAP). Meeting this SAP requirement means completing a degree or certificate in a timely manner, maintaining a satisfactory grade point average (GPA), and completing the courses you attempted each year. Each college sets its own SAP policy for financial aid purposes and the requirements for a satisfactory grade point average (GPA) as well as the necessary number of completed courses per semester. In addition, SAP policies provide detailed information on how an incomplete grade, withdrawal, repeated classes, change of major, and transfer of credits from another institution may impact your satisfactory academic progress. *Maintaining satisfactory academic progress is one of the most important components of remaining eligible for financial aid each year you are in college*.

Institutional SAP policies will include three important guidelines:

• When your college will evaluate your SAP progress (the end of the semester *versus* the end of the academic year).
• Any consequences if you fail to maintain satisfactory academic progress such as scholastic probation.
• The appeals process for reinstatement of financial aid if you do not meet mandatory SAP requirements.

A Final Message: Student Loan Default

There are many financial aid opportunities to help pay for a college education, and *borrowing money* from the federal government to pay for a college degree should be taken very seriously. You need to be aware that you are totally *responsible for repaying* any student loans that you borrow for educational expenses, and there are negative consequences that can adversely affect your life if you default on student loans. Loan repayment usually begins six months after you graduate from college or six months after you drop below half-time enrollment. Defaulting on a student loan means failure to make monthly loan payments for 270 consecutive days. There are six different ways in which defaulting on a student loan can negatively impact your life:

- Your federal and state income tax refunds can be withheld.
- You cannot renew professional licenses such as medical, legal, real estate, or cosmetology.
- You will have a negative credit history.
- Your wages will be garnished (kept by the government) until your student loan is repaid in full.
- You may lose eligibility for deferment, forbearance, and flexible repayment plans.
- You may lose eligibility for additional federal student aid to continue your education.

For more information regarding obtaining student loans, defaulting on student loans, or any of the information presented in this chapter, please visit www .studentaid.gov. It is our hope that this chapter will help you identify and secure the financial assistance necessary to make your educational dreams come true. The following web resources are provided to further assist in finding and understanding financial aid, completing necessary application forms, and advice on planning for a college education.

Important Web Resources

Glossary of Financial Aid Terms
https://studentaid.ed.gov/sa/glossary

Financial Aid (always check with your college's financial aid office or student services area
www.fafsa.ed.gov
www.studentaid.gov
www.studentloans.gov
www.finaid.org
www.mappingyourfuture.org

Planning and Paying for College
www.collegeboard.org
www.aie.org (Also includes a scholarship search engine.)
www.salliemae.com

Scholarship Search Engines
www.scholarships.com
www.fastweb.com
www.scholarsite.com

PART II

Succeeding in College

CHAPTER FOUR

STEP 4: ~~Surviving~~ Thriving in the First Year of College

Vijay Kanagala, Josephine J. Gonzalez, and Jose Adrian Leon

Congratulations! You are going to college! What a proud moment for you, your family, and everyone who supported you through the college application process. During the past couple years in high school, you may have certainly mastered the art of balancing multiple expectations. In addition to doing well academically and hopefully enjoying high school, you may have had to plan and execute your college application process with absolute precision. Your college application process may have needed your undivided attention and may have included numerous detailed tasks such as exploring college options; meeting with admissions counselors; attending college fairs; visiting college campuses to meet students, staff and faculty; taking the SAT or ACT; filling out college applications; writing and rewriting your college admissions essay; gathering supplemental documents; requesting recommendation letters; meticulously submitting each application online or mailing application packets to each institution; developing a financial plan to pay for college expenses; and perhaps even interviewing for either admissions or scholarships or both.

While applying for admission to colleges is an exciting phase and a *rite of passage* in your formal educational journey, it can also be a time-consuming and stressful period in your life if you do not have the required support network and guidance to do all that is needed for a positive outcome—the coveted letter of admission to one of your top choice colleges. After an agonizing wait, your wait is finally over. You have received an offer of admission from one of your top choice colleges. Perhaps you have been accepted by multiple colleges. If you have multiple options, you should carefully weigh pros and cons of attending each institution before you make your final decision. You may want to revisit a college campus, if you are able, to make sure you like that college. You will be spending four-plus years of your life there, so your decision is very important. You can ask more specific questions during such a visit, questions you may have thought irrelevant earlier about campus/social life, living in the residence halls, library facilities, transportation, and majors. Irrespective of whether you received any scholarship in your financial aid package or not, you should compare all admissions offers, cost of education, and living expenses to decide which institution makes the best financial sense to attend without compromising your educational goals.

Once you have decided, do not wait till the deadline. Be proactive and let the admissions office of your top choice college know your decision to accept their offer. Most colleges will require that you pay a deposit as part of your acceptance decision (usually by May 1). If you have multiple admission offers, you should notify the colleges you do not plan to attend that you are declining their offers of admission. You should be aware that most college offer admissions to students on a conditional basis; that is, you should successfully complete your senior year of high school, so make sure to focus on your academics and graduate high school.

The moment you received your offer of admission, you went from being a prospective college student to becoming a first-year college student just like that! As you head to college either during the fall semester or fall quarter of the academic year, this chapter will give important information and essential resources that will ensure that you not just survive but *thrive* during your first year of college.

TRANSITIONING FROM HIGH SCHOOL TO COLLEGE

Your transition from high school to college as a first-year student can be daunting for any number of reasons. It could be that you are the first in your family to attend college, and, therefore, you do not know what to expect of what lies ahead of you. The traditions and the values at the college you plan to attend will be new, and it will take time to adjust to your new environment. It can be challenging to make friends with other students who may or may not share social and cultural identities similar to you. To aid with this transition, almost all colleges host an on campus welcome and orientation session for new students. These sessions are planned for the summer between high school graduation and before you enroll for college classes (during the months of June and/or July), and they are usually a mandatory requirement for all first-year students at many colleges. Parents and families are also invited to attend. Colleges have multiple orientation sessions, so you have the option to select dates that are convenient for you and your family to attend this two-day event. We recommend that you make plans to attend orientation early. Your successful integration into the campus begins with orientation. These events are usually hosted by a college office called the orientation and new student programs office (or a similar name).

WHAT TO EXPECT AT ORIENTATION?

Orientation is an exciting opportunity for you to get to know your future home for the next four-plus years. It can also be intimidating if you have never lived on your own or away from your family before. Before you depart to campus, make sure you have gathered all of the necessary documents and forms. Double check if you have registered yourself for all the required activities; there will be several activities that your parents or family members can opt into or opt out of based on their interests and needs. Your college will give you a detailed orientation schedule at check-in on the first day. While there may be minor differences in schedules and events depending on a college and its traditions, you can expect to participate in the following events during orientation.

Welcome Meeting with Orientation Team

Your college's orientation team is your lifeline during your visit to campus. They are dedicated staff who are your welcome crew and want to ensure that you have a pleasant and productive visit to campus. This team will have several orientation leaders who are current students (sophomores, juniors, and seniors) on campus and are a great resource to ask any questions you might have. They have been through what you are about to experience. Plus, if you like meeting people and have a great experience at orientation, you can apply to work as an orientation leader next year.

Student Picture ID and Set Up Email Account

You will soon realize that nothing is possible on a college campus without your student picture ID. Your student ID may serve as your key/access card to enter your residence hall, to check out books at the library, or to use as a debit card at the campus store. You will have to be careful not to lose your card. You will also need to set up your institutional email id to communicate with your professors and college staff.

Meet with Your Academic Adviser

You will briefly meet with your adviser to discuss your major, course requirements, and select your courses for fall semester. Depending on your college, this individual may be a faculty member in your major or a staff member whose primary role is academic advising. If you are undecided about your major, you will be assigned an adviser who can assist you in selecting the courses that meet the general education requirements across all majors, such as English, math, psychology, and science courses. Sometimes advisers may also provide you with your four-year college plan so you know what courses you need to take each semester. Before you meet your adviser, you may have to take your math and English placement tests to ensure that you are placed in the appropriate course.

Register for Fall Classes

To ensure that you hit the ground running the first day of school, your academic adviser will either register you during your advising meeting or provide you with information so you can self-register for all your fall classes online. By registering for classes, you will know details such as course number, course title, the room and building where the course is taught, the day and time when class will meet, and the name of the professor who will be teaching the course ahead of time. This will give you an opportunity to go visit the classroom or stop by and say hello to the professors, if they are teaching on campus in summer.

Student Disability/Accessibility Services

Every college has a student disability/accessibility services office to assist students who have visible and invisible learning disabilities. If you have already been diagnosed with special needs and know that you will need an accommodation in fall, you should contact this office ahead of time to set up a consultation appointment to ensure that you are able to have a barrier-free learning environment and experience.

Multicultural and Identity Centers

Your formal orientation program may or may not include a visit to your college's multicultural student center and the different identity centers such as the women's center or the lesbian, gay, bisexual, transsexual, and queer (LGBTQ) center. Make time during your visit to stop by and say hello. The staff in these offices often serve students with marginalized identities and provide a great sense of community when you return to campus in fall. During your visit, ask about each center's welcome orientation and the different programs and services they provide to students throughout the year. These are also great offices to look for work study positions.

Residential Life and Dining Services Information Sessions

At this session, staff members from your college's residential life and dining services departments will provide details about on-campus housing facilities, dining facilities and meal plans, and share the cost for on-campus room and board. Housing and meal plan contracts may be shared and are due late June/early July. Pay close attention to these contracts because they are legally binding and are usually for the nine-month academic year. These documents also outline your responsibilities as a member of the community and provide all policies and procedures governing student code of conduct. Some colleges require all their first-year students to live on campus. Be aware of this requirement before you sign up for off-campus housing.

Health and Insurance Forms

Your college may require that you maintain an electronic health record such as immunization records and laboratory reports at the student health center on campus. It is important to provide accurate and complete information about your health history in case it is necessary in an emergency situation. You may also need to show proof of health insurance. Make sure your emergency contact information is current and accurate.

Tour Campus Facilities

Orientation leaders typically lead scheduled tours of campus facilities so you have a general idea of campus geography. It can be overwhelming to remember all the facilities and buildings on campus; you will gradually learn to recognize buildings as you spend more time on campus. We recommend that you prioritize and try to remember where you will live, dining facilities, your classroom buildings, your adviser's office, tutoring or the academic success center, and the library. It is okay if you forget; you can always ask someone.

TRANSITIONING AND ADAPTING TO THE WORLD OF COLLEGE: THE FIRST-YEAR EXPERIENCE

Do you remember the first time you rode your bike without training wheels? It must have been an exciting yet nerve-racking experience. You had to ensure that you were riding in a safe location. You had to put on safety gear such as a helmet and perhaps even elbow and knee pads. You had to be certain that your bike seat was adjusted and customized to the right height, check that the brakes were functioning, and you had to learn to not only focus as you start pedaling but also pay attention to your surroundings.

Attending college is similar to learning how to ride a bike without training wheels. It can be very exciting and downright stressful. The bike represents freedom, adventure, courage, and much more, and it is analogous to your first year in college. Perhaps, for the first time in your life, you are going to have to make decisions of your own and on your own. You may have been looking forward to this next chapter of your life. You will have support all around you, but you are still the driver of your destiny. Just as when you first started riding your bike without training wheels, someone probably held your seat and provided support until you gained balance and were able to ride away. At times, falling off your bike and tending your wounds need to occur before you finally feel confident and are prepared to ride the bike again.

Similarly, this is the reality for many college students, especially Latinx first-generation STEM college students. Many aspects of your college life will be seamless if you are well prepared, but there will always be some aspects of your academic learning that are unpredictable and possibly chaotic. These experiences may at times result in feelings of isolation, frustration, and loneliness. In these instances, you can choose to teach yourself, and you can trust others (faculty and staff) around you to help guide you. Colleges provide you with the tools and the skills to successfully address these unpredictable and chaotic experiences.

While attending college is a four-plus-year affair for many students, college administrators and educators agree that the first-year college experience is possibly the most important and critical one of those years. For students of color and students with other marginalized identities (women, LGBTQ, or different ability), the first-year college experience is even more vital. To be certain that first-year students like you are successful and will remain in college, colleges often make extra efforts to introduce as many resources as possible during your first few weeks of your first year. It is also an attempt to successfully integrate you into the college's academic, social, and cultural experiences. By adopting such a strategy, your college wishes to enhance your awareness of all the resources that are available for you to take advantage of so you can thrive as a college student.

THRIVING IN YOUR FIRST YEAR OF COLLEGE

Attending college and thriving in college are interconnected. You need a specific set of tools and the knowledge to successfully navigate the world of college. Oftentimes, first-generation college students and students of color from low-income backgrounds, despite the best high school preparation, face innumerable obstacles in college to survive, let alone thrive. As a first-year college student, finding a sense of belonging in a classroom and on campus can be difficult. You are in a new environment. You are surrounded by new people, new cultures, new traditions, and new expectations. The newness around you can be overwhelming. There could be other reasons why you may be experiencing difficulty. For example, you may find it challenging to connect with your professor(s), or the course material is not as you thought it was going to be. You may be feeling homesick. It could be that English is not your primary language. This may be the first time in your life you are being taught by someone who does not look like you. Likewise, you could be the only Latinx student in your classroom. There can also be sense of "I am not enough" with respect to your academic preparation that you may feel at the pit of stomach.

As a first-generation college student, you are not alone! It can be intimidating when all your peers pull out their MacBook pros or when you are reminded of the years of AP biology and statistics your peers had in high school. Everything happening in the classroom can feel foreign. In this section, we provide tangible tools and strategies that we hope will assist Latinx college students interested in STEM disciplines and careers to thrive during their first year of college.

Get a Planner/Notebook

Being organized is a key to being successful in college, and time is a currency in college; that is, time is a very, very valuable commodity in college. Therefore, time management is an important skill to develop early in college. Check your student government or student life office for free planners. You may have received one at orientation. If not, you can purchase one at your campus bookstore. You may have a digital app on your cell phone to organize your calendar. Utilizing a planner/digital calendar will help you organize both your academic and social responsibilities.

Attend All Your Classes

It is very important that you attend all your classes, especially the first day of class. Make sure to schedule them in your planner/calendar so you do not miss a scheduled class meeting. During the first class, each professor will give you a course syllabus, set expectations, provide you with important dates for assignments and tests, and clarify questions. Once you receive your academic syllabus, make time to review it carefully. Find a buddy in your class to discuss the assignment and expectations. Treat the syllabus as your ticket to success. If you do not understand the expectations or an assignment, make note of your questions and follow up with the professor either during your second class or visit them during their office hours, which are listed on the syllabus. This demonstrates to the professor that you care about the course and your education.

Get to Know Your Professor(s)

Depending on the class size, your professor may or may not recognize you. Make an effort to set up a meeting with your professor. Introduce yourself, share a little bit about your background, your hopes and fears for the class, and ask them what is the best way to get in contact with them if you have questions about the class or assignments. This proactive effort on your part will come in handy later on in the semester/future when you may need an extension on a class assignment or need a recommendation for a scholarship or work-study position on campus. This is also a great way to connect with faculty if you are interested in working with them on a research project.

Visit Your Academic Adviser

Remember the academic adviser you met with during summer orientation. Make sure to stop by or make an appointment, and reintroduce yourself to your adviser. If you are not comfortable asking questions about courses and requirements to your professors, you can ask your adviser for assistance.

Develop Good Study Skills

Learning may have come effortlessly for you in high school, or you may have had challenges. Either way, college is a fresh start. Studying for college classes is much different than what you may be used to in high school, and it requires that you develop good study skills from the beginning. The sooner you understand this difference and adapt your learning, the more likely you will be successful in college. Your college faculty expect you to be creative, critical, and thoughtful. Use your planner. Set aside specific times for studying during the course of the day. Assess when you learn best. Are you a morning person? Or do you do your best learning at night? Depending on each course, you can set aside time to work on class assignments, read, and attend review sessions. It is important that you identify a place on campus that you can use regularly to study. This could be your college library, a lounge in your residence hall, your academic success center, or an on-campus coffee shop. Cultural and identity centers also offer great spaces to study and are often the best kept secrets.

Form a Study Group

Depending on your learning style, you can ask a group of students in your class or your residence hall to study together. This strategy allows you to hold each other accountable for your learning and develop a sense of community. Building community with your peers in and outside the classroom gives you the opportunity to take ownership for your learning. Whether you are forming or joining a study group with your peers or thinking critically about the material covered in class, owning your learning will give you the tools to overcome feelings of doubt. It will remind you what brought you here in the first place.

Get Involved on Campus!

The more involved on campus you are, the more likely you are to thrive. Being involved can occur in multiple ways. Colleges offer a variety of clubs and organizations where students can find community and common interests. These clubs and organizations could be either discipline related, such as the Society for Advancement of Chicanos and Native Americans in Science (see Chapter 10 for more national organizations), or it could be based on your identity as a Latinx student. Find out if your college has a Latinx student union, Alianza Latinx, or students of color-based club or organization on campus. Being involved in these organization allows you to develop your communication and leadership skills, qualities that are valuable in STEM careers.

The hardest part of going to college is being away from your family, community, and support networks. Sooner or later you will begin to miss the food you are used to eating, access to social and cultural events from your home community, language, and the people you used to hanging out with. College is a great place to step out your comfort zone and cultivate a better understanding of self and values. Participate in events taking place on campus. This can include programs your resident assistant (RA) plans, an event on campus, or volunteer opportunities off campus. Finding a balance between academics and your social life is important for your well-being. Learning is possible inside and outside of the classroom. Building community and solidarity with students, faculty, and staff members on your campus will remind you that you are not alone. While you may feel alone at times, know there are people on campus who are concerned about your well-being and are ready to support you.

Create Community!

Overall, we believe the learning process does not need to be painful. We do not believe experiencing feelings of isolation, frustration, and loneliness are necessarily needed in order to thrive in college. It also should not be treated as a badge of honor. Mentors can also be a huge help in finding and creating a sense of belonging. This can be a peer, your supervisor, or a professor. Any of these individuals can help you transition to campus and meet new people. Meeting new people and putting yourself out there can be nerve racking. Whether you are an introvert or extrovert, develop skills to enable you to meet and form acquaintances. These acquaintances can slowly become good friends who can be part of your social network. It is not a matter of how many people you know or how many clubs you are part of—you have to ask yourself what and who makes you feel whole, seen, heard, and motivated. Involve your parents, family, and community members from home in your college journey. Take time to reflect. What are some of your areas of strength? What have you learned about yourself since starting college? What brings you happiness about being in college? What are some challenges you are experiencing? Having thoughtful and honest conversations with yourself can help bridge both your mind and heart and help you thrive in college.

Know Your Career Counselor

Students wait to think about their careers until they are in their junior or senior year of college. Often this is late because the student may have missed many opportunities that are available through the college's career center. While you do not have to visit with a career counselor the first week of classes, we recommend that you schedule an appointment and visit the career center to know all the services they offer. They may include helping write your cover letter for a summer position, developing your resume, or simply knowing about summer internship opportunities. Counselors may also be able to help you develop a career plan, set realistic goals, and make sure you are pursuing the right major if you are interested in a specific STEM career.

STEM SPECIFIC ACADEMIC SUPPORT SERVICES

Knowing and utilizing the numerous student services that may be available to you is the key to your success in college. There are many different campus services that provide additional academic, social, cultural, and financial support. In order to get the most out of your college experience, make sure to learn about all the resources your college offers. The professional staff members within the campus services want to see you succeed and will try their best to make sure you are provided with the best support you can possibly have. Your college experience can be vastly different depending on how often you choose to use these campus services. In this section, we share information about three college program and services: academic support services, TRiO programs, and learning communities focused on STEM disciplines. Chapters 6 and 9 offer examples of specific institutions and programs related to STEM across all 50 states and Puerto Rico. You should also reach out to your adviser and/or faculty mentors at your college to inquire about other programs that may be specifically related to your major.

Academic Support Services

Within your first year of college, you should learn and develop a sense of how you work academically depending on how much time you invest in your education. The biggest transition you may experience is understanding that college is different from your high school academic experience. There are academic support services at your college that can help provide you with support with being academically successful inside the classroom. For example, within most academic support services, you can find either a tutoring center or a supplemental instruction office that will offer instructional facilities outside the classroom. These centers hire upper class students (sophomores, juniors, and seniors) who have passed the course you may be having challenges with to teach and help you with course assignments. Many students choose to create study groups and have study sessions with one another. Entering your first year of college can be academically challenging, and by using academic support services on your campus, you can begin to understand how higher education works. There are many different academic support services across various colleges across the country. Each one provides a unique opportunity for students to achieve success throughout their college education.

TRiO Programs

Colleges may have outreach and student services programs that are specifically designed to serve students from disadvantaged background. The federal TRiO program (TRiO) is one such federally funded initiative that serves and assists low-income, first-generation college students and individuals with disabilities to progress through the academic pipeline from middle school to post baccalaureate programs. Specifically, you should be aware of the Student Support Services Program (SSSP), and the Ronald E. McNair Post-Baccalaureate Achievement Program (McNair Program).

The SSSP provides you with opportunities for academic development, assists you with basic college requirements, and motivates you toward the successful completion of your degree. The goal of SSSP is to increase the college retention and graduation rates of its participants.

If you are interested in pursuing graduate school and are able to demonstrate strong academic potential, you may be eligible to participate in the McNair program. By participating in this program, you will receive mentorship and guidance to pursue doctoral studies through involvement in research and other scholarly activities. (U.S. Department of Education, 2017).

In addition to providing a learning community, these programs offer valuable resources to ease the cost of attending college. They resources may include funding for textbooks, paying for group tutoring services, mini scholarships to attend conferences, and funding to join professional organizations. Not all colleges have a TRiO program, so you should inquire with your student services office on campus to see if a similar program is available at your college that can support your academic pursuits.

STEM Learning Communities

Colleges across the country have been intentional that students who pursue STEM disciplines are successful. To meet this goal, students are introduced to the concept of "learning communities." Usually a learning community consists of a small group of students who enroll and take one, two, or three courses together in the same or related major. For example, your college may have a learning community for students who are interested in environmental issues. What this means is that students who want to major in either environmental engineering, environmental science, or natural resources can all consider to be part of the environment and sustainable resources learning community. Many colleges have specific STEM-related learning communities depending on the majors that are offered. You can ask your adviser what learning community options, if any, you may be able to join.

Students who are part of a learning community may also consider living in the same residence hall to further enhance in- and out-of-class interactions. These residence halls may have special designations and criteria for you to join and are called living/learning communities. By intentionally creating a community for first-year students, STEM learning communities allow students from different backgrounds but with similar academic interests to interact. By taking common courses, students in learning communities organically form study groups. These groups establish expectations for collective success and introduce every student in the learning community to college resources. It also provides opportunities for students to mentor each other and allows for greater faculty interactions with your specific major.

Final Message About Thriving in Your First Year of College

As we mentioned earlier in this chapter, the first-year college experience is vital for your success as a Latinx college student. How well you do in your first year will not only set the foundation for the remaining years in college, but it will have an impact on your career trajectory in the future. Latinx college students pursuing STEM disciplines and careers are on the rise, and you have the opportunity to make a big difference for yourself, your family, your country, and STEM through your educational contributions. We hope that the various strategies and programs outlined in this chapter provide you with the necessary tools to feel confident, engaged, and successful during your first year in college.

REFERENCE

U.S. Department of Education (2017). *Federal TRiO programs—Home page.* Retrieved from https://www2.ed.gov/about/offices/list/ope/trio/index.html

CHAPTER FIVE

STEP 5: Choosing a STEM Major

Dimitra Jackson Smith and Frankie Santos Laanan

Welcome to the journey into choosing a science, technology, engineering, and mathematics (STEM) major! Choosing a STEM major and career can be both exciting and overwhelming. We understand this completely! Anxiety can emerge from not being sure you have the right math and science academic preparation or the skills necessary to enter STEM careers, yet getting into STEM careers can be exciting because these fields offer many financial and high-paying career opportunities. STEM careers are also exciting because STEM education and the associated skill sets are vital to the future success of our country, the economy, and the future of our nation. In a STEM career, you have the potential to make significant discoveries and innovations that will have an impact on the Latinx community and even the world.

As you consider a STEM degree, you should keep in mind that earning a college degree, especially in STEM, can significantly affect your entire lifetime earnings. Individuals who hold a bachelor's degree earn about $2.27 million over their lifetime. Those with "master's, doctoral, and professional degrees earn $2.67 million, $3.25 million, and $3.65 million, respectively. Those with bachelor's degrees who work either in management or STEM fields earn more, on average, than people with advanced degrees of any level who work in fields like education, sales, and community service" (Bumsed, 2011, para.3).

The main purpose of this chapter is to guide students to choose majors specifically in science, technology, engineering, and mathematics. These are the very fields in which Latinx students are not well represented, and your participation can help break barriers to access and representation in important STEM careers that will shape the future of this nation. In many cases, you will be the first or among the first to pursue a career in certain STEM areas.

STEM EDUCATION, PREPARATION, AND CAREER EXPLORATION

The most pressing challenge that Latinx students face in choosing a STEM major is to determine what they should know and be able to do by the time they finish high school. Unfortunately, these choices can be confusing. In every state, there are different STEM standards and different curricula (National Research Council, 2013; STEM Smart Briefing, 2013). As a result, many individuals do not view STEM as a viable career option (National Research Council, 2013). For those who manage to remain open to STEM career options, understanding how to choose majors for specific careers and/or for graduate school preparation is essential.

The U.S. Census Bureau has identified some of the fastest growing STEM-related occupations between 2008–2018. These occupations include biomedical engineers, network systems and data communications analyst, financial examiners, medical scientists, epidemiologists, physician assistants, skin care specialists, biochemists and biophysicists, dental hygienists, veterinary technologists and technicians, computer software engineers, medical assistants, physical therapists assistants, veterinarians, occupational therapist aides, environmental engineers, computer system software engineering, survey researchers, physical therapists, and environmental engineering technicians (Employment Projections by Occupations: 2008–2018).

Preparing for a Science Major

The 2015–2016 PayScale College Salary Report (PayScale, 2015–16) indicates that science majors can wind up in a diverse array of careers with extremely high earning potential. The best high-paying jobs appear to be for those who major in chemistry, biology, physics, and geology. These majors can lead to jobs such as regulatory affairs director, quality assurance director, principal scientist, project manager in pharmaceuticals, senior geologist, and hydrogeologist, among others.

If you are a high school student planning to enter a degree program in the physical and biological sciences, you should be aware of the high school preparation you must have to enroll in college. The physical sciences fall in four broad areas: astronomy, physics, chemistry, and the earth sciences (geologic, hydrologic, and atmospheric sciences).

As one example, the University of California-Santa Cruz outlines the following science preparation, found online at http://undergrad.pbsci.ucsc.edu/resources/prospective/science-prep.html:

1. Continue taking math courses throughout high school. Be consistent taking math courses every year of high school, and avoid having a year without any math courses. This keeps you current and involved in mathematics. Any break that includes no math will set you back.

2. Be prepared to start calculus. Majors in physical and biological sciences require calculus.

3. Be ready for college-level chemistry. Many majors require general chemistry. A solid background in high school chemistry can help you with the general chemistry sequences and will help in learning the basic concepts covered in biology courses.

4. Consider taking statistics. This is especially true if you have already covered your math and general chemistry courses. Statistics are used heavily in the sciences as well as the social sciences.

5. Take and pass Advanced Placement (AP) courses with the highest grade possible. "Advanced Placement (AP) is a program of college-level courses offered at many high schools. Courses are available in many subject areas, including English, history, humanities, languages, math, psychology, and science. The focus is not on memorizing facts and figures. It is on engaging discussions, approaching and solving problems together, and learning to write well" (Advanced Placement, n.d. para.1). The benefits of taking AP courses are that you will gain skills and study habits that are needed to succeed in college. You will also improve your writing, problem-solving, and time-management skills. You may also be able to move through college faster and qualify for college scholarships. AP courses ultimately help you to get accepted to college. Colleges want to know that you are willing to take a challenging class, even if it lowers your grade point average. This makes you stand out in the admission process. It also shows that you are taking the initiative to prepare yourself for college-level work. AP classes do not just earn you high school credit. You may also earn college credit if you take an AP exam at the end of the course *and* earn a score of at least 3 on a scale of 1 to 5. Colleges and universities consider a score of 3 an indicator of your ability to do successful college work (Advanced Placement, n.d.)

6. Ensure community college courses are equivalent to the college to which you plan to transfer. Some students will begin their STEM careers in community colleges and then transfer to a four-year institution. Do not enroll in any course without first checking for a course-to-course equivalency.

Preparing for a Major in Technology

Computers, cell phones, tablets, and computer games have become a part of our everyday lives. Careers in technology are some of the highest paying. According to World Wide Learn (n.d.). you can land an information technology (IT) job as a programmer or analyst with a bachelor's degree in computer sciences or a related area, though some jobs will require only an associate's degree. Having work experience is also beneficial, and in some companies, solid work experience can be enough to land you a job.

The top 10 paying technology majors (Learn.Org, n.d.) include the following, with average annual salaries in specific careers listed in parentheses.

1. Information technology and management ($123,081). IT managers supervise information technology departments and make sure all systems run smoothly. Cybersecurity, also referred to as information technology security, focuses on protecting computers, networks, programs, and data from unintended or unauthorized access, change, or destruction.

2. Software engineering ($97,742). Software engineers develop and test computer hardware and systems. A graduate degree is preferred.

3. Database administration ($94,430). Database administrators ensure database systems are secure, organized, and work properly. Most database administrators work for search portals, Internet service providers, government agencies, and data processing firms.

4. Video game programming ($92,151). Programmers work with various software systems to program games for computers, consoles, and other gaming devices.

5. Web development ($78,848). Web developers create and program content for websites.

6. Computer programming ($78,624). Computer programmers write and test computer programs.

7. Network engineering ($78,389). Network engineers are responsible for the design and the implementation of local area networks (LAN) and wide area networks (WAN).

8. Game design ($75,065). Game designers create video games for computers, consoles, and other gaming devices.

9. System administration ($72,904). System administrators design, install, and maintain computer systems. Some system administrators are also responsible for supporting entire networks.

10. Network management ($68,347). Network managers oversee a variety of different networks, including computer networks and fiber optic networks. Students who earn a degree in network management may end up working as operators, administrators, or planners.

According to World Wide Learn (n.d., para 1), to prepare for an IT degree program you should:

- Gain extensive experience using computers. You may want to take computer classes, join groups of people who work with computers, or surf the Internet as often as you can.

- Join chat rooms or receive email newsletters that discuss the changes in technology and the latest breakthroughs in computer science. It is important to stay current with the latest technologies in the industry.

- Take the right high school classes that prepare you for the field. Typically, liberal arts colleges require a minimum number of math, science, social studies, and English courses prior to admission. Make sure you meet these prerequisites before you send in your application fee.

- Understand the role of technical institutes and colleges. Some students choose to attend a technical institute, sometimes called technical colleges. These provide specialized training in different career fields, including computer technology. Programs take anywhere from less than two years up to four years to complete and result in a certificate, a diploma, or an associate's degree. Here students get hand-on training, and there are opportunities for internship experiences. Technical institutes may not require GE courses, but they might require you to have some proficiency with computers and networks.
- Join your school's computer clubs to gain proficiency.
- Get a job in the computer industry. Whether the position is sales or service oriented, the job can give you valuable computer experience and information.

To be successful, you should also have problem-solving skills and be able to identify, locate, and fix problems in a timely fashion. Because you will often be working with people who are not computer and technology-savvy, you will need good people skills and excellent communication abilities, whether it is in-person, over the phone, or via email. You will be spending a great deal of time in front of a computer screen. This means you need to have good manual dexterity, typing skills, and hand-eye coordination. To succeed in technology careers, you can always benefit from additional skills such as problem-solving, logical thinking, critical thinking, creativity, and technical writing.

World Wide Learn (n.d., para.3) indicates that IT degree programs vary widely depending on the college issuing the degree. Examples provided include the following types of certificates and degrees:

Certificate in Information Technology. These are usually six- to 12-month courses that certify students as proficient in one particular area of information technology. Programs are available through accredited online and distance learning institutions. Certificate courses allow IT professionals to stay current in their fields and are appropriate for people who already have experience but wish to extend their knowledge into another specialty area.

Associate Degree in Information Technology. These are usually two-year programs that prepare you for an entry-level career as a help desk operator or computer user. These degrees require students to pass a certain number of general education (GE) classes before the degree can be conferred. Specific courses in information technology such as computer interfaces, basic communications networks, and web design, among others, are also required to graduate with an associate's degree.

Bachelor's Degree in Information Technology. The bachelor's degree program in IT is similar to the associate's degree program, but it usually requires four academic years of study to complete. The first two years of study usually include introductory courses in IT and GE requirements. The last two years focus on the more specific and advanced aspects of the IT field.

Preparing for an Engineering Major

Engineering is a high-paying career with high demand. Among the highest paying are biomedical engineering, software engineering, environmental engineering, civil engineering, petroleum engineering, nuclear engineering, chemical engineering, electronics and communications engineering, computer science engineering, electrical and computer engineering, systems engineering, and aeronautical engineering (Goudreau, 2012; Study.com, n.d.).

Your interest to pursue a degree in engineering should be matched by early preparation academically. It is never too early to start preparing. You can start as early as early as middle school. Pre-university course options include courses such as algebra II, biology, calculus, chemistry, computer science, language arts, pre-calculus, physics, second language, and trigonometry. Through these middle and high school courses, you will have early exposure to university level work. For more information, visit: http://tryengineering.org/explore-engineering/become-engineer.

Potter, Whitener, and Sikorsky (2015) outline three important steps you should take to become successful in engineering.

Step one is to find the right engineering field for you. You will need at least a bachelor's degree, and a master's degree is essential if you wish to stay competitive. You can try out your future career through engineering summer camps, internships, or volunteer jobs. These will give you hands-on experiences that allow you to sense whether a particular kind of engineering is indeed the best fit for you.

Step two is to make sure you have the right preparation for college-level work. For this, you will need to take courses that really challenge you in high school, including the most rigorous AP college-prep courses. Courses to consider taking in high school include:

"*Math*: Algebra I, algebra II, geometry, probability and statistics, calculus courses.

Science: Physical science, biology, applied biology/chemistry, chemistry, and advanced physics.

Writing and Communication: Engineers must effectively communicate their design ideas, so English, writing, and speech classes are also an important part of pre-engineering coursework." (Potter, Whitener, and Sikorsky, 2015, para. 2)

Step three is to prepare for a career in engineering. Remember that a career in engineering will be a very competitive field, so you need to do everything you can to make yourself competitive. Employers look for two things: the right coursework and the right relevant experience. Take the right courses, and get involved in hands-on learning experiences such as internships, research opportunities, summer jobs, and summer career programs to develop your engineering experience. Also consider positioning and promoting yourself on social media with a LinkedIn profile to keep an updated list of accomplishments, classes, and experiences.

Do not forget about exploring professional opportunities in Latinx websites such as Society for Advancement of Chicanos/Hispanics and Native Americans in Science (SACNAS). Also explore the website of the Society of Hispanic Professional Engineers (SHPE) where you can upload your resume. Make sure to update your resume periodically. Become involved in the local chapter of these organizations at your institution, and plan early to attend their regional and national conferences. Sometimes you can apply for scholarships to attend these conferences. Networking is very important to be successful in a STEM career.

Preparing for a Math Major

Mathematics is the foundation for many high-paying jobs such as treasurer in certain job settings, physicist, astronomer, actuary, mathematician, economist, robotics engineer, biochemist, and civil engineer (Sokanu, n.d.). Other fields that are lucrative include data scientist, quantitative analyst, mathematics professor, financial analyst, statistician, and financial adviser. Some students may choose a minor in mathematics to complement another major. Having a minor in mathematics can show a well-rounded education and make you competitive in the job market. A minor in mathematics for high school teaching is a track that can also be pursued. As the number of Latinx youth increase, more Latinx STEM teachers will be needed. The National Education Association (NEA) has an interest in engaging and increasing the number of Latinx K-16 and graduate students in STEM fields of study.

Every concentration in the mathematics major requires a high level of competency in general math, particularly algebra, trigonometry, geometry, and even calculus and statistics. Your best preparation is to take a math course in every year of high school to build your skill level. You should have at least four years of high school mathematics before entering college, including algebra, geometry, and precalculus. Ideally, math, engineering, and science majors should be ready to take calculus upon arrival at college. Developmental courses in mathematics are offered at many colleges to help students who need additional preparation. Be sure to check the college website for information about course requirements well in advance. You should also seek advice from high school counselor or faculty adviser to get accurate information to plan an appropriate course of study. Some colleges have specific math advisers who assist with course selection and major requirements.

Writing and communications courses are also essential. Success as a professional depends on clearly written communication and writing skills. Advanced Placement

(AP) and International Baccalaureate (IB) courses in any discipline can prepare students for college-level work. In addition, if you take the AP or IB exam, you may be able to get college credit to apply toward your degree. This means you can get into your advanced coursework sooner.

CHOOSING A STEM MAJOR: ADDITIONAL FACTORS TO CONSIDER

There are many factors to consider as you ponder your decision to pursue a STEM-related career path. The information below will help you in choosing a STEM major.

1. **Understand and master the skills needed to enter STEM fields of study.** Key skills can be organized into three clusters: cognitive, interpersonal, and intrapersonal. These skills include critical thinking, problem solving, communication, teamwork, and learning to learn. These foundational skills need to be mastered and are essential for life and work (National Research Council, 2013; STEM Smart Brief, 2013). Also included in the clusters are the following essential skills and abilities:
   A. Analytical skills to research a topic, develop a project plan and timeline, and draw conclusions from research results.
   B. Science skills to break down a complex scientific system into smaller parts, recognize cause-and-effect relationships, and defend opinions using facts.
   C. Mathematic skills for calculations and measurements.
   D. Attention to detail to follow a standard blueprint, record data accurately, or write instructions.
   E. Technical skills to troubleshoot the source of a problem, repair a machine or debug an operating system, and computer capabilities to stay current on appropriate software and equipment (Understanding Science, Technology, Engineering, and Math 'STEM' Skills, 2016).

2. **Have a good foundation in math and science content.** STEM-related courses are needed to acquire a solid foundation in math and science. Do not be discouraged if you do not fully grasp math and science concepts at the onset. These concepts are developed gradually over time. It is essential that you begin taking math and science related courses as soon as possible. However, it is never too late to take math and science courses. These courses include but are not limited to algebra, statistics, biology, geography, physics, chemistry, computer technology, computer-assisted art, research methods (in any discipline), calculus, economics, electronics, environmental science, and political science.

Many colleges and universities will have their own math and science course sequence, and you should get assistance from college advisers and counselors to determine the order in which you should take courses. In short, examining the order in which you should take specific courses at specific institutions of choice is as important as mastering math and science content knowledge. This will help you stay on track and obtain the necessary math and science knowledge in the recommended sequence.

3. **Keep learning and stay engaged in learning opportunities.** Students need to engage in learning opportunities where they can apply skills, knowledge, and content-level understanding (STEM Smart Briefing, 2013). For example, you should take advantage of opportunities to engage in paid and unpaid internships in the business and industry. With the help of a mentor, adviser, or counselor, you should seek internships in your community that will help you develop the precise skills you need to succeed in your chosen STEM major. Another way to do this is through undergraduate research opportunities (UROs), which means that you will work on research with a faculty member. In fact, "the effects of UROs tend to be the strongest among Hispanics/Latinos" (Russell, Hancock, and McCullough, 2007, p. 549). These opportunities can be paid/unpaid and/or credit/no credit. UROs are usually offered at specific colleges and universities, and the requirements for participation are specific to a particular institution. The benefits of UROs are numerous. (Russell, et al., 2007; Jackson-Smith, 2015) indicate that UROs can allow students to:
   - Engage in hands-on research.
   - Develop confidence and awareness of how to conduct research.
   - Strengthen research skills and abilities.
   - Become aware of master's and doctoral STEM programming.
   - Increase understanding of STEM related careers.
   - Transition and adjust to college life and academic demands, which have been highlighted as a challenge for Latino students (Taningco, 2008).

4. **Explore STEM-related career options.** This is one of the most important things you can to prepare to choose a STEM major. If you do not understand STEM major requirements, you may change majors and leave STEM all together (Blickenstaff, 2005). To enter a STEM career, you must be on a STEM educational path. If you do not pursue a science-related educational path, the likelihood of obtaining a science-related career is unlikely. Long forgotten is the childhood question: "What do you want to be when you grow up?" While this question may seem cliché, it is a key question when embarking on a STEM career path. Thinking about what type of professional you would like to be encourages you to think about your interests, what you like to do, what you do not like to do, what excites you, what motivates you, what makes you want to wake up in the morning, what courses you are good at, what skill sets come naturally to you, and what areas you need to work on. Thinking about these different areas can assist you in focusing on your experiences and interests.

Additionally, there are many career opportunities in STEM that are not widely known. You will hear many individuals say: "If I only knew what I know now . . ." This does not have to be you! Now is the time for you to learn more about STEM so that you can get into the right STEM career. STEM preparation can prepare you for careers you might not have thought you could enter. For example, did you know that you could be a dolphin trainer with a degree in a STEM field? It is true! A bachelor's degree in biology, marine biology, zoology, or animal science is preferred.

5. **Identify a good mentor or adviser.** To choose a STEM major, you will need assistance from people who are experienced and knowledgeable. Mentors and advisers are by far the most helpful in terms of providing essential information regarding STEM pathways. Mentoring is generally defined as a process by which a more experienced and knowledgeable person assists in the professional development of a less experienced person, such as the protégé or mentee (Muchinsky, 2009; Crisp and Cruz, 2009; Noe, 2006).

Professional mentors provide information regarding the courses and the skills you need. Mentors can also keep you informed on recent changes that are occurring both in a specific STEM career and within the STEM workforce in general. Professional mentors can also inform you on traditional and nontraditional/alternative career paths. For example, postsecondary vocational certificates and college credit for life experiences programs are examples of nontraditional/alternative career paths. Professional mentors also serve as role models. In this capacity, protégés can emulate the behaviors of the mentor to replicate the mentor's success (Pellegrini and Scandura, 2005). Science teachers are good role models. Science teachers have a major influence on students depending on the quality and the amount of time spent together. Science teachers can assist students through experiences in science classrooms and extra-curricular activities. They also provide information regarding content of college-level science courses, and teachers can motivate students to stay on science related career paths. Other professional mentors include leaders within STEM business and industry sectors, faculty members, and community leaders, to name a few.

STEP-BY-STEP STEM CAREER PLAN

Now that you have the essential background information to consider on your journey to pursue a STEM-related career path, consider developing a step-by-step plan to pursue a career in STEM.

Step 1: Become Educated about STEM Skills, Credentials, Majors, and Careers

A. Educate yourself and develop a clear understanding about different STEM-related skills, credentials, majors, and careers. New information is always coming up, so make sure that you remain updated on current developments.

B. Educate yourself on math and science content areas. Take as many math courses as possible. Remember to refer to the sequence of courses and when they are offered in your major. The course sequence may vary by institution.

C. Learn about the different STEM majors, including how to prepare for them, the skills and education they require, and the careers these majors can lead to.

D. Educate yourself on the various traditional and nontraditional/alternative career paths (vocational certifications and college credit for life) For example, according Koebler (2013), there are two STEM economies. The first is the professional STEM economy that functions mostly in the corporate sector and requires graduate degrees. The second draws from high schools, workshops, vocational schools, and community colleges. These STEM jobs are in construction, installation, manufacturing and healthcare (Koebler, 2013; STEMJOBS, 2015).

Step 2: Acquire a Strong STEM Preparation

A. Learn about and participate in different learning opportunities that allow you to apply your STEM-related skills and content knowledge. For example, you can participate by working with a faculty member on a research project, engage in an internship, become a member of a STEM club, or volunteer to work in a STEM-related field. For Latinx students, the Minority Science and Engineering Improvement (MESA) program has been very successful, and you should definitely consider getting involved in if your college has a MESA program. Program components include 1) MESA School Program to support pre-college students in middle and high schools to excel and go on to pursue college STEM majors; 2) MESA Community College Program, which provides STEM academic preparation and career advising for students wishing to transfer from a two- to a four-year institution; and 3) MESA Engineering Program, which assists students in completing bachelor's degrees in engineering and computer science. Learning opportunities can also come in the form of UROs and internships in business and industry. Other programs serving Latinx students include those that are in place at Hispanic-serving institutions to assist students earning STEM degrees to transfer from community colleges to four-year institutions. The Upward Bound Math and Science program helps students strengthen math and science skills and pursue STEM fields of study (White House Initiative on Educational Excellence for Hispanics, n.d.).

B. Find a mentor or adviser who can provide information regarding the STEM workforce, traditional and nontraditional pathways, and important courses to take as you pursue your major focus of study. These individuals serve as role models who can provide both STEM information as well as encouragement, validation, and emotional support.

Step 3: Explore the Diverse Array of STEM Careers

A. Once you understand the world of STEM and have developed a strong STEM preparation, it will be easier for you to explore the diverse array of STEM careers, and there are many! Review college catalogs, websites, books, and magazines, and talk with STEM professionals who are already working in your chosen field. Use social media to learn more about STEM majors and careers, and visit with counselors and advisers to ask questions about career options.

B.   When possible, volunteer to work as an intern with a STEM professional. This process can result in you learning and gaining knowledge regarding different STEM careers, and you will also know more about the important skills you need to develop. You will pick up knowledge about required math and science courses, and hopefully you will have engaged in some learning opportunities and have developed and formed relationships with mentors and advisers.

This chapter has provided the key things you need to consider on your way toward choosing a STEM major in college. Congratulations! You are now ready to explore the many STEM-related majors and career options with greater confidence.

REFERENCES

Blickenstaff, J. C. (2005). Women and science careers: Leaky pipeline or gender filter? *Gender and Education, 17*(4), 369–386.

Bumsed, B. (2011). How higher education affects lifetime salary. *U.S. News & World Report.* Retrieved from http://www.usnews.com/education/best -colleges/articles/2011/08/05/how-higher-education-affects-lifetime-salary

Career Wise. (2006). *Understanding science, technology, engineering, and math (STEM) skills.* Retrieved from https://www.careerwise.mnscu.edu/careers /stemskills.html

Crisp, G., & Cruz, I. (2009). Mentoring college students: A critical review of the literature between 1990 and 2007. *Research in Higher Education, 50*(6), 525–545.

Goudreau, J. (2012, May 15). The 15 most valuable college majors. *Forbes.* Retrieved from http://www.forbes.com/sites/jennagoudreau/2012/05/15/best -top-most-valuable-college-majors-degrees/#5418aa246ddb

Jackson-Smith, D. (2015). The summer was worth it: Exploring the impacts of a science, technology, engineering, and mathematics focused summer research program on the success of African American females. *Journal of Women and Minorities in Science and Engineering, 21*(2), 87–106.

Koebler, J. (2013, June 10). Study: Half of STEM jobs don't require bachelor's degree. *U.S. News & World Report.* Retrieved from http://www.usnews.com/news /articles/2013/06/10/study-half-of-stem-jobs-dont-require-bachelors-degree

Learn.org. (n.d.) *Top 10 paying technology majors.* Retrieved from http://learn.org /articles/Top_10_Paying_Technology_Majors.html

Muchinsky, P. M. (2009). *Psychology applied to work: An introduction to indus- trial and organizational psychology* (9th ed.). New York: Hypergraphic Press.

National Research Council. (2013). *Monitoring progress toward successful K-12 STEM education: A nation advancing?* Washington, DC: The National Acad- emies Press.

Noe, R. A. (2006). An investigation of the determinants of successful assigned mentoring relationship. *Personnel Psychology*, *41*, 457–479. doi:10.1111/j.1744-6570.1988.tb00638.x

PayScale. (n.d.). *2015–2016 Pay Scale*. Retrieved from http://www.payscale.com/college-salary-report/common-jobs-for-majors/physical-and-life-sciences

Pellegrini, E. K., & Scandura, T. A. (2005). Construct equivalence across groups: An unexplored issue in mentoring research. *Educational and Psychological Measurement*, *65*, 323–335. doi:10.1177/0013164404268665

Potter, A., Whitener, A., & Sikorsky, J. (2015). *3 easy steps to prepare for an engineering career in high school.* Retrieved from https://www.envisionexperience.com/blog/steps-to-prepare-for-an-engineering-career

Ready, Set, Go. Success in School and Beyond (n.d.). *Advanced placement.* Retrieved from http://readysetgo.state.mn.us/RSG/AP/

Russell, S. H., Hancock M. P., & McCullough, J. (2007). Benefits of undergraduate research experiences. *Science (Washington)*, *316*(5824), 548–549.

Sokanu. (n.d.). *Highest paying jobs that involve math.* Retrieved from https://www.sokanu.com/careers/collections/highest-paying-jobs-that-involve-math/

STEMJOBS. (2015). *8 high paying STEM jobs that don't require a bachelor's degree.* Retrieved from http://stemjobs.com/dont-require-a-bachelors-degree/

STEM Smart Brief. (2013). *Preparing students for college and careers in STEM.* Retrieved from http://www.successfulstemeducation.org/sites/successfulstemeducation.org/files/Career%20and%20College%20Readiness%20Brief.pdf

Study.com. (n.d.). *How much more do college graduates earn than non-college graduates?* Retrieved from http://study.com/articles/How_Much_More_Do_College_Graduates_Earn_Than_Non-College_Graduates.html

Study.com. (n.d.). *What are technical schools?* Retrieved from http://study.com/technical_schools.html

Taningco, M. T. V. (2008). Latinos in STEM professions: Understanding challenges and opportunities for next steps. A qualitative study using stakeholder interviews. Tomas Rivera Policy Institute. Retrieved from http://files.eric.ed.gov/fulltext/ED502064.pdf

Try Engineering. (n.d.). *Become an engineer.* Retrieved from http://tryengineering.org/explore-engineering/become-engineer

U.S. Census Bureau. (2015). *Census bureau: State and county quickFacts.* Retrieved from http://www.census.gov/quickfacts/table/PST045214/00

U.S. Census Bureau. (n.d.). *Employment projections by occupations: 2008–2018.* Retrieved from https://www2.census.gov/library/publications/2011/compendia/statab/131ed/tables/12s0618.pdf

U.S. Department of Education. (n.d.). *White House initiative on educational excellence for hispanics.* Retrieved from http://sites.ed.gov/hispanic-initiative/

World Wide Learn. (n.d.) *What does it mean to study information technology?* Retrieved from http://www.worldwidelearn.com/online-education-guide/technology/information-technology-major.htm

CHAPTER SIX

STEP 6: Continuing on to Graduate School in STEM

Leslie A. Coward, Kimberly A. Koledoye, and Stella L. Smith

Students who are considering a career in science, technology, engineering, and mathematics (STEM) should also think about pursuing an advanced degree: either a master's, doctorate, or professional (medicine) degree. A good way for you to make academic and career decisions is to align your career choices with your personal interests. If you are interested in STEM, there may be many reasons why you might consider pursuing the path to earning a STEM undergraduate or graduate degree. Occupations in STEM are among the highest paying, fastest growing, and most influential jobs driving economic growth and innovation (National Governors Association for Best Practices, 2011). Individuals employed in STEM fields enjoy low unemployment rates, financial prosperity, and career flexibility. Thus, STEM education is a powerful foundation for individual and societal economic success (National Governors Association for Best Practices, 2011).

Currently, there is a shortage of STEM graduates. The low number of students pursuing STEM degrees is one cause of the STEM shortage in the United States. The percentage of students who choose to pursue STEM degrees is lower than those students who choose to pursue non-STEM majors (Chen and Weko, 2009). The number of underrepresented minorities (URMs) such as Latinx and African American students completing STEM bachelor's degrees is substantially lower because fewer URM students decide to pursue STEM degrees in the first place. Of those URM students who do choose to pursue STEM degrees, these students are less likely to remain in STEM majors than their Asian American and Caucasian counterparts (Chen and Thomas, 2009). Therefore, the United States needs more students to earn STEM degrees! As a STEM graduate, you will be in high demand in the workforce and can reap all the benefits granted to STEM degree earners.

What Is Graduate School?

Graduate school is the next step in higher education after an undergraduate student has completed his or her bachelor's degree. A student can pursue a master's degree or a doctor of philosophy degree (PhD). A master's degree is usually earned within two years, during which a student will take on a specialized course of study, focusing narrowly on a specific topic. A doctor of philosophy, also called a terminal degree, is the highest degree a person can earn. The doctorate degree can take a minimum of three years beyond the master's degree. You should not to be discouraged by the additional time it takes to earn an advanced degree, as there are countless benefits to pursuing a master's and doctorate degree.

Many master's degree programs focus on developing a student's theoretical knowledge with a strong focus on research. These programs require students to complete a graduate thesis in a specialized area where the student works independently on a research project. This path of study often leads to students going on to undertake PhD studies as well.

A second route for a master's degree programs is the nonthesis option. For example, a student may choose to pursue a master of business engineering (MBE), master in engineering business management (MsEM/MSc), master of science in technical management (MS), or a master of public health (MPH) degree that may require the student to take fewer courses and complete qualifying exams in place of a thesis. These types of degrees may focus more on the profession and involve lectures, seminars, and practical work application. Students who pursue the nonthesis option are generally looking to improve employment prospects, expand their skill sets, or increase their wages.

A PhD is a degree for specialized scholarly expertise. Students in doctoral programs are trained to become expert in their fields. Many doctoral programs require students to enroll in full-time studies, although part-time programs are also available at some institutions. Doctoral programs in STEM are designed to prepare students to be future researchers, teacher educators, or practitioners. Whether students choose to pursue research or become practitioners, their studies culminate in a dissertation research study.

Graduate school is a full-time job; it is different than undergraduate school. The professor's expectations will be higher. Professors want students to develop their creativity and form critical and innovative ways of thinking, while at the same time understanding the theoretical foundations of their chosen field. There is a lot of autonomy in a student's educational development, especially in doctoral programs.

You must be fully committed to the program you choose if you want to be successful. Although universities offer part-time programs, it does not change the amount of time and commitment that you must spend studying and interacting with fellow students and professors. Graduate studies are focused on the development of a particular field. You are expected to expound on the general norms of your chosen profession and critically evaluate your area of study.

Pursuing a graduate degree can be beneficial to professional growth, especially in the sciences. A master's or doctorate degree improves your chances of advancing within a particular field of employment and can lead to future wage increases and promotions. Some employers, however, might view a person with an advanced degree as overqualified or too expensive to employ. Career advancement is not guaranteed with a graduate degree; therefore, it is important that you fully investigate your degree paths and evaluate whether a master's or doctorate degree will be beneficial in the future.

Questions to consider:
Why am I thinking about graduate school?
Am I ready for graduate school?
Will graduate school assist me with my career paths?

How Should You Prepare for College or Graduate Programs?

Preparing for graduate school in STEM fields is much like preparing for academics in any field, with a few minor differences. You will need to set goals and monitor your progress. You will need to decide what to study and then determine what steps you need to take to be accepted into an appropriate program. Making this decision early will ease the transition from high school to college and then from undergraduate to graduate studies. You should do your due diligence by researching the different program options and requirements at the various institutions you are considering. Once the requirements are clear, you can make realistic plans to achieve your desired goals. In addition to setting clear goals, there are several strategies that can help you prepare to study STEM.

Regardless of your academic plans, you should work hard to achieve extraordinary grades in your courses. Students with good grades will have more doors open to them in the academic world and professional workforce. Undergraduate admissions officers want to be confident that the students they accept will be able to successfully complete the degree requirements of a particular program. A student with a high GPA in both high school and college, who has also performed well on their entrance exams, is someone college admissions officers will feel more secure about selecting to pursue graduate studies. High school students preparing for college should be focused on taking the types of classes that will prepare them for studying STEM fields. These classes will be higher level mathematics and sciences. School counselors can help students identify the appropriate classes. Students who complete high-level mathematics and science courses in high school are more prepared to enter just about every field of study, not just those in a STEM area, so enrolling in a higher level of courses can be beneficial to any student interested in pursuing a degree in higher education.

Graduate-level STEM programs are seeking the same assurances as those at the undergraduate level, but these programs can sometimes admit only a few students annually, making the program highly competitive. Thus, it is imperative that you have a strong GPA and performances on graduate school admissions exams such as the GRE, MCAT, or DAT. Fortunately, for both high school students and undergraduates, there are test preparation courses that can help students achieve their desired scores. You should contact your advisers or counselors to learn more about these opportunities.

In addition to maintaining a strong GPA, current undergraduate students pursuing STEM degrees should seek opportunities to further their experiences in STEM fields. Many professors allow students with high academic performance to assist them with their research projects. You should also speak with your professors about joining their research teams. Students who participate in research with their professors are far more likely to know their program's faculty. This will be beneficial when looking for a faculty mentor, someone who will help students explore new and different fields of research while guiding them along their academic careers. In addition, mentors can also be a professional reference for you when you are considering moving on to your next endeavor and can provide well-informed letters of recommendation. Securing a supportive mentor can make all the difference in a student's academic career, so you should not hesitate to seek out professors who might be open to the idea of mentoring. Many students are dissuaded from seeking mentors because they do not feel they have much in common with their faculty members. These feeling should be avoided because any STEM student has at least one thing in common with their professor: an interest in STEM.

Another method of developing or expanding experiences and preparing for STEM undergraduate/graduate school is to join STEM-focused clubs, teams, and organizations. Many high schools and colleges have STEM teams that compete against other schools. Students who gain experience in these organizations will have a broader understanding of their future career options, as well as an increased understanding of STEM principles overall. Students who participate in high school STEM programs are far more likely to gain entrance to universities. These students are also good candidates for scholarships. Similarly, undergraduates who participate in STEM teams and organizations not only heighten their knowledge base but also find opportunities to win monetary prizes and recognition for their efforts. These organizations expose you to like-minded peers who are following the same path. Finding peers who can offer guidance or become study partners will help you avoid isolation during challenging times of study. Engaging in study groups, peer tutoring, and simple companionship with other STEM students will help with the completion of a STEM degree. In addition, affiliation with professional associations allows you to become familiar with faculty from other institutions where you may wish to pursue your graduate studies, as well as industry representatives where you may want to pursue employment opportunities.

Finally, you should look for scholarships and grants that can help you pursue your education. There are numerous funding sources specifically for students studying in one of the many STEM fields. There are also STEM scholarships and programs specifically for students of color. Many STEM programs have built-in faculty mentoring programs, peer tutoring, research projects, and financial support for graduate students. You should investigate what programs exist at the colleges you are considering. Selecting a college with STEM programs encapsulated in supportive supplemental programs will heighten your ability to successfully complete your degree. These suggestions will help you increase your chances of entering academic STEM programs as prepared as you can possibly be.

Choose the Right STEM Program

When you are selecting the institutions at which you will pursue your graduate studies, there are multiple factors to consider. Researchers (American Council on Education, 2006) have found that Latinx students in STEM are more successful when the institution understands the financial concerns, provides academic guidance, and has social support structures needed by minority students. Five factors to support Latinx students' choice to pursue graduate studies in STEM have been identified to support their academic growth and completion: standard program requirements, program and institution selection, academic structures and social integration, program diversity and campus climate, and location and cost (see Figure 6.1). Evaluating these factors can assist you in identifying a program that is a good fit for your career path and academic goals.

Each program's requirements can be identified on its college department's website. However, detailed information regarding the program may require you to probe deeper or utilize educational reporting websites for more specific information such as student demographics, financial resources, and community diversity.

Figure 6.1   Components for Graduate School Selection

Program Requirements

This is an overview of minimum requirements for acceptance into graduate STEM programs. Many master's and doctorate degrees require at least a 3.0 GPA to qualify for graduate school admission to the university. The 3.0 GPA may be required for a student's grades in their overall undergraduate degree, the last 30 hours of undergraduate coursework, all science and technical courses, or some specific courses. The graduate school will advise applicants of how it will assess the GPA requirement.

You may also be required to take the General Record Examination (GRE) as part of the academic requirements for graduate school. The minimum GRE scores are not always published. When researching programs of interest, you can ask the graduate adviser or review demographic information of students who have been accepted into the department. This information may reveal the average or minimum GRE of the entering class.

Graduate programs also require students to submit three letters of recommendation. These letters should come from professors and/or professionals in the chosen field. Professors and professionals should be able to talk confidently and in-depth about your undergraduate research work, scientific writing, and communication skills, as well as your analytical and technical ability to pursue a graduate degree.

Supplying strong GPAs, GRE scores, and letters of recommendation are the basic requirements needed to apply to a graduate school program. Each program will identify more specialized criteria required for its department. Department requirements may be more selective than those of the university's graduate admissions office. For example, science and mathematics departments may require students to have a 3.3 GPA, or at least a 3.0 in all upper level science and mathematics courses instead of one general GPA requirement. This is why it is important to research both graduate school and department requirements when exploring different programs.

Program and Institution Selection

The program you select can have an impact on the direction of your career. When thinking about applying to graduate school, students tend to look at national rankings first. National rankings are worth considering, but they do not show the whole picture about the institution or the specific degree program of interest. All graduate programs are not created equal. This is why it is important for you to research and identify programs that align with your academic and professional goals in order to discover which program will be the best fit for you.

You are not expected to know the answers to all your questions right away. In fact, it is common for URM students to wonder where to begin or not understand the process to matriculate in a graduate program. Therefore, it is important for you to develop an intended career direction and select an adviser to help you determine what type of institution will be most beneficial academically, professionally, and personally. The only way to know which program this will be is by asking questions and researching the program itself as well as its current students, recent graduates, and faculty areas of research.

Questions to consider.
Does it matter what type of university I select?
Which university should I attend?
Is this school a match for me?
Does the university offer a degree in my area of interest?
Are there professors doing research in areas of interest to me?

Unlike selecting an undergraduate school, selecting a graduate program should focus on the department rather than the institution. You should consider what the department has to offer in terms of degree specialization, areas of research, and financial assistance.

Every university is different. Just because one program provides a specialization in the engineering department, another university may provide the same degree in the science department. For example, a master's degree in medical anthropology and sociology may be offered in the school of medicine at one university and the college of arts and sciences at another institution. Therefore, you should ensure that the university offers the degree of specialization that is of interest to you and a program that is aligned with your professional and academic goals.

It is also important to understand the emphasis of the program. For instance, the goal of one program may be for students to pursue careers in global health, but this may not work for a student more focused on regulatory affairs and global energy policy. You must investigate the program's goals to know if the school is focused more on theory or practical application. One way to determine this is to research if people who attend the program go on to work in areas of research or work for corporations instead. The information is not always printed in black and white; you may have to read between the lines to understand if the goals of the program will align with your own professional and personal goals.

Researching programs can raise more questions for you as you begin to explore specialized fields of study that you were not aware of prior to investigating graduate programs. Therefore, you must speak with professors and academic advisers or participate in graduate school information sessions offered by professional associations. Professors, advisers, and mentors can help you develop clear career goals, understand the different areas of specialization available, and identify programs that may be a good fit for their academic and professional advancement.

Other factors to consider when selecting a graduate program are class size and type of institution. Pena (2008) advised that small classes contribute to minority students attaining degrees in STEM. A smaller class size allows students to have greater access to faculty. In addition, students have an opportunity to build their scientific identity by developing intentional relationships with faculty, which in turns builds their academic confidence and scientific interest.

Universities with a Hispanic-serving institutions (HSI), historically Black colleges and universities (HBCU), Asian American and Native American Pacific Islander-serving institutions (AANAPISI), and/or minority-serving institutions (MSI) designation are known to be more supportive and successful in graduating URMs. These college and university designations indicate that these institutions typically have a significant number of Latinx American, African American, Asian American, or combination of ethnic minority students represented at multiple levels of the institution. Although Hispanic-serving institutions represent a small but growing percentage of universities in the country, they enroll and graduate a significant portion of Latinx students. Researchers have found that HSIs, specifically, have diverse student populations and offer more resources such as increased funding, learning communities, and cultural programs that contribute to the academic success of Latinx students (Godoy, 2010).

The type of program, class size, and type of institution are all factors to consider when selecting a graduate program that will contribute to Latinx students graduating with master's or doctorate degrees in a STEM field. Therefore, to be successful in a STEM graduate program, you must look beyond the institution's name and good reputation, its national ranking, or its HSI, MSI, and HBCU status to select the graduate STEM program that is right for you. The only way for you to know if the institution is a good fit for your career path is to properly investigate the program and ensure that it aligns with your academic and professional goals.

Academic Structures and Social Integration

At the undergraduate level, there are resources and programs to help students be successful in their studies and reach graduation in their program. Support structures are not as readily available for graduate students. Graduate students have to establish their own learning communities, build relationships with professors, and actively participate in professional organizations.

Academic structures and social integration support the development of Latinx graduate students in STEM fields (Tinto, 1993; Pender, Marcotte, Domingo, and Maton, 2010). Academic structures, such as peer-to-peer interaction that connect students with other Latinx students, professors, and administrators, support students' educational matriculation. Developing relationships with faculty mentors and actively participating in professional associations increase skill competencies and analytical thinking, thereby enhancing retention and achievement in STEM fields (Hernandez and Lopez, 2004; Camacho & Lord, 2011; Bonous-Hammarth, 2000; Maton et al., 2011). Since academic support structures are not pre-established in graduate school, you must actively seek help and not be afraid to ask for assistance as you adjust to the rigors of participating in a graduate school program.

Social integration also influences Latinx students' success in graduate programs (Maton et al., 2011; Gardner, 2008). Social integration teaches students about the unwritten rules and the professional norms in their respective areas of study, and it increases a student's commitment to their chosen field. In addition, social integration into the department can alleviate feelings of inadequacy and provide emotional support. Integration can occur as you expand your involvement in and knowledge of your field. Similar to academic integration, developing faculty relationships is key, so that you can be part of the fabric of the department and be connected to the work you are doing.

The academic structures and the social integration of a particular institution are difficult to identify through Internet research alone. Determining if you are able to cultivate academic and social support structures must include interviewing current students and recent graduates. Inquire about students' academic and personal experiences as part of the program, the type of support they received, any mentoring experiences they have had, and their participation in faculty research. This line of inquiry can help develop a clearer picture of departmental characteristics to determine if the program is a good fit for you.

Program Diversity and Climate

When debating which program to choose, consider program diversity and climate. Graduate departments generally do not have a very diverse population of graduate students and faculty, as you may have experienced at the undergraduate level. Latinx students in STEM programs often find that they are the only Latinx or minority student in their respective graduate department. However, the lack of diversity should not dissuade you from selecting a program that may be an overall good fit for your career path. You can form relationships with a diverse body of students as you strive to accomplish goals of attaining STEM degrees together.

Depending on your goals, you can spend two or more years in a graduate program. Graduate programs can be both isolating and collaborative environments. These programs are a place for you to learn your profession through group work with professors and fellow students, but the experiences can also be very isolating as you stretch your education to develop a scientific identity. In both cases, students can and do persist toward graduation when they feel supported and part of the program. Therefore, you should thoroughly investigate the program regarding diversity among faculty members and diversity of students who are accepted and have graduated from the program (Figueroa and Hurtado, 2013; Donnelly and Jacobi, 2010; Tolson and Esters, 2012).

Program diversity may signify a supportive academic climate and have a positive impact on a student's persistence towards graduation (Ramirez, 2013; Nunez et al., 2008). In addition, it sends the message that the department values diversity and is supportive of diverse populations. Whether or not a program is supportive of diversity may not be reflected in the number of minority students, faculty, staff, or administrators. Programs may support diversity in other ways; for instance, a department may assign students an academic mentor within the program or connect students with Latinx faculty members from other departments.

Faculty mentors are an important part of program climate in graduate studies as they promote career development and provide access to professional networks and opportunities. There are a variety of factors to consider beyond diversity statistics to determine if a program supports diversity, but you must ask questions and research prospective programs to determine if and how it supports the persistence of Latinx students.

Location and Cost

Location, the cost of post-baccalaureate education, and the availability of financial aid play a large role in Latinx students pursuing a graduate degree in STEM. Many Latinx students tend to select institutions that are located close to home because of cultural practices or familial obligations (Desmond and Lopez-Turley, 2009). Keep in mind that although institutions located close to home may provide you with needed support and lower tuition costs, it may also result in increased familial pressures and obligations and lead you to select a program that is not the best fit. Moreover, familial obligations oftentimes distract you from your studies and are known to have an adverse impact on degree completion.

Questions to consider:
Can I live in this city or town for the next two to five years of my life?
What social and cultural diversions are available where the university is
    located?

A benefit to exploring STEM programs in different locations is the availability of increased resources as well as educational, research, and professional opportunities. Researchers have found that students who attend graduate programs that are located in or close to communities with large Latinx populations continue to persist toward graduation (Ramirez, 2013). Students who attend programs located in culturally rich environments learn to flourish and build on the strength of their community, which helps them continue their matriculation in graduate studies (Peralta, Caspary, and Boothe, 2013).

Students attending graduate programs located away from home will have higher financial costs. However, graduate programs have monetary resources for students, specifically Latinx students in STEM fields. Graduate school does not have to be costly to you. Many full-time master's and doctoral programs offer financial aid packages. The type and the amount of financial aid that may be available to you varies based on the type and the location of the graduate program. Although student loans are available for graduate studies, other forms of institutional aid consist of scholarships, graduate or teaching assistantships, and fellowships. Institutional aid may provide substantial funding to cover program costs and even some living expenses. Oftentimes these awards are renewable and available for multiple years. In addition to these sources of funding, faculty members have access to funds through grants and research projects. However, you must be willing to ask for assistance in identifying financial resources beyond student loans (Malcolm and Dowd, 2012) or risk severely limiting your opportunities to attend a graduate school that may be a good fit for your career path.

Roadmap to Graduate Degrees in STEM: Education Plan

Obtaining a graduate degree is a journey of self-improvement and can change the trajectory of life opportunities for students, their families, and their communities. The most successful students in graduate school are able to focus their academic research in areas that are of interest to them. These students pursue their graduate studies to make a difference in a specific area of research and ultimately the greater community. Students in graduate school demonstrate self-efficacy as they envision themselves as researchers and scholars in a STEM profession, and they follow a path that will make that dream a reality. When figuring out how to get a graduate degree, you need to have an educational plan to ensure you choose a career path that is best suited for you, your interests, and your talents.

Questions to consider:
What field of study am I passionate about?
Does the prospect of discovery and innovation thrill me?
Do I have a desire to understand the world around me?

These questions might not seem like the typical questions to consider when looking at graduate study, but they are essential in determining the program where you can make the most impact, both personally and professionally. You do not need to figure out the answers to these questions on your own. There are resources available through high school counselors and college and university advisers who can help you determine the direction of your career path. For instance, when considering graduate studies, try visiting career services, participating in professional organizations, and talking to faculty members who can assist you in exploring areas of study and specific programs. You can work with a career counselor or an academic adviser to identify their strengths and preferences to determine the best field of graduate study. Another benefit of working with career services is that they can help you learn about possible career options you might not otherwise have known about or considered.

One of the best ways for you to learn your strengths and develop new skills is by volunteering with student organizations. Serving in a leadership capacity, volunteering, and getting involved not only helps you learn about yourself, but it also develops your technical and nontechnical competencies such as analytical and organizational skills that are essential in graduate studies.

Another way you can determine your areas of interest is to talk with professors and other students in graduate programs. Ask questions about what it is like to be a graduate student. How did they pick their graduate program, their areas interests and research, and what steps did they take to get there? Learning about the stories of those who are working in your area of interest can help inspire you to dream big and develop your own plan for success.

Skillsets for Advanced Studies

There are specific skillsets that help support students on their journey to advanced studies. Developing these skillsets in your undergraduate work will make you a stronger applicant for graduate school. Some beneficial skillsets that you should begin to develop are listed below.

Redefining success. In high school and undergraduate work, getting the correct answer is fundamental. However, when you transition to graduate level work, critical and creative thinking becomes essential. There is no correct answer, but rather you need to be able to evaluate information effectively.

Manage your time. Effective time management skills are essential to your success. You must learn to prioritize and focus on a task in the moment to complete it and move on to the next item. You should develop a system of time management that works best for you. Also, you should be sure to use a planner or calendar software to remind you of important deadlines and dates.

Communicate technical material well. Communication skills are also essential in graduate school. Whether it is in the work you complete as a teaching assistant or research assistant, or the ability to communicate the technical language of the STEM field, language is a necessary skill. The best way for you to increase your communication skills is to practice, practice, and practice some more! You should take presentations in high school and undergraduate classes seriously and volunteer to speak at other events to develop this key skill. Also, you should be able to articulate your research interests in a well prepared "elevator pitch" that defines why you are interested in your field of study.

Select courses and professors strategically. Earlier in the chapter, the importance of keeping a high GPA was discussed. A strategy you can use to do this is to strategically choose classes and professors to ensure that you will be successful. In addition, taking multiple courses from the same professors will provide you with an opportunity to develop meaningful and rich relationships with your faculty. These professors can be a resource for you later when applying to and attending graduate school because they may be more willing to provide strong references or access to research and internship opportunities.

Seek support programs. Thinking about graduate school can be overwhelming. You should seek out help from student support programs that provide guidance to those considering graduate school. For example, there are federally funded programs, such as the McNair Scholars, and independent organizations, such as the PhD Project, to help students demystify the graduate school process.

Network with everyone, start conversations, and volunteer to help others. Learning to network is key to success in graduate school. Relationships with peers provide you with access to opportunities to which you might not otherwise have access. You can start honing your networking skills by attending events sponsored by the university, professional associations, or student organizations, and making sure to take the time to purposefully meet new people. You can also meet with professors who work in your area of interest to interview them about how they were able to secure their current position.

Seek meaningful research/internship experiences. Obtaining meaningful research fellowships, research apprenticeships, and internships is critical in maximizing your graduate school experience. As an undergraduate student, you can begin to build relationships with faculty who you would like to work with when you begin graduate school. In addition, faculty might have opportunities for you to participate as undergraduate research assistants, which will provide you with invaluable experience and connections.

A Timeline for Success

Once you have narrowed down your field of study and have identified programs that are of interest to you, it is important to have a roadmap or plan for applying to graduate school. Be sure to prepare a timeline with specific deadlines, and follow up with the school close to those dates in case the deadlines have changed. Applying on time is critical to being considered for most financial aid packages. A suggested timeline developed based on information provided by the Committee on Institutional Cooperation (CIC) is below. You should customize this timeline based on your specific goals.

Things to Do during the Summer before Your Senior Year in College

The summer before your senior year in college is a critical time in your process for applying to graduate school.

- *Research Graduate Programs*: If you have not already done so, explore graduate schools that have programs that are of interest to you. Contact those schools and ask for information about the admission requirements for the program. Each graduate program will provide a unique experience, so choosing a graduate experience that is consistent with your lifestyle and goals is important. Use this time to critically evaluate the program to determine what the best fit is for you.

- *Prepare for the Graduate Record Examination (GRE)*: Use this time to prepare for the GRE. There is free software available on the GRE website. You can also purchase review books from any book vendor or attend a preparation class to prepare you for the exam. Be sure to take a practice exam in a simulated testing environment. You want to make sure the first time you take a full exam is *not* when you are taking the test for real. Seek out advice from students who have already taken the exam or who are currently studying for the exam about tips and strategies to be successful. Even if your graduate program does not require the GRE, it is good to take the exam and have that score just in case you decide you want to attend a graduate program where the application requires the GRE.

- *Draft Your Personal Statement*: Take some time to think about your personal and professional goals and the things you might want to include in your personal statement. Check with the graduate schools you are applying to ensure you are providing the information that is required in the personal statement; each school/program may have a different prompt/question that you have to respond to for the personal statement. Some things to consider when writing your personal statement include:

  - Professional Goals: Why do you want to attend graduate school? How do you envision your work in this area and degree to impact your community and help you develop a global/broader perspective?
  - Personal Accomplishments: Interests and talents.
  - Community Involvement: Extracurricular activities, volunteering and civic organizations.
  - Academic Accomplishments: Honors and achievements.
  - Professional Experiences: Work experience and professional affiliations.

Things to Do in the Fall Semester of Your Senior Year

- *Apply to Graduate Programs*: Narrow down your graduate program choices. Review the requirements for admission at each program, and map out how you will complete the applications by the deadline. Pay close attention to the requirements when completing the applications and, ensure you follow the directions provided. Note that most applications will require letters of recommendation and official transcripts from your undergraduate institution. Make sure to budget enough money for the application process. You have to pay an application fee before you can submit the application. Sometimes, graduate school or the graduate program is able to grant application fee waivers on a first-come, first-serve basis, so make sure you ask! Requesting transcripts to be sent to multiple institutions can get expensive. You can ask if the graduate program admissions committee will consider an informal transcript during application review. Some programs allow you to submit formal transcripts after you have been accepted into the program but before you are officially enrolled.

- *Take the GRE*: Continue to study for the exam until your test administration. Register to take the GRE early. Make sure you register for an early exam date to ensure your score is received by the graduate schools that you are applying to by the application deadline. Make sure to have your GRE scores sent to the graduate program to which you are applying.

- *Finalize Your Personal Statement*: Continue to revise your personal statement, and share it with professors, mentors, career services, and the writing center. Use their input to revise your personal statement. Strong personal statements can be very valuable to make a case for you during admissions decisions.

- *Request Letters of Recommendation*: Identify faculty members who will write strong letters of recommendation for you. Provide these faculty members with your resume and personal statement so they can reference your experiences, strengths, and areas of interest when they write your recommendation letter. Give them ample time to write these letters.

- *Financing Your Education*: Submit your Free Application for Federal Student Aid (FAFSA) form to access funding for graduate school. FAFSA is used to determine eligibility for funding through grants and scholarships as well as student loans that must be repaid. You can submit your FAFSA application online beginning October 1 at https://fafsa.ed.gov/.

Things to Do in the Spring Semester of Your Senior Year

- *Follow Up on Graduate Applications*: Contact the graduate programs where you applied to ensure that all application documents have been received. If possible, schedule a visit to the graduate schools to which you applied and meet with current students, faculty, and staff in those programs. You can expect to receive a letter of admission, including information about funding and research/teaching positions around mid- to late March. You should accept or decline offers of admission around late April or early May.

Funding Sources for Latinx and Minority Students

As mentioned earlier in this chapter, graduate studies do not have to be costly. Many graduate programs provide some level of funding, but there are additional financial resources available to Latinx students. There are scholarship and grant opportunities available from both private and governmental funding sources to pay for graduate school. Below is a list of selected funding opportunities and resources that can help you find funding for multiple programs in STEM fields. This list is to assist you in identifying financial resources and is no way comprehensive of all of the funding that is available. These scholarships, research grants, and internships include various levels of funding. Some of these resources are available one time, and others are renewable and available for multiple years during the course of a student's graduate studies. More detailed information about financial resources can be found by visiting the websites listed within the chart. These sources are not attached to a particular institution, so you should also check with your school's financial aid office to determine if other funding opportunities are available.

Table 6.1 List of Scholarships

Name of Scholarship	Website	Deadline	General Information
Support for Hispanic Students in STEM			
Society of Hispanic Professional Engineers Foundation	http://www.shpefoundation.org/scholarships	May 1	Latino students studying engineering.
Hispanic Scholarship Fund	https://hsf.net/en/scholarships/	Multiple deadlines available through third-party links.	Multiple scholarship offers for all fields of study.
Gates Millennium Scholars Program	http://gmsp.org/	August	Scholarships available for all majors and for any university.
Hispanic Association of Colleges and Universities	http://www.hacu.net/hacu/Scholarships.asp	Deadline published annually.	Scholarships for students who demonstrate financial need; website includes a list of additional scholarships available with other organizations.
Hispanic Dental Association	http://www.hdassoc.org/hda-foundation/scholarship-program/	May 15	Scholarships for students interested in studying dentistry.
League of United Latin American Citizens, in conjunction with General Electric	http://lulac.org/programs/education/scholarships/index.html	March 31	Awards are available for Hispanic students studying business or engineering; website also provides a list of additional scholarships available with organization affiliates.
National Action Council for Minorities in Engineering	http://www.nacme.org/	Multiple deadlines available through member institutions.	Scholarships for minority engineering students.
National Association of Multicultural Engineering Program Advocates	http://www.namepa.org/student-scholarships	Multiple deadlines available through member institutions.	Scholarships for freshmen students entering an engineering program and students transferring from a community college to a four-year engineering program.

Organization	URL	Deadline	Description
National Alliance for Hispanic Health	http://www.hispanichealth.org/signature-programs.html	March 15	Large scholarship/internship awards for high school seniors and additional scholarships to students with a declared STEM major.
Funding Sources for Diverse Populations			
Alfred P. Sloan Foundation Graduate Scholarship Program	http://sloanphds.org/	Deadline published annually.	Graduate scholarship awards and funding opportunities for research, professional conferences, and fellowships.
Alliances for Graduate Education and the Professoriate	http://www.nsfagep.org/		Provides a list of scholarship sources and internship opportunities for minority students.
American Association of University Women	http://www.aauw.org/what-we-do/educational-funding-and-awards/	Multiple deadlines.	Provides list of educational scholarship and fellowship funding for graduate women.
Ford Foundation Diversity Fellowships	http://sites.nationalacademies.org/PGA/FordFellowships/	Deadline published annually.	Provides sponsorship at the predoctoral, dissertation, and postdoctoral level by the National Academy of Sciences.
MS PhD	http://www.msphds.org/	Deadline published annually.	Provides mentoring assistance for minority PhD students in earth systems science and engineering.
Southern Regional Education Board Doctoral Studies Program	http://www.sreb.org/page/1074/	March 1	Offers awards to students pursuing Ph.D. and plan to become college and university professors.
General Graduate/Scholar Funding Sources			
Alfred P. Sloan Foundation	http://www.sloan.org/	Deadline published annually.	Graduate scholarship awards and funding opportunities for research, professional conferences and fellowships.

(continued)

Table 6.1 (*Continued*)

Name of Scholarship	Website	Deadline	General Information
Council for International Exchange of Scholars	http://www.cies.org/	Multiple deadlines.	The Fulbright Scholar Programs provide funding for teaching/research grants to U.S. faculty and experienced professionals, teaching, independent, and post-doctoral research, and professional foreign exchange for scholar programs.
Grants.net	http://sciencecareers.sciencemag.org/funding	Multiple deadlines available through third-party links.	Searchable database maintained by AAAS and *Science Magazine*.
Integrative Graduate Education and Research Traineeship (IGERT)	http://www.igert.org/	Multiple deadlines.	Sponsored by the U.S. National Science Foundation, IGERT provides support for interdisciplinary training and educating PhD scientists and engineers at member institutions.
Western Regional Graduate Program	http://wiche.edu/wrgp	Deadline published annually.	Helps with tuition costs so students pay only in-state costs for enrolling in a member graduate program.
Funding Sources for Life and Health Sciences			
Howard Hughes Medical Institute	http://www.hhmi.org/about	Deadline published annually.	Supports early career scientist in biomedical research and science education with post-doctoral appointments to support new and innovative research.
Life Sciences Research Foundation	http://www.lsrf.org/home	October 1	Post-doctoral research support in the medical research and life sciences area.
McKnight Endowment Fund for Neuroscience	https://www.neuroscience.mcknight.org/	Multiple dates.	Support for master's and Ph.D. degree-holders in the neuroscience of brain disorders and memory and cognitive disorders professional areas.

Name	URL	Deadline	Description
Tylenol Scholarship	http://www.tylenol.com/news/scholarship	Deadline published annually.	Awards competitive scholarships to students in the health and life sciences who have demonstrated leadership and involvement in community activities.
Funding for Sciences and Engineering			
AAAS Career Resources	http://www.aaas.org/careers		Provides information for students regarding internships, fellowships, and other opportunities for scientists.
American Society for Engineering Education	http://www.asee.org/fellowship-programs	Multiple deadlines.	Provides external links to various science and engineering funding opportunities.
National Defense Science & Engineering Graduate Fellowship	http://ndseg.asee.org/	December	Offers three-year graduate fellowships to students training in science and engineering disciplines of military importance.
NOAA National Estuarine Research System Graduate Fellowship	http://www.nerrs.noaa.gov/Fellowship.aspx	November 1	Fellowships to conduct research to address natural and social science priority issues, working with disciplines such as biology, ecosystems engineering, anthropology, biogeochemical, etc.
National Science Foundation Graduate Research Fellowship Program	http://www.nsfgrfp.org/	October and November (depending on major).	Funding for master's and Ph.D. students, supports students in NSF-supported STEM disciplines.
Naval Research Intern Program	http://nreip.asee.org/	December	10-week paid internship opportunity for undergraduate and graduate students.
Smithsonian Institution	http://www.smithsonianofi.com/	Multiple deadlines.	Provides information about various fellowship, research, internship, and research-study opportunities with the Smithsonian system.

SUMMARY

Latinx students are underrepresented in STEM fields. Global competition in technical fields coupled with Hispanic non-whites being one of the largest growing demographic in the United States makes the case for Latinx students to pursue advanced degrees in the area of STEM. STEM access and success is important to universities, industries, and the nation. Careers in STEM will continue to grow, and Latinx students must be trained with the technical skills necessary to fill future positions in these industries. Attending a graduate program in a STEM field is an opportunity for students to participate in future scientific and technological advances that will lead the country in areas of employment, innovation and development, and research.

The information contained in this chapter is meant to encourage and guide Latinx students to take on the rewarding work of pursuing graduate studies in STEM fields. Initially, graduate school can seem inaccessible to you if you do not understand the benefits of pursuing another degree, what graduate school requirements entail, or the process of preparing for an advanced degree. Therefore, you need information about what questions to ask, how to evaluate program requirements, and how to determine if pursuing graduate studies is the right decision for them. It is important for you to explore your options and decide early in your academic career whether you plan to continue on to graduate school. You need to prepare early for graduate school in much of the same way you prepared for high school and college. You need to know why you want to pursue a master's or doctorate degree and what steps to take next.

In review, graduate school builds on students' understanding of the norms of their professions and provides them with the requisite skills to become experts within their disciplines. Therefore, you need to decide on a career path, contemplate the importance of attaining a graduate degree in your area, understand the differences between the master's or doctorate degrees in your field, factor in the length of time your chosen program will take, and consider the mental and financial commitment required to pursue advanced studies. Academic preparation begins early. In addition to the standard requirements of GPA and GRE scores, you need to engage in research and conversations with professors and faculty mentors. Faculty members can help you develop an understanding of the vast options that are available to you through graduate work. Moreover, by actively participating in organizations and undergraduate research programs, you will position yourself for academic success at the graduate level.

Additionally, you should be proactive and develop an educational plan. As part of the graduate school process, you must know yourself and develop your professional goals and career plans for advanced studies. You must do the research to effectively evaluate which graduate programs are aligned with your career interest, support diversity, provide academic and social integration, and fall within your desired range of location and cost. You should pursue advanced degrees in STEM despite assumptions of financial limitations. A myriad of financial resources is available for Latinx students wanting to pursue graduate degrees in STEM—advanced degrees do not have to be costly.

In closing, multiple factors that contribute to the academic success of Latinx students in STEM have been presented and discussed in this chapter. You must do the research to determine which graduate program is a good fit for your career path, whether that career path falls within academia, research, or industry. Hopefully the information provided for continuing on to graduate school in STEM and the identification of factors that support Latinx students in graduate programs has better equipped you to make an informed decision about choosing the graduate program that will serve you best.

REFERENCES

American Council on Education. (2006). *Increasing the success of minority students in science and technology.* Retrieved from http://www.acenet.edu/news-room/Pages/Increasing-the-Success-of-Minority-Students-in-Science-and-Technology.aspx

Bonous-Hammarth, M. (2000). Pathways to success: Affirming opportunities for science, mathematics, and engineering majors. *Journal of Negro Education, 69*(1), 92–111.

Camacho, M. M., & Lord, S. M. (2011). Quebrando fronteras: Trends among Latino and Latina undergraduate engineers. *Journal of Hispanic Higher Education, 10*(2), 134–146.

Chen, X., & Weko, T. (2009). Students who study science, technology, engineering and mathematics (STEM) in post-secondary education. *Stats in Brief: NCES 2009-161.* Washington, DC: U.S. Department of Education, National Center for Education Statistics.

Committee on Institutional Cooperation. (n.d.). *Applying to graduate school: Tips, timeline, and tools of the trade.* Retrieved from http://www.cic.net/docs/default-source/diversity/gradschoolguide.pdf

Crisp, G., & Cruz, I. (2009). Mentoring college students: A critical review of the literature between 1990 and 2007. *Research in Higher Education, 50*(6), 525–545.

Desmond, M., & Lopez-Turley, R. N. (2009). The role of familism in explaining the Hispanic- White college application gap. *Social Problems, 56*(2), 311–334.

Donnelly, A.E. & Jacobi, J. (2010). *Attracting, retaining, and preparing a diverse academic engineering workforce: The AGEP model for success.* Paper presented at the IEEE Educon Engineering Conference, Madrid, Spain.

Dowd, A. C., Malcom, L.E. & Bensimon, E. M. (2009). *Benchmarking the success of Latino and Latina students in STEM to achieve national graduation goals.* Center for Urban Education, Los Angeles: University of Southern California.

Figueroa, T., & Hurtado, S. (2013, November). *Underrepresented racial and/or ethnic minority (URM) graduate students in stem disciplines: A critical approach to understanding graduate school experiences and obstacles to degree progression.* Paper presented at the Association for the Study of Higher Education in St. Louis, MO. https://www.heri.ucla.edu/nih/downloads /ASHE2013-URM-Grad-Students-in-STEM.pdf

Gardner, S. K. (2007). I heard it through the grapevine: Doctoral student socialization in chemistry and history. *Higher Education, 54*(5), 723–740.

Gardner, S. K. (2008). What's too much and what's too little? The process of becoming an independent researcher in doctoral education. *The Journal of Higher Education, 79*(3), 326–350.

Godoy, C. (2010). *The contribution of HSIs to the preparation of Hispanics for STEM careers: A multiple case study.* [EdD dissertation]. Philadelphia, PA: University of Pennsylvania.

Hernandez, J. C. (2000). Understanding the retention of Latino college students. *Journal of College Student Development, 41*, 575–588.

Hernandez, J. C., & Lopez, M. A. (2004). Leaking pipeline: Issues impacting Latino/a college student retention. *Journal of College Student Retention, 6*(1), 37–60.

Hunter, A., Laursen, L. S., & Seymour, E. (2007). Becoming a scientist: The role of undergraduate research in students' cognitive, personal, and professional development, *Science Education, 91*, 36–74.

Koebler, J. (2011, December 15). 12 Scholarships for Hispanic Students Interested in STEM. *U.S. News & World Report.* Retrieved from http://www.usnews .com/news/blogs/stem-education/2011/12/15/12-scholarships-for-hispanic -students-interested-in-stem

Koledoye, K. A. (2013). *Differences in STEM degree attainment by region, ethnicity, and degree type.* (Doctoral dissertation). Retrieved from https://ezproxy .shsu.edu/login?url=http://search.proquest.com/docview/1507564277 ?accountid=7065

Malcom, L. E., & Dowd, A. C. (2012). The impact of undergraduate debt on the graduate school enrollment of STEM baccalaureates. *The Review of Higher Education, 35*(2), Winter, 265–305.

Maton, K. I., Wimms, H. E., Grant, S. K., Wittig, M. A., Rogers, M. R., & Vasquez, M. J. T. (2011). Experiences and perspectives of African-American, Latina/o, Asian-American and European-American psychology graduate students: A national study. *Culture Diverse Ethnic Psychology, 17*(1), 68–78. doi: 10 .1037/a0021668

National Governors Association for Best Practices. (2011). *Innovation America: Building a science, technology, engineering, and math: Education agenda an update of state actions.* Retrieved from http://www.nga.org/files/live/sites /NGA/files/pdf/1112STEMGUIDE.PDF

Nuñez, A., McDonough, P. M., Ceja, M., & Solorzano, D. (2008). Diversity within: Latino college choice and ethnic comparisons. In C. A. Gallagher (Ed.), *Racism in post-race America: New theories, new directions,* 267–281. Chapel Hill, NC: Social Forces.

Pender, M., Marcotte, D. E., Sto. Domingo, M. R., & Maton, K. I. (2010). The STEM pipeline: The role of summer research experience in minority students' Ph.D. aspirations. *Educational Policy Analysis Archives, 18*(30).

Peralta, C., Caspary, M., & Boothe, D. (2013). Success factors impacting Latina/o persistence in higher education leading to STEM opportunities. *Cultural Studies of Science Education, 8*(4), 905–918.

Ramirez, E. (2011). "No One Taught Me the Steps": Latinos' Experiences Applying to Graduate School. *Journal of Latinos and Education, 10*(3), 204–222.

Ramirez, E. (2013). Examining Latinos/as' graduate school choice process: An intersectionality perspective. *Journal of Hispanic Higher Education, 12*(1), 23–36.

Tinto, V. (1993). *Leaving college: Rethinking the causes and cures of student attrition* (2nd ed.). Chicago: University of Chicago Press.

Toldson, I. A., & Esters, L. L. (2012). *The quest for excellence: Supporting the academic success of minority males in science, technology, engineering, and mathematics (STEM) disciplines.* Washington, DC: Association of Public and Land-Grant Universities.

University of Central Florida (2015). *McNair Scholars Program—Funding.* Retrieved from http://mcnairscholars.com/funding/

PART III

Choosing a Career in STEM

CHAPTER SEVEN

STEP 7: Choosing a Career in STEM—STEM Majors

Rosa M. Banda and Alonzo M. Flowers III

"The hardest thing is not making a decision. It is thinking about the results of what you have decided."

—Anonymous

There are many life decisions that often determine our life paths as young adults. Among those, one of the most important and impactful decisions students make is choosing an appropriate college major and career pathway. Part of this decision is choosing the appropriate college or university to attend. Students also consider the "personality fit" (Holland, 1997) between who they are, what they are interested in, and how these are connected to their career choice. The end of your high school experience and the beginning of your undergraduate are important times in your life. It is at this time that you will make very important decisions that will impact your future career selection.

Considering the quote cited above, the decision to select a college major that will subsequently impact your career selection is not necessarily the most difficult choice you will make. Rather, what is hardest is an understanding of the *results of your decision* to pursue a specific career. This is where career planning becomes important. For example, if you choose a STEM major, do you really understand all the preparation that is needed and what this major can do for you in your future professional career?

This chapter seeks to provide information on science, technology, engineering, and mathematics (STEM) career pathways to allow you to make a better-informed decision in regard to your career planning. The shortage of students (particularly women, students of color, and other underrepresented student populations) who choose to pursue a career in STEM majors is well known (National Academy of

Science, 2007; National Science Foundation [NSF], 2009). Despite universities' repeated attempts and purposeful designed programs to increase student interest to pursue a STEM career, there has not been much success. This remains a matter of national interest (Museus, Palmer, Davis, and Maramba, 2011).

We aim to provide you with detailed and concrete information about the choices that a career in STEM will afford you after your college graduation. This chapter provides you with the *end result* of what your college major should materialize. First, we offer practical advice in regard to what you should consider before you choose a major in college let alone a STEM major. We then offer concrete information in relation to the following subsections: careers in science, careers in technology, careers in engineering, and careers in mathematics. Before the end of the chapter, we provide a list of online resources so you can further explore and learn about what STEM careers entail.

POINTS TO CONSIDER BEFORE YOU CHOOSE A MAJOR

This section details three important points to consider before you choose a college major. First, you *must* be genuinely reflective about what "dream big" means and looks like for you. Second, you must "assess your skills" in an accurate and realistic manner. Third, you must develop "plans to succeed" to create an opportunity to access the necessary resources and important individuals who can help you toward successful completion of your undergraduate degree and your entrance into a STEM career.

Figure 7.1.—Gearing for success in motion offers an illustration of the interlocking and dependent processes critical for your success to help in your decision to choose a college major. The sprocket wheels illustrate the interrelatedness of the importance of dreaming big, assessing your skills, and planning to succeed as a constantly rotating process that requires you to self-monitor your career path. Essentially your aspirations, goals, and desires are the key mechanisms that control the direction of your gears that align your determination to succeed. It is vital to continually assess your skills as you progress to the career planning process.

Dream Big. Part of being able to "dream big" is to visualize yourself in *your* future. What makes you happy? What genuinely interests you? How do you see yourself? Are you doing what you love? Oftentimes, the end result of a decision is your ability to picture what your future looks like. Such a vivid vision allows you to set goals and implement a plan to reach your desired potential. To dream big in STEM, you should consider the following questions:

- *Why* are you choosing a particular STEM major? What draws you to this major? What do you hope to get out of this field?

- Are you willing to make the sacrifices to attend college, and do you have the perseverance to stick with your plans all the way toward completing your degree in STEM?

- Do you see yourself as a STEM professional, for example, as a future scientist, astronaut, engineer, or mathematician?

Figure 7.1   Gearing for Success in Motion

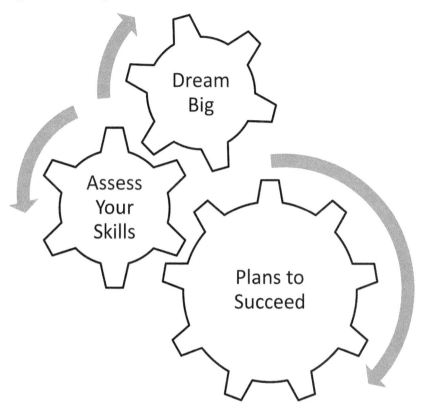

- Is there an *actual* student (undergraduate or graduate), professor, or professional in STEM you can speak to in order to better understand their experiences in STEM?

- How do other students' authentic experiences in STEM majors and professional settings align with the way you see yourself as a STEM student and future professional? Is a STEM major really for you?

- What do you plan to do as a future STEM professional? How do you believe you can make an impact in STEM?

An example of the depth and importance of hopes and dreams for your future is the experience of Sally Ride, the first female American astronaut in space. She stated:

I would like to be remembered as someone who was not afraid to do what she wanted to do, and as someone who took risks along the way in order to achieve her goals. (National Aeronautics and Space Administration [NASA], 2014)

Ride majored in physics at Stanford. By happenstance, she read an advertisement in her college newspaper where NASA sought participants for an astronaut program. While in space, she operated a robotic arm that helped put satellites into space (NASA, 2014). With her physics degree, Ride dreamed and visualized more than being just a physicist. She dreamed big, and so should you!

Assess Your Skills. Is a STEM major the right fit for you? You need to determine if you are *actually* good at math and science. You should also carefully assess your skills to reflect an accurate and realistic understanding of what you *know* you are good at. Jacobs and Hyman (2009, para. 10) stress that "[u]nder no circumstances should you major in something you don't have the skills and gifts for." Be, in other words, certain that you possess the necessary skills to be successful in your pursuit of a STEM major. Part of assessing your skills is taking into account how successful you have been in your high school math and science courses. If you have done well in high school math and science courses, you have a good idea that this is something you are good at doing, but if you have not done well, perhaps STEM is not a good fit for you.

Regardless of major choice, it is important to assess your skills. For instance, Dr. Daniel Hale Williams, an African American doctor, was the first surgeon to perform open heart surgery in 1893. Dr. Williams *had* to *accurately* assess his skills before he attempted a medical procedure that had never been conducted. In other words, Dr. Williams had to think carefully about whether he indeed had the skills to perform the surgery successfully. Ultimately, Dr. Williams saved the life of James Cornish. Such a feat would not have been possible had he inaccurately assessed his skills. An accurate assessment of skills, coupled with one's ability to dream big, are critical precursors to the manner in which people set goals as a means to execute the necessary plans to succeed.

Plans to Succeed. You must plan to succeed, and you must be persistent in staying the course to achieve your short- and long-term goals. In other words, you must not give up on your plans to succeed in STEM. The result of your ability to dream big and to accurately assess your skills are reflected in short-term, incremental goals that ultimately create your individualized plans to succeed. Adriana C. Ocampo, a planetary scientist and lead program executive for NASA, disclosed in an interview about how she visualized becoming a scientist as a young student who went to college to help achieve her dream. Ocampo (NASA, 2015, para. 3) shared, "Space exploration was my passion from a very young age, and I knew I wanted to be a part of it. I would dream and design space colonies while sitting atop the roof of my family's home in Argentina." Dr. Ocampo's clearly visualized plan is a reflection of a map to her career. Throughout her career, she utilized resources and maintained relationships with professional organizations as a form of networking. You can do the same. Plan for your success!

CAREERS IN SCIENCE

Before you can dream big, assess your skills, and create plans to succeed, you must be well-informed. You should also have a concrete understanding of the types of jobs that will be available to you once you attain your STEM degree. The sciences ". . . are all about exploration and delving into the unknown" (CollegeXpress and Ward, 2015, para. 1). As abstract as that may sound, there are many career paths that remain concrete in nature. Whether you choose to pursue a major in earth and environmental science or physical science, there are many jobs available upon graduation.

Table 7.1 notes various careers as well as the required subjects to be studied in school, minimal education attainment, median salary, and key skills set needed to successfully perform the job. The careers highlighted show a breadth of career options that you can choose from if you attain an earth or physical science degree.

Table 7.1   Careers in Science

STEM Area	Career	Subjects to Study in High School	Minimum Education	Median Salary
Earth and Physical Science	Climate change analyst	Physics, algebra, geometry, calculus, English; if available, environmental science, computer science, statistics, political science	Bachelor's degree	$62,920
Earth and Physical Science	Environmental scientist	Biology, chemistry, physics, geometry, algebra II, calculus; if available, environmental science, statistics	Bachelor's degree	$62,920
Earth and Physical Science	Geographer	Chemistry, physics, computer science, geometry, algebra II, pre-calculus, calculus; if available, statistics, environmental science, applied technology	Bachelor's degree	$74,760
Physical Science	Astronomer	Chemistry, physics, computer science, algebra, geometry, calculus; if available, earth science, statistics	Doctoral degree	$95,500
Physical Science	Chemistry teacher	Biology, chemistry, physics, geometry, algebra, pre-calculus, English; if available, foreign language	Bachelor's degree	$54,270
Physical Science	Pilot	Physics, computer science, algebra, geometry, algebra II, English; if available, applied technology, foreign language	Bachelor's degree	$70,000

Source: Data Collected from Science Buddies: *Careers in Science.* (2015). Retrieved from http://www.sciencebuddies.org/science-engineering-careers#lifesciences.

The careers range in area of interest and focus from a geographer to an astronomer to a pilot. While these careers are distinctly different, the required skill set such as deductive skills, analytical skills, and abstract thinking remain an underlying commonality. It is imperative for you to pay particular attention to the required courses needed to successfully plan for these careers. As indicated on the chart, for example, an environmental scientist must take courses in physics, chemistry, geometry, and environmental statistics in order to successfully prepare for this field of study. Assessing your academic skill set is an important step in gearing up your career planning process in science.

Careers in Technology

Much like the previous section that explores careers available in science, this section provides you with information about the careers in technology. Because we live in a technologically savvy world, there is an abundance of career opportunities if you choose to pursue a major in technology. This, in other words, suggests that "demand for computer professionals with the right qualifications is at an all time high" (Career Profiles, 2015, para. 1). As such, being qualified in a rapidly changing technological world works to your advantage if you attain a technology degree.

Much like Table 7.1 that discloses careers in science, Table 7.2 denotes career options in technology. A similar outline highlights the required subjects to be studied in school, minimal education attainment, and median salary to successfully perform the job. When you choose to major in and attain a degree in technology, there are various career paths you can follow. The careers range in area of interest and focus from a computer science engineer to a data scientist to a computer programmer. For careers that fall under this realm, the underlying and connecting skill sets needed include analytical skills, logical thinking, and being detail-oriented. Again, the required high school courses that will be required to plan for these careers include applied technology, statistics, and computer science. Such classes, if not offered at your high school, can be taken via dual credit courses with your local community college. Your high school counselor would be a contact person to help you with dual credit courses. Assessing your academic skill set is a vital step in gearing up your career planning process in technology.

Careers in Engineering

This section explores the careers available to you if you choose to pursue an engineering degree. You may choose to pursue a civil, mechanical, petroleum, industrial, electrical, environmental, biomedical, computer, or geotechnical (to name a few) engineering degree. Because there is a national shortage of engineers, you should know that there are many jobs to be filled in every engineering career field. The shortage of engineers remains the " 'New American Dilemma" (National Action Council for Minorities in Engineering [NACME], 2013), which suggests that plentiful career choices await you.

Table 7.2   Careers in Technology

STEM Area	Career	Subjects to Study in High School	Minimum Education	Median Salary
Computer Technology	Computer hardware engineer	Physics, chemistry, computer science, algebra, geometry, algebra II, calculus, English; if available, electronics	Bachelor's degree	$98,610
Computer Technology	Computer programmer	Physics, computer science, algebra, geometry, calculus	Bachelor's degree	$72,630
Computer Technology	Computer software engineer	Physics, chemistry, computer science, geometry, algebra, algebra II, calculus, English	Bachelor's degree	$96,600
Computer Technology	Computer systems analyst	Chemistry, physics, algebra II, pre-calculus, calculus, English; if available, computer science, statistics, applied technology	Vocational/associate's degree	$79,680
Computer Technology	Data scientist	Biology, physics, geometry, algebra II, pre-calculus, calculus, English; if available: computer science, statistics	Bachelor's degree	$103,000
Computer Technology	Database administrator	Biology, chemistry, algebra, geometry, algebra II, pre-calculus, English; if available, business, computer science	Associate's degree	$75,190

Source: Data Collected from Science Buddies: *Careers in Math and Computer Science.* (2015). Retrieved from http://www.sciencebuddies.org/science-engineering-careers#mathcomputerscience.

Much like Tables 7.1 and 7.2 that disclose careers in science and technology, respectively, Table 7.3 explores career options in engineering. Identical to the first two tables, Table 7.3 also offers an examination of the required school subjects, minimal education attainment, and median salary. Your choice to pursue and attain an engineering degree affords you a wide range of career paths with much availability, given the shortage of engineers in the U.S. workforce. With that said, the careers range in area of interest and focus from aerospace, architect, and civil to energy. For engineers, the common skill set found amongst them is creativity, problem-solving skills, and detail-oriented mindset. The mind of an engineer, in other words, works with a solution in mind for a given problem. Like degrees in science and technology, there are course requirements that aspiring engineers must take into account in high school. Such course requirements include advanced math, physics, calculus, and other high-level mathematics. Assessing your academic skill set, particularly as it relates to your ability to be successful in advanced level mathematics courses, is a vital step in gearing up your career planning process in engineering.

Table 7.3   Careers in Engineering

STEM Area	Career	Subjects to Study in High School	Minimum Education	Median Salary
Engineering	Aerospace engineer	Chemistry, physics, computer science, algebra, geometry, calculus, English; if available, applied technology, statistics	Bachelor's degree	$102, 420
Engineering	Architect	Physics, chemistry, geometry, algebra II, pre-calculus, calculus, English; if available, art, applied technology (CAD)	Bachelor's degree	$73,340
Engineering	Biochemical engineer	Physics, chemistry, biology, algebra, geometry, calculus	Bachelor's degree	$90,580
Engineering	Civil engineer	chemistry, physics, computer science, geometry, algebra II, pre-calculus, calculus, English; if available, statistics, environmental science, applied technology	Bachelor's degree	$77,990
Engineering	Energy engineer	Biology, chemistry, physics, geometry, algebra II, pre-calculus, calculus, English; if available, computer science, statistics, applied technology, business	Bachelor's degree	$90,580
Engineering	Photonics engineer	Chemistry, physics, algebra, geometry, calculus; if available, applied technology	Bachelor's degree	$90,580

Source: Data Collected from Science Buddies: *Careers in Engineering.* (2015). Retrieved from http://www.sciencebuddies.org/science-engineering-careers#engineering.

Careers in Mathematics

Choosing to major in mathematics, much like science, technology, and engineering, also gives you viable options for your future career path. The Mathematical Association of America (2015) noted that, according to CareerCast, being a mathematician was voted to be the best job for 2014 on the premise of environment, outlook, stress, and income. The latter was also taken into account in a study conducted by PayScale. The study disclosed that mathematics was the common thread that connected 15 of the "highest earning college degrees" (Mathematical Association of America, 2015, para. 1) primarily due to the interdisciplinary analytical and problem-solving skills that mathematics requires.

Table 7.4 explores careers in mathematics. This table also examines the subjects needed to be studied in school, minimal education attainment, and median salary needed to successfully perform the job. Your decision to pursue and attain a mathematics degree offers you various career options. Such careers range anywhere from an economist to a math teacher to a statistician. The common skill set found among most mathematicians include excellent, sporadic spatial skills as well as analytical and abstract thinking. The pursuit of a mathematics degree suggests that you are relatively successful at computing high-level forms of mathematics. Like other science, technology, and engineering majors, those who choose to major in mathematics must have taken high school courses that include, but are not limited

Table 7.4   Careers in Mathematics

STEM Area	Career	Subject to Study in High School	Minimum Education	Median Salary
Mathematics	Actuary	Geometry, algebra II, pre-calculus, calculus, English; if available, computer science, statistics, business	Bachelor's degree	$91,060
Mathematics	Economist	Geometry, algebra II, pre-calculus, calculus, English; if available, computer science, statistics, environmental science, business	Bachelor's degree	$90,550
Mathematics	Math teacher	Physics, geometry, algebra II, pre-calculus, calculus, English; if available, computer science, statistics, child development, foreign language	Bachelor's degree	$ 54,270
Mathematics	Mathematician	Physics, computer science, geometry, algebra II, pre-calculus, calculus, English; if available, statistics	Bachelor's degree	$ 101,040
Mathematics	Statistician	Chemistry, physics, biology, computer science, geometry, algebra II, pre-calculus, calculus, English; if available, statistics, environmental science, economics	Bachelor's degree	$73,880

Source: Data Collected from Science Buddies: *Careers in Math and Computer Science*. (2015). Retrieved from http://www.sciencebuddies.org/science-engineering-careers#mathcomputerscience.

to, algebra II, calculus, and physics. Success in these high school courses give you a good sense of your STEM academic skill set necessary to gear up your career planning process in mathematics.

HELPFUL ONLINE RESOURCES

While the chapter offers concrete examples of the career path you may choose if you pursue and attain a STEM degree, there is much more information about many more jobs within your respective career path. The limited space in this chapter, in other words, offers you a solid, though snapshot explanation of the careers

Table 7.5   Additional Online Resources to Explore a STEM Career

Website	Description
https://www.science pioneers.org/students /stem-websites	The Science Pioneers site provides a good catalog of STEM careers through an interactive format.
http://www.pathwaysto science.org/whatwepost .aspx	This website promotes STEM education and career opportunities for underrepresented groups via news items and fellowship opportunities, to name a few.
http://tryengineering.org/	This website introduces students to the world of engineering. It includes lesson plans for educators and interactive engineering-based activities for students.
http://www.discovery education.com//students/ ?campaign=flyout _students	This site has all types of resources for science, math, English, and social studies. The site also has interactive games, puzzles, activities, contests, STEM career information, and virtual labs.
http://thefunworks.edc.org /SPT—homegraphic.php	This site promotes STEM career development via diverse interests for middle and high school youth.
http://www.science buddies.org/	This website has over 1,000 ideas for science fair projects, project guides, project kits and detailed profiles of STEM careers.
http://stem-works.com/	This website includes helpful articles and job information in STEM fields. STEM-Works also includes activities and games that will inform the student about interesting STEM areas of study.
http://www.bls.gov/k12/ index.htm	On this website you will find careers that relate to your STEM interests and learn fun facts about STEM careers.
http://www.discovere.org/	Discover Engineering—the careers and companies at the leading edge, games, activities, interesting facts, and videos all for students to learn more about engineering.
http://www.exploratorium .edu/explore/	An online resource and video library for hundreds of topics in math and science.

available, high school courses needed (or preferred), minimal salary, and key skills set required to successfully navigate a career in STEM. Because we recognize the need to provide further assistance for you to continue to explore in-depth your own STEM-related career aspirations, we offer a list of online resources (see Table 7.5) with a brief explanation of the resource to assist you. In addition to these online resources, we encourage you to launch your own investigation into other websites that can help you further explore various career options in STEM.

In addition to the online resources referenced in Table 7.5, we previously noted and suggest that you also seek out high school counselors, teachers, academic advisers, individuals who currently pursue a STEM-related discipline in postsecondary education, and a STEM professional who actively works in the field to further enhance the options available if you choose to pursue a STEM major in college. Different perspectives offered from various individuals can provide you with a deeper understanding if you choose to pursue a STEM major in college. Moreover, discussions with STEM professionals also provide you a much more concrete and tangible understanding of a particular career—an understanding that is not possible with *only* the exploration of online resources. In other words, networking with people within the realm of STEM careers serves as a critical resource that allows for a more complete understanding of the multifaceted process that is career planning. As such, we encourage you to seek various online and real-life outlets so that you can make a well-informed decision about your possible decision to pursue a STEM major in college and, subsequently, the career options available to you after the attainment of your degree.

CONCLUSION

As an emerging young adult, the decisions you begin to make about college and career may seem daunting at times. As you consider what to choose as a college major, it is important for you and your family to do some careful thinking and planning for your future. First, it is important for you to "dream big" about your future. Visualize who you want to be and where you see yourself in the future. Next, you must "assess your skills" in an accurate and realistic manner. What do you enjoy that you are relatively good at? Last, devise your "plans to succeed" in such a way that you develop and visualize a roadmap that is comprised of both short-term and long-term goals.

Your decision to pursue a STEM major in college and subsequently enter the STEM profession begins with your ability to "dream big" in regards to your future. While you may already know what your interests are and what you are good at, it is more difficult to imagine the what you can *actually* do with the attainment of a STEM degree. This chapter is designed to help you to understand the potential outcomes of choosing a STEM field of study. We offer you a critical and practical examination of STEM careers, high school course requirements, minimal education, median salary, and key skills set required for success. We also offer additional online resources to help further your own investigation of the STEM-related career that best suits your interests and aspirations. We also offer you a snapshot look at what STEM career options are available, *if* you *choose* to dream to pursue such aspirations.

REFERENCES

Career Profiles. (2015). *Computer and technology careers*. Retrieved from http://www.careerprofiles.info/computer-careers.html

CollegeXpress, &Ward, T. (2015). *Science majors and potential jobs.* Retrieved from http://www.collegexpress.com/interests/science-and-engineering/articles/studying-sciences/science-majors-and-potential-jobs/

Holland, J. L. (1997). *Making vocational choices: A theory of vocational personalities and work environments*. Odessa, FL: Psychological Assessment Resources, Inc.

Jacobs, L. F., & Hyman, J. S. (2009, December 16). *10 questions to ask before picking a major.* Retrieved from https://www.usnews.com/education/blogs/professors-guide/2009/12/16/10-questions-to-ask-before-picking-a-major

Mathematical Association of America. (2015). *Careers*. Retrieved from http://www.maa.org/careers

Museus, S. D., Palmer, R. T., Davis, R. J., & Maramba D. C. (2011). Racial and ethnic minority students' success in STEM education. *ASHE Higher Education Report, 36*(6), 1–14.

National Academy of Science. (2007). *Rising above the gathering storm: Energizing and employing for a brighter economic future*. Retrieved from https://www.nap.edu/read/11463/chapter/1

National Action Council for Minorities in Engineering (NACME). (2013). Minorities are answer to U.S. shortage of engineers. *NACME Press Releases.* Retrieved from http://www.nacme.org/news/press-releases/41-minorities-are-answer-to-u-s-shortage-of-engineers

National Aeronautics and Space Administration. (2014). *Who was Sally Ride?* Retrieved from https://www.nasa.gov/audience/forstudents/5-8/features/nasa-knows/who-was-sally-ride-58.html

National Aeronautics and Space Administration. (2015). *Adriana Ocampo: Science program manager, NASA Headquarters*. Retrieved from http://solarsystem.nasa.gov/people/profile.cfm?Code=OcampoA

National Science Foundation, Division of Science Resources Statistics. (2009). *Science & engineering degrees by race/ethnicity: 1997–2006,* (NSF 10-300), Table 1.

PART IV

Sharing Stories

CHAPTER EIGHT

Testimonios

Vijay Kanagala and Laura I. Rendón

Previous chapters of this book introduced you to what is science, technology, engineering, and mathematics (STEM), and why STEM majors and careers are important for you to pursue as a Latinx student. Each chapter provides you with valuable information such as how to prepare and choose a college and STEM program, how to pay for college, key strategies for you to be successful in college, advanced STEM degrees and graduate school options, and the importance of academic rigor and developing research skills in college to foster professional confidence in order to pursue STEM careers.

In this chapter, we share with you *testimonios*—stories of inspiration and determination of 14 Latinx individuals who are doctoral students, scientists, college professors, administrators, and managers who successfully pursued STEM degrees and careers using many of the strategies that we outlined in previous chapters. Making use of *testimonios*, we are able to provide you with compelling stories and transformative lived experiences that tell the truth of the myriad ways in which other Latinx navigated the complex pathways to college and careers in STEM.

Many of these Latinx individuals were first-generation college students. Some of them came from low-income backgrounds. All of them had a deep and unwavering conviction and desire to be successful in college. You will notice, as you read these *testimonios*, that not everyone's path to and through college was clearly laid out. At times the world of college and their personal world collided because the academic, cultural and social norms and practices were remarkably different from their home culture. Some had unimaginable life obstacles to overcome. Others endured disappointing and invalidating encounters and were able to learn, be resilient, and persevere through those experiences. Therefore, we feel it is important for you to understand and know what it means to pursue a STEM degree and career as a Latinx student from another Latinx individual who has either already experienced or is experiencing the different aspects of going to college we discussed earlier in this book.

We hope as you carefully read through each *testimonio*, you too are able to witness the palpable joy and pride each Latinx contributor discovered while pursuing their passion; the enormous challenges that were overcome; the priceless mentoring each one of them received from high school teachers, counselors, college faculty and staff; and most importantly the unwavering love and support they received from their *familias*. We are confident that these *testimonios* will resonate with your life experiences and will fuel your confidence and your own passion to pursue STEM degrees and careers.

TESTIMONIO 1

Stephany Alvarez-Ventura

Key Fields of Study: Agroecology, Environmental Studies
Program Manager, School of Environment,
Arts and Society (SEAS)
Florida International University, Miami, FL

It is important for students to work with their advisers in finding a proper schedule to fit the needs of the research project without compromising their well-being. Needless to say, the toughest part of achieving a master's degree was not conducting field research with 2 million bees but going home with stings on my hands and caring for my two children during every single sleepless night for two years, while still achieving a 3.9 GPA.

From a non-English speaking immigrant child to balancing motherhood while earning a master's degree in science, my journey captures the various elements that foster the development of a successful career. Eligibility, readiness, barriers, and affordability are common challenges, but my story also reveals some of the social dynamics that affect many young Latinas entering college. The acknowledgement of such challenges marks an opportunity for those around us to serve as the inspiration and force to achieve success.

Who are those that can help us reach such milestones? How can we recognize those who push us and follow their guidance? While educators and policymakers have recognized the urgent crisis facing young Latinx students, our community can utilize stories such as mine to recognize the power one individual can have on a student's success.

I have come to recognize three types of inspirations in our lives:

#1 La Familia:

My story began in the mid-1980s where the sugar crisis in the Dominican Republic fueled my parents' decision to leave our homeland in search of the American dream. I was only 3 years old then, but a faint memory recalls the first years of learning a new version of Spanish, let alone the English language! I was sent home the first week of preschool due to a miscommunication with my Cuban teacher. A boy slapped me across the cheek, yet when I exclaimed "*me dio una galleta!*" to my teacher, she was thrilled that he shared his "galleta" with me. Enraged, I showed her what a "galleta" meant to me with a jab to the face and quickly found myself in the principal's office, only to learn that "galleta" means "cracker" to Cubans.

For English, the television served as my educator, rambling off words that seemed to be spoken through a muzzle. My body and my mind always jittered with energy, moving too fast for teachers I didn't understand. I always entered a different realm where daydreams fostered creativity since I was forced to sit for hours on end. My father worked every waking moment of the day yet felt hopeless that his master's degree in marketing was no match for my third-grade English reading homework. He would tell me stories of his own discipline in learning not for the love of it but to get out of trouble and challenge authority. My mother has always been there to remind me to take every opportunity presented and to fight hard in the face of adversity. While our family can serve as a direct inspiration in our lives, we also need help from others to develop the aptitude for success.

Entering fourth grade, I had Mr. De Valle as a teacher. He was a short man with a thin nose and a firm demeanor who did not allow students to use language as an excuse for poor performance. He repeated every instruction in Spanish while setting high expectations, and he challenged each student individually. Up to this point, I had not fully connected with my teachers—perhaps due to cultural and language barriers. Also, Mr. De Valle was wittier than me and foresaw my mischievous ways. I met his persistent challenge, learning to focus my attention on instruction and leave distractions outside the classroom. The rest of my adolescent years were met with ease in the classroom. A's and B's became common place, and I received many awards for my educational and sports-driven goals.

Growing up in Miami, Florida, has its many benefits and challenges. For one, there is a wonderful mix of different cultures from which to learn. Unfortunately, it also meant segregation between racial and ethnic groups in high school. I served on both the board of student mediators and was selected to participate in my school's Hispanic Ambassadors Program, where I often found myself in the midst of tension between such groups. These opportunities helped me to develop social and mediation skills, as well as leadership skills. My first resume was developing, and I seized an opportunity to work for a large financial banking institution during my junior year in high school, believing I would enter the financial industry upon high school graduation.

Having extracurricular activities allowed for additional networking time with my tenacious school counselor. Although I had perfected my English by this time, she walked me through the entire college application process to ensure that I would apply. She also helped me fill out my FAFSA and Florida Bright Futures grant applications. Little did I know that these dreadful pieces of paper would cover my *entire* university tuition! Unbeknownst to me, she also submitted my high school volunteer project, *Blow-drying Elderly Women's Hair*, to the Redland's Country Club, where I was recognized with an additional $1,000 scholarship. Knowing and working with school counselors is a critical opportunity for Latinx students, particularly those whose parents never attended college or cannot help with college applications due to language limitations.

THE BEGINNING OF STEM

At this stage, I still did not recognize the power the early mentors had on my life. They played a great part in bringing me to the university campus. However, it would be my university mentors who ultimately helped me decide on a science career. A second type of inspiration developed during this time.

#2 Los Mentores:

The first semester in college is pivotal in who you will become. I decided to bypass the two-year college and applied to a four-year university, Florida International University (FIU). Now the fourth largest university with 54,000 students and the first in offering degrees to Hispanics, FIU was the perfect choice for me since it was close to home and accepted all my scholarships. During college orientation, however, we were herded like cattle to meet with a general adviser. These advisers help you chose a major and select a plan of study for which classes to take. Selecting a major can be overwhelming, especially when you are evaluating potential income versus interesting topics. It is important to spend some time narrowing down which majors to choose and looking at common classes between them. I was one of these students on the fence in choosing a science, technology, engineering, and math (STEM) field or continuing in finance given my banking experience.

Entering the fall semester, I met with Professor Robert Ratner, my English instructor who spoke in a raspy voice and wore a curly silver mullet. Our entire semester assignment was to create a binder of essays on a subject we were passionate about. The purpose was to help students figure out a major with enjoyable topics and evaluate career options that fulfilled their passion. STEM was not my passion, but I was very interested in pollution and how it affected the environment. I had the drive to make a difference in this field and found myself at the doorstep of the adviser for environmental studies, Dr. Jack Parker. He was more than an adviser to me. He was one of the founding faculty members for the university who pushed for the development of the environmental studies program and is a prominently known environmentalist.

People tend to choose the path of least resistance. Not Parker. I tried selecting the nonscience path to an environmental studies degree, but he wouldn't have it. He said that he knew I could do the science and would make a difference in my field, which, like many others, was lacking in Hispanic women. While this helped to persuade me some, his next words made the difference: "If you do the science, you will have more job opportunities and get paid more." DONE! CHECK. LET'S DO THIS! It was the extra push that guided me down the right path.

OVERCOMING THE CHALLENGES OF WORK/LIFE BALANCE

I continued to work in the banking industry for a total of six years between high school and my undergraduate degree. I also married my high school sweetheart during this time. Planning a wedding while in my first year of college was a bit overwhelming. I had to be willing to compromise and let my family help so that I could study. While love is important, my new husband was the complete package. He was not only handsome and hard-working, but he was also an honorable person who supported my endeavors in the STEM field. Balancing a full course load, a part-time job, and a growing social life can be very stressful, but a work/life balance is a very important skill to manage. You can either tell yourself, "No puedo," or become that person that everyone says, "No se como lo haces." I chose the latter and, oftentimes, found myself studying while on the road to our campsite or doing my homework during the NBA finals at family gatherings. I would soon learn that finding this balance could be extremely challenging.

#3 La Comunidad

As we grow to represent a larger proportion of the U.S. population, let us not forget the wonderful culture that binds us. The ability to accomplish so many things is only possible with family and community support. As a woman, and more specifically a Latina, much is expected of you. As a woman, you are expected to cook, clean, and serve your husband. As a Latina (as in many other cultures), you are responsible for taking care of your parents, siblings, and extended family. Society also expects you to be successful in school and earn your own income.

For many, this is where the rubber meets the road. The Latinx community must learn to understand the various challenges affecting college-age adults. Families are prepared to support going to college financially or ideologically but may find challenges working through the daily logistics and the emotional and physical separation from you. Families should work out schedules around your classes and understand when you cannot take *abuelita* to the doctor, pick up your sibling, or pick up your phone. Likewise, it is on the student to call/text every few hours to let them know you are alive. Latinx parents worry a lot and may not understand that you studied all night and slept in all day. This is a very common phenomenon I witnessed with many of my college friends.

With the help from both our families, my husband and I bought our first home by my 20th birthday. Two years later, we were blessed with a beautiful daughter. Pregnancy can be a challenge when you are taking organic chemistry and are sleepy all the time. When I was eight months pregnant, my environmental science labs involved taking water samples from filthy canals and trekking through the Everglade swamps in kayaks to study ecological restoration. My work landed me an opportunity to intern at the U.S. Environmental Protection Agency (EPA) Office of Ground Water and Drinking Water. I made the difficult decision to leave my 1-year-old daughter, husband, and family to gain experience in water policy in Washington, D.C. It was a tough summer, but it was possible only with the help and the support of a loving family. I was offered a position as an environmental science tech with the EPA but decided to return to Miami to pursue higher education.

THE ROAD TO A MASTER'S DEGREE

Experience begets experience. Once you learn *how* to learn and *how* to take opportunities, the pursuit of knowledge becomes an ever more integral part of yourself. I began wanting to learn more about the interconnectedness between our food system and impacts to the environment. I stumbled upon a small but growing agroecology program at FIU. My two professors, Dr. Krish Jayachandran and Dr. Mahadev Bhat, were pleased with my work in their classes. A master's degree was not at the top of my mind, but they presented me with an opportunity to receive a full research assistantship to earn a master of science degree in environmental studies at FIU. I was pregnant with my son and had to make an important choice to pursue higher education or live comfortably at home with my two, very young children. Again, my mother has always pushed me beyond the boundaries, reminding me each time to take the opportunity presented and face the challenges with confidence.

My son was born through cesarean three weeks before I began my master's degree. I was taking classes, developing a research proposal, and helping to manage the agroecology program. My advisers and my family were a major source of support during this time. It is important for students to work with their advisers in finding a proper schedule to fit the needs of the research project without compromising their well-being. Needless to say, the toughest part of achieving a master's degree was not conducting field research with 2 million bees but going home with stings on my hands and caring for my two children during every single sleepless night for two years, while still achieving a 3.9 GPA.

Networking and building a professional community of support is critical for aspiring Hispanic professionals. The American Association for Hispanics in Higher Education (AAHHE) is one such network that binds Hispanic professors and administrators to PhD students and young professors. This group understands that Hispanic students starting college are entering a new world and often struggle to find guidance. They work to help build mentorship support between faculty and students so that you do not feel alone. Under a collaborative effort between AAHHE, Texas A&M University, and the U.S. Department of Agriculture (USDA), a Career Preparation Institute was launched with a national thesis competition. With an extra push from my adviser, Dr. Bhat, I submitted my thesis and earned the first-place prize. I also met with Dr. JoAnn Canales, the director for the program, and a great leader and advocate for mentorship to Hispanic students pursuing higher education. I had the opportunity to serve as co-chair and chair for the program, gaining insight to becoming a successful professional in a STEM field. Students must learn the hard science skills but need also to understand individual personality types and how to work with others.

Hard work pays off, and timing is everything. I finished my degree at the precise moment a position opened up for the agroecology program, for which I was qualified. The most rewarding aspect of my position as program coordinator is the ability to mentor other students of color in choosing agriscience as a STEM field and the opportunity to travel with students around the world to help them learn and train for such positions. My advisers, and now colleagues, are my inspiration to continue beyond the comfortable boundaries of my current position. My advisers have put student learning and success above all responsibilities, and my success is only a ripple of what they have created, and one I continue to reflect. While some may call it success, my limits are set higher, and I can visualize a dream where success is a continuous measurement of those you inspire. I plan to pursue a PhD in science and someday manage higher educational programs in agroecology. I am no one to admire, not yet at least. I just live the American dream; one where you achieve so many personal milestones through a lot of hard work and support from *la familia, los mentores, y la comunidad.*

TESTIMONIO 2
Alejandro Araiza

Key Field of Study: Mathematics
STEM Adviser
Northwest Lakeview College, San Antonio, TX

I owe this degree and this story specifically to my mother. She, with so much effort, fought through academics and battled through personal life obstacles to accomplish her degree. As my biggest influence, I thank her each day for the sacrifice she made and cherished each time she showed me her degree. My mother wore it like a badge, and it became a symbol in our house that I did it, too. You can too.

As a student, I have always found my education important, and I have always done all that I can to improve it. My intellectual growth is important to me because it gives me the opportunity to contribute towards creating a better future and making a difference in our society. I grew up in a family of eight siblings, where hardship was constantly present. However, through the midst of it all, I have seen my siblings, for the most part, grow into successful individuals. I assume that I am not the only one who can relate to having hardship. I know that other people who can relate would agree that it is not a walk in the park. I believe that hardships do not define a person, but they do have an impact on your life. Those impacts can be for better or worse.

By growing up in a single parent household, I saw my mother accomplish so much and demonstrate remarkable strength. Education was prominent in our family ever since my mom graduated with her bachelor's degree at Southwest Texas State. Once she completed her bachelor's degree, my ambition grew, and I began to gain so much determination and desire to complete higher education. I owe this degree and this story specifically to my mother. She, with so much effort, fought through academics and battled through personal life obstacles to accomplish her degree. As my biggest influence, I thank her each day for the sacrifice she made and cherished each time she showed me her degree. My mother wore it like a badge, and it became a symbol in our house that I did it, too. You can too.

Now, it wasn't an easy start but definitely the most interesting. I did well in high school, not the greatest, but I was acknowledged as being in the top 10 percent and could have gone to any university in Texas with that honor. During my senior year, I won a scholarship to visit a prestigious college on the East Coast and experience college life for a few days. I had never travelled outside of Texas before, and to venture all the way to Maine truly opened my eyes. I was changed forever with the beauty of the East Coast, the majesty of the college campus, and the college life. I was also captivated with the people. Once I graduated from Burbank High School, I took a pilgrimage of sorts to Brunswick, Maine. I chose to attend Bowdoin College, a small, vibrant residential college specializing in liberal arts with majors that were central to the world's issues of today. During my first year at Bowdoin, I struggled to maintain the appropriate grade point average to pass my classes and ultimately failed. After about two semesters of struggling, I finally decided it was in my best interest to go home and transfer back to a community college. Having to start over with my educational journey was a difficult pill to swallow.

Dealing with failure was tough, and it brought a lot of things to the surface personally that made me want to give up. Faced with that reality, and still standing here today as a graduate student poised to purse a doctoral degree, the growth of grit and perseverance have been my greatest progress in my development. In addition to my development of grit, I have also made tremendous progress in my focus and passion. I started attending Palo Alto College in San Antonio, Texas, in early 2009 and started to see the difference between attending Bowdoin and Palo Alto College. There were changing demographics, but there was also a sense of family in every stage of the educational pipeline. It was through this sense of *carino* that I found my first job. I salvaged my strengths and one day, through engagement with an educational leader, Carmen Velasquez, I began working in the advising center. The advising center advised students on numerous majors, and it was in that office that I found my niche, my major. My aspirations became cultivated as a peer adviser. I began to recognize how important going into the STEM field would be for my family. Working in the STEM field was tied to making more money, but it was also a field that allowed me to gain an increased understanding of power and resistance in my life. My loss of motivation quickly turned into an advocacy for higher education within a matter of semesters. I chose a major in mathematics after seeing how math problems would take up my time and make me think when life became too much to think about. The complexity of my life at the time was in need of a distraction, and going to school was that distraction. I decided not to walk the stage during the conferring of my degree at the University of Texas at San Antonio (UTSA) in 2014 because I wanted to walk with my graduate degree. Right after I was conferring this degree, I was notified I would also be conferred a degree from Palo Alto College. That was when I realized that a community college degree was just as important as the university degree I would obtain. To this day, I have not opened my degrees, which sit on a bookshelf in my room. This is not because they are unimportant, but because I am afraid they will rip and tear. The minute I get my first director position, I will proudly showcase these awards, which took many obstacles to obtain.

Right after graduating with my degrees, I was motivated to find employment. I found a position at Palo Alto College as a scholarship adviser and aimed to motivate as many male and female students of color to apply. Currently, I am working as an adviser in the STEM field at Northeast Lakeview College. I am also a club adviser for a club called HOME, which motivates male students of color to attend and stay in college through mentorship. On a daily basis, I have increasingly become a resource for many students. My students need the same power that I lacked when I was attending Bowdoin. I posed myself with the question that if I was still in Boston, would I be able to shape minds in the same way I was in San Antonio? I wish to encourage students who have been silenced due to lack of knowledge of the importance of educational equity necessary for the reinvestment of this economy.

Within the next few years, I will be finishing my graduate degree in higher education, and then my next degree will be required of me. I will be the first in my family to go to school for my doctorate. I will follow in the footsteps of a person I look up to highly, Dr. Victor Saenz. He has provided me with books and journals, and has dialogued about the national imperative of the importance of Latinx males attending college and graduating. I would like to earn my doctorate degree from University of Texas at San Antonio (UTSA), but I would also like to venture to another university as well. Next year, when I start my practicum for my graduate program, I hope to intern with the president of Palo Alto College, Dr. Michael Flores. During his time at Palo Alto College, he has been a role model for all male students of color by breaking barriers. There are not that many male presidents of color in the United States or in Texas. His motivation to create initiatives such as PAC Males on campus has driven male students of color to keep attending college and pursue STEM-related majors. Dr. Flores worked initially in the institutional research department of the college at Palo Alto. This position allowed him to maintain data in college recruitment, enrollment, and ultimately persistence. His hard work was recognized in Dr. Saenz's latest book, *Ensuring the Success of Latino Males in Higher Education: A National Imperative*. His ability to increase one of San Antonio south-side community college's persistence rates has vastly changed the outlook of this specific community for the next 30 years. As an intern, I hope to look at the data the south-side has provided as a cross-sector network and a narrative to a proactive response to low educational rates.

If you ask me the main reason why one ought to pursue a STEM degree, it is because STEM degrees do have long-term consequences. STEM is an addicting major that broadens your mind continuously and seeks ways to keep it growing. There is a huge problem in our community with not enough students wanting to participate in STEM events, projects, or even enter STEM majors. There are many ways public, private, and charter schools can get students to have an appetite for STEM. At Palo Alto College, there are events such as Discover PAC, which motivate students early to learn about the programs community colleges offer in STEM fields. UTSA has National Health Professions Day and offers fellowships that pay students to learn and gain a better interest about STEM. Also, the underrepresentation of minorities in the STEM fields leads to a bigger picture. Without minority STEM male and female influences, our job outlook is dim. The context by which we live is based on STEM-related jobs. Our doctors and engineers are all STEM majors. Each time I advise a new student about a STEM-related field, I remind them that they are a huge asset to this city, state, and, most importantly, the world. Who knows if I am advising the next person to find the cure for cancer, AIDS or even someone who wants to help a third-world country fight a deadly illness? My goal in life is to continue changing lives through STEM advising because somehow, while changing other people's lives for the better, they have also changed mine.

If I had any advice to give Latinx students pursing a STEM degree, it would be to design a future for yourself with how STEM could be improved over the years. I would tell them not to think small but to have the biggest dreams and never stop setting goals. It is important to never underestimate one's self. If someone sets you back, you must continue to press on. STEM skills are marketable to employers and should be showcased in a variety of ways. Social media and technology are huge career fields right now with a promotable future. I would let Latinxs know that "Si Se Puede!" This country is growing in vast ways, and if they come up with new endearing paths for future Latinxs to walk, then that is the main goal. If I could go back in time and tell myself anything, it would be to start my education at a community college first. At this point, I could be 26 years old in my first year in doctoral school, but my setbacks are tattoos I wear with pride. There are stories to tell, and one day I will tell my future children that I worked hard for them to be able to achieve their goals, and they must continue with their aspirations.

TESTIMONIO 3
Diana Del Angel

Key Field of Study: Environmental Studies
Gulf Research Program Science Policy Fellow
National Academies of Sciences, Engineering, and Medicine

If I had to summarize my life journey, which led to my career, I would say it was fueled by a need to know. Even as a young girl, I always wanted to know. What happens when you put a snail, a grasshopper, and a fuzzy worm in the

*same jar? Perhaps if I probe a lock with a toothpick, I can figure out how
it works? Curiosity can get you stung by insects or punished by
your abuela, but curiosity can also reroute your career life.*

The first time I was fascinated by a scientific concept, as far as I remember, must
have been when I was 6 or 7 years old. While my parents were at work over the
summer break, I stayed at my grandparents' house. It was the best. My abuelos
gave us the freedom to roam the yard, climb trees, make mud cakes, and play with
ant farms. One day while sorting through books at my abuela Santitos' house, I
discovered one I found particularly interesting. It was a biology book, most likely
a high school science book, belonging to one of my aunts or uncles. I liked it because
of its vibrant images of plants and animals. Reading through the material proved
to be somewhat difficult but not completely impossible. The particular page that
caught my attention focused on how plants produced energy by absorbing energy
from the sunlight. Plants absorb a select portion of light and reflect some of the light
back. Sunlight is composed of various colors, incidentally the colors of the rain-
bow, which combine to make white light. I would later learn that light is a small
section of the spectrum of electromagnetic radiation emitted from the sun; most
of that radiation is not visible to the human eye. Within the visible range of electromagnetic radiation, we find the colors of light, from the shortest to the longest
wavelengths: violet, blue, green, yellow, orange, and red. Plants use light from either
side of the visible spectrum violet/blue and yellow/red and convert it to food for
the plant to live and grow. The green part of the light spectrum is not absorbed;
instead, it is reflected. It turns out all objects will reflect the light of its correspond-
ing color. The reflected wavelength from the leaves reach our eyes; therefore, we
can see that leaves are green. Not only that, but black objects absorb all the wavelengths of the visible spectrum, absorbing more energy than objects of other colors,
especially objects that are white, which reflect all the color wavelengths back. This
idea was astonishing—a wave of excitement swept over me, almost like the feeling you get when opening a present on Christmas Day. This experience inspired my
first science project in elementary school.

If I had to summarize my life journey, which led to my career, I would say it was
fueled by a need to know. Even as a young girl, I always wanted to know. What
happens when you put a snail, a grasshopper, and a fuzzy worm in the same jar?
Perhaps if I probe a lock with a toothpick, I can figure out how it works? Curiosity
can get you stung by insects or punished by your abuela, but curiosity can also
reroute your career life. Initially in college, I was a psychology major and had not
considered a science degree as something in which I might be interested. Most, if
not all, bachelor's degrees require a science course to graduate, so in my second
year, I took biology. Professor Nash was such an enthusiastic biology instructor.
After he explained a concept, he would look up from the overhead projector, sweep
his comb-over back in place to reveal his face with an expression, which I inter-
preted to mean something like "Can you believe this? Isn't it amazing?" I am not
sure if it was his enthusiasm for the subject, or perhaps it was my own, but I loved

learning about the natural world. It was entertaining and interesting, so I decided to change my major. I chose an environmental science degree because I wanted the opportunity to learn about Earth systems, natural resources, chemical and physical science, and about ocean and coastal environments. To me, it was practical to understand everyday processes of the surrounding world.

My undergraduate experience was truly some of the busiest times with multiple jobs, fieldwork, and homework. One of my undergraduate assistant jobs involved mapping vegetation along the Rio Grande River and adjacent coastal plains. We used a global positioning system (GPS) to navigate to sites and, once there, we would record the species of vegetation found, the approximate percentage of each vegetation relative to other vegetation, and the percentage of cover compared to bare ground. The south Texas coastal plains are a beautiful and diverse landscape, with low thorny trees and shrubs, expansive low marsh covered with a sea of *Batis maritima,* a short succulent with small bulbous leaves, to the beautiful flowers such as beach evening primrose found in the beach and dunes adjacent to the mouth of the Rio Grande River. This experience gave me the opportunity to visit sites I would have never visited on my own because they were hard to get to, and sometimes roads were not in place to reach such places. What may seem like a long stretch of nothing is actually a beautiful environment that reminds me of home.

Appreciating nature is much like appreciating art. It can be beautiful and inspiring even if you don't know much about it. However, when we learn of the elements and the historical conditions that make this scene possible, it becomes an interesting piece that we can analyze and discuss its purpose in society. It was the vegetation mapping experience, exploring and trekking through the south Texas plains, along with other similar field experiences, which inspired my appreciation and love for coastal wetlands: the individual plants found there, the sandy and muddy flats, and wetland smell of sulfur.

As a young woman, some of my best summers were spent at the beach. Beaches are synonymous to vacations, relaxation, and fun. To me, beaches are some of the best places on Earth. My "home beach" was South Padre Island, the southernmost beach one of the world's longest barrier island, Padre Island, which stretches approximately 113 miles from Corpus Christi to Port Isabel, Texas. It was one of my favorite places. I was concerned, as I learned in classes, that many beaches were being lost or eroded. Beaches are formed of sediments that are not coalesced, and the energy of waves and currents can move these sediments to and from the beach. Sometimes sediments are removed, run out, become trapped, or simply are not enough to offset sea level rise, and beach erosion takes place. During a class field trip to Bolivar Peninsula, we visited areas with wide beaches and backed by wide and grassy dunes. Other beaches in Galveston Island had been so eroded that the house originally placed behind a dune was standing on stilts in the Gulf of Mexico waters. What makes these islands different? Will my South Padre Island look like Galveston in the future? What will happen if the sea level continues to rise? Why are dunes very large in certain sections of a beach and not in others? I did not have answers to any of these things. If I could continue to a graduate degree, these were the things I wanted to find out.

I was initially convinced I would not go to graduate school. When my undergraduate professor asked if I planned to seek a graduate degree, I responded that as much as I loved school and would like to learn more, I could not afford to pay for graduate school. Dr. Heise explained to me that there are such things as graduate assistantships. These assistantships cover your tuition and provide a monthly stipend while you work on your graduate degree. News to me! From that moment on, I seriously considered a graduate degree and began to look at potential schools. I am deeply grateful for Dr. Heise's guidance. As a first-generation science student and first-generation college student, I was extremely lost. I had no idea where to find scholarships, internships, or what graduate school would entail. She considered me for an undergraduate assistant to do work in the field and in the lab. She encouraged me to apply to scholarships, internships, and graduate school. She took me to my first national science conference and showed me to how to make a scientific poster. These activities were the foundation to what much of graduate work depended on, and my life might not have been the same without her advice.

Following my undergraduate mentor's advice and with the help of a fellow student, I submitted applications to three graduate programs. Ultimately, I decided to attend Texas A&M University Corpus Christi (TAMUCC). Picking up where I left off, I wanted to learn more about barrier islands, sand exchange between beaches and dunes, sea level rise, and coastal change. If you read a biography of my graduate adviser, Dr. James Gibeaut, you will find most of those keywords in it. I was very excited to start graduate school and be able to study, in depth, that which I found most interesting. It was also a challenge. In graduate school, you trade textbooks for peer-reviewed articles and hours of studying for hours of trying to figure out where to start your thesis. My first semester, in seminar class, we had to write a proposal for our thesis project. We all had an idea of what we wanted to research, but how were we going to do it and why? Both are difficult questions to answer if you do not have the proper background. At the end of the semester, after we received feedback for our proposals, I was stunned. I had never been so heartbroken and disappointed at the comments I received on a paper. Most of my grades as an undergraduate were A's with some compliments and praises from my professors. This time it was way different—the comments stated the background was nowhere near sufficient, the methods needed strength and revision, the citations did not reflect the author was knowledgeable of the topic, and, finally, this proposal was poorly written and would never "fly" in any sort of professional or academic setting. My chest was heavy, and I could not help but think that, perhaps, I had made a mistake. How could I flunk my first semester? From the day, we received our reviews to the day grades were released, I moped, along with a fellow student and colleague (who also did not do so well), considering what kind of job I would look for after I shamefully flunked out of graduate school. Once grades were posted, I did not even want to look, but we had to face it. Was it an F? Perhaps a D, if my professor was compassionate. Final grade for seminar class: A. I was shocked! Is that an A for "attempted"? Yes, I believe so. One of the objectives of this class was for the student to write a proposal. I guess it did not have to be a good proposal. Part of graduate school is holding yourself and your peers to the highest scientific standards, and it must not be taken as an insult but as part of the process in developing transparent and sound projects. Since then, I have received many more criticisms and suggestions to my reports, and by the same token, I have done the same. Definitely a lesson learned.

For my thesis, I wanted to focus on my "home beach" of South Padre Island. Given my past interests, I wanted to evaluate some of the previous questions I had about barrier islands and erosion. My classes were on the themes of coastal processes and hazards. I learned about climate change and to develop statistical models. For my thesis project, I used field survey data and geographical information systems (GIS) to build a model for dune growth in South Padre Island. GIS is a platform for manipulation of maps and other spatial data. This tool allows the users to illustrate certain features of the environment, calculate areas, measure length and other geometric measures on a map, in addition to identifying patterns and correlations of the environment with many other types of data (i.e., economic, demographic, and soil data). Using GIS software, I was able to map beach and dune features and calculate the volume of sand in the dunes and how it had changed over time. The process of developing a thesis was definitely a challenge. I was lucky that my adviser fostered independence to seek my own project and identify my own methods.

As a graduate assistant at the Coastal and Marine Geospatial Lab, one of my favorite activities was conducting beach and dune topographic surveys. Topographic surveys use an electronic digital theodolite. You may see an electronic digital theodolite at a construction site where a surveyor looks through the scope of an instrument sitting on top of tripod towards another person holding a rod with a triangular piece on top (usually orange or yellow) which holds a prism. These tools are used to measure the distance and the angles between the instrument and the prism and can be used to measure the topography along a cross-section of beach, extending from behind the dunes to the waterline. Collecting topographic data of the beach and dune at the same location over time provides a documentation of beach behavior and can be used for analysis of beach and dune losses after a storm.

One of the first beach surveys I did as graduate student was on Galveston Island, a month after Hurricane Ike made landfall on the upper Texas coast on September 13, 2008. Hurricane Ike landed as a category 2 storm bringing winds of approximately 110 mph and a storm surge of 15 to 20 feet, causing major destruction—uprooting trees, washing up boats and debris, and flooding thousands of homes. The damage was astounding. Barrier Islands, although popular tourist destinations and beautiful places, are narrow (1 to 5 miles wide) and low-lying segments of unconsolidated land, which separate the mainland from the ocean. Because of their dimensions, structure, and location, they are vulnerable to impacts of storm and hurricane forces. Bolivar Peninsula, where I had admired the dunes and beach during my undergraduate field trip, had been completely submerged by the elevated water levels of the storm, washing away many homes. In Galveston Island, homes were missing windows, had collapsed foundations, and exposed septic tanks. The surveys we collected did not focus on the homes or the people but on how much sand was lost from the beach and the dunes. The beach washed away, and the dunes, if not completely gone, were scarped, as if the sea came to bite a big chuck of sand from the face of the dune. Witnessing the physical destruction of a hurricane on a barrier island is overwhelming and an enduring sight. This became another experience that, I believe, has shaped my work and research interests. Further GIS analysis of the impacts of the storm on the upper Texas coast revealed 20 to 90 feet of beach after the storm. The beach did recover some, from 10 to 70 feet of beach, gradually in the three years that followed. It is this type of analysis that is useful for community planning.

I had the privilege to continue to do research at TAMUCC after I graduated. I find that working at the university is rewarding because you have a chance to give back and help other students who are trying to figure things out. As a researcher at the Coastal and Marine Geospatial Lab, I had an opportunity to work on a number of projects regarding coastal hazards, storm assessments, barrier islands, and wetlands in Texas and in the U.S. Gulf of Mexico Coast. One of the products of this lab, which I feel embodies all my research interests both old and new, is the Geohazards Map of South Padre Island. The map features areas that are more or less susceptible or in need of mitigating effects relative to sea-level rise, erosion, and storm-surge flooding. These maps consider current environments and what we know about barrier island processes to create a map of areas with potentially hazardous conditions.

A big part of the learning experience as a professional comes through volunteer opportunities. It is worthwhile to share your skills and knowledge outside of your work place. For example, I have had the pleasure of being a guest speaker at a local aquarium and sharing with the public the issue of beach erosion in Texas, what we can do about it, and what it costs. I have also had a great experience serving on a city advisory committee for waterfront management and safety. This committee is composed of a diverse group of professionals: engineers, scientists, waterfront condo owners, tourism board members, environmentalists, and other community representatives, who come together to discuss issues pertinent to the community and provide advice to the city council. We all learned from one another through our discussions, realizing we all want a safe and healthy beach, but we have different approaches and knowledge. These discussions gave me an idea for an event I was planning, a state-wide beach and dune forum. I did not want the forum to be the typical academic type of forum, but one that included local and state coastal managers, tourism board, local nonprofits and environmental groups, engineers, students, and researchers. Putting these people together in one forum took me back to when I was a kid, and I would place different kinds of insects in the same jar. Where you might expect a big conflict, in fact, turns out to not have one at all. The forum was a great opportunity to share the work each of us is doing, and it was a place to discuss some of the relevant issues on our beaches today and what are some potential solutions. In time, my work has evolved from solely following personal research interest to a service-oriented coastal and marine science professional.

In hopes to gain experience outside the academic realm, I recently applied to and received a science-policy fellowship. This one-year fellowship seeks to build leadership and capacity by providing recipients with a valuable educational experience at the science-policy interface. As part of this fellowship, I am working with the Florida Department of Environmental Protection and learning how the state manages its coastal resources. It is an exciting opportunity to gain a different experience in understanding and solving coastal issues, as well as exposure to a new set of coastal and marine environments, such as coral reefs. Although it has been eight years since I received an undergraduate degree, I still feel like I am in the early stages of my career, mainly because I am still looking to experience new opportunities. There are many possibilities to contribute to the protection or improvement of coastal and marine ecosystems, and I could not tell you now, exactly, what my endpoint will be.

In the end, I hope to give back to my community and take my gained skills and experiences back to South Texas. I hope to improve environmental conditions and coastal conservation through the use of science and advocacy. I look forward to living close to home, so my future kids can play at their abuelas' house while their parents are at work, for it is a fact that no one gives you as much freedom to explore as our abuelos do.

TESTIMONIO 4

Julissa Del Bosque

Key Fields of Study: Biology, Medicine
Undergraduate Student
The University of Texas at Austin

Committing to a STEM field of study does take time and perseverance. Don't let anyone or any event stop you from reaching your maximum potential. If you get knocked down, you get back up because you know someone else is getting back up just like you. It shouldn't matter if statistics show a small number of Latinxs enter careers in the STEM fields. If your passion and your purpose falls in the STEM spectrum, show everyone around you that you took what life threw at you to get you where you are today. You are worthy to aspire and dream beyond what you think is possible. At the end of the day, if you have the drive, your purpose will have no limitation, and it will only lead the way for a very rewarding life.

Being able to call myself a STEM major was not something I decided overnight. Majoring in biology was in the making long before I even imagined the possibilities it would create for me. The foundation of even imagining that I could excel in any major started from the story of my parents.

Mathis, Texas, is a small town you've never heard of; it is located about 30 minutes south of Corpus Christi. If you are headed to Corpus Christi and blink, you will miss this tiny town. It is a town where everyone knows each other's business, and gossip is your main source of entertainment. It is a place where time seems to move more slowly, and to have any kind of fun, you better catch a ride into Corpus Christi. This little town is not a town with money but a town of hardship and struggle. Mathis is the town where my mother and father grew up. They both grew up in the projects, and everyday my parents did not know from where their next meal would come. My father became a migrant worker to help support his family, and both of my parents wanted so much more from life.

When I visit Mathis, I cannot imagine my parents' lives and how they did the seemingly impossible. You can easily become comfortable, remain content, and not strive for more, failing to realize there is an entire world past the Mathis city limits. Their story does have a happy ending, and I am more than honored to say both of my parents are first-generation high school graduates and college students with bachelor's degrees. My parents beat the odds and did not conform to the small-town mindset of doing things the way it has always been done and never leave. I try over and over to picture my parents living there and relate it to their accomplishments, but I do not think I will ever truly understand.

Their story inspired me to continue the tradition and go to college. I know my hardships and adversities are not nearly the same as my parents, but their struggle, their courage, and their successes are the foundation of who I am. Their dreams of becoming more and their fight to refuse to conform to the "Mathis norm" instilled in me a strong mindset to overcome the obstacles life throws my way. Fight for what you want no matter how many times life might put you down, and know that the "get up" is the part that builds up the person you are becoming. Hearing the stories and experiencing snapshots of my parents' journeys through pictures is simply that: stories. Their story. Little did I know that the beginning of my story, of finding out who I am, deciding I wanted to major in biology, and discovering what I am capable of achieving would begin at the age of 13.

At 13, I was confident I would play soccer at the collegiate level, and an athletic scholarship would assist with covering the finances for my education. I put in countless hours improving my skills and dedicating my free time to becoming the best athlete that I could be, but then I tore my anterior cruciate ligament (ACL) in my left knee, and everything changed. I had to recover, strengthen, and catch up. Even then I knew I would never be the same player I was before. I had a total of five surgeries over the next four years, with all of these years becoming a blur of hardship. I could not comprehend how my life had turned into shambles.

Many thought I was crazy for continuing to play, but I had been playing soccer since I was 4 years old, and I could not imagine my life without it. I refused to let my injuries dictate when my career would end. When you have been involved in something that long, it is hard to let go. Initially I asked, "Why me?" Why was I spending more time in hospitals and in rehabilitation than at school, with my friends, or on the soccer field?

I struggled and started to lose the fight and inspiration that was instilled in me by my parents' story. It was my mother who stayed beside me, and in my struggle, she reminded me of what it is to fight and persevere. Without her constant reminders, I believe I would not be sharing my story now. Over time the "Why me?" changed to "Why NOT me?" and I realized that was not an original thought; it was the same thoughts my parents had which molded them into the people they are today. They may have questioned their situations and the possible outcomes, but they fought on, and their fight has become the moral of our stories.

We often hear the saying, "Life happens," but do we ever stop to understand what life really just threw our way? One moment in our lives, in my case five back-to-back knee surgeries, shakes us into the realization that we stand in this world with only choices to define ourselves. We have no control with what life gives us, only what we choose to make out of it. I was stubborn and only saw the negative and how unfair life was to me. No one could tell me differently that those five years would alter my life in a positive way.

I thought my life would forever be over once rehabilitation life consumed me. Doctors, coaches, therapists, family, and mentors came in and out of my life constantly. These people, who at first were merely titles, are the ones who made the difference in my life. These people, ultimately, were the glue that held me together and kept me going. That's when I knew I wanted to be a doctor who could come into someone's life and fix the pieces back together. I wanted to enter someone's life without knowing them and leave a lasting impression.

Committing to a STEM field is a big step, but being a Latina is another. To be the doctor that I imagined myself becoming, I knew selecting biology as my major was the best option. Doing some research, I knew biology major coursework would align with the prerequisites for medical school, so it was a done deal, and I decided biology would be my field of choice. This was not an easy one by any means, but it was a choice I knew had to be made to create opportunities for years to come. That one single choice would be the start to a whole new beginning. Not everyone will have a clear picture that points to the STEM field. I was very blessed that a negative time in my life opened my eyes to the STEM field. If you can believe, have a passion, and can imagine yourself in the STEM field, then there should be no reason why you should ever stop persevering.

Fast forward past my epiphany moment of deciding to become a doctor to actually putting the steps together to make it happen. At 18, I was barely wrapping my head around the idea that I was finishing high school. I had great grades in high school and was accepted into any public University in Texas, but deciding where to go was not that easy. I could face five surgeries, but I could not commit to what would be next in my life. Not knowing what was yet to come was the scariest. Committing to one thing and not being happy was another thing. I knew I was not going to waste the life my parents created for me. Their hardships lingered in the back of my mind as making a decision where I would continue my education was drawing near.

My parents always made sure I never worried about finances. I was constantly reminded to find a school where I would be proud of going and embrace every aspect it had to offer. Lastly, my parents always said, "Do not let the price of tuition scare you. If you want to go there, we will find a way." Hearing that put more pressure on me. I knew my surgeries had put a burden on my parents, so how could I even imagine committing to a big four-year university?

When I turned down going to a big university, people thought I was crazy to pass that up, but it wasn't my time. I decided to attend a two-year college and take a nontraditional route to take on my career goal in milestones. I could be smart and save money now, so when I was farther along in my STEM field, I would have less debt. I could not pass up becoming core complete (what we know as the basics) and debt-free when I saw friends struggling with finances while taking simple math and English.

The deal was done, and I had my mind set. I would get my basics out of the way and be in and out. You would think by now I would have learned that life throws many things your way when you least expect it. I always heard there is so much free money out there to pay for your schooling, but I never believed that money could be for me. It was not a question of whether I was smart enough, but rather was I worthy. Here came my mother again, reminding me that anyone who puts in effort, dedication, and has determination is worthy of anything they want. So, I took a leap of faith and applied for scholarships. What did I have to lose?

I was blessed with a scholarship that paid for my associate's degree, and my whole mind-set of only getting my basics was out of the picture. When I saw that email in my inbox, I knew Northwest Vista College in San Antonio, Texas, would be my home for the next two years.

Community colleges have this stigma that you receive a cheap education and that it is so much easier. Let me get it straight that my chemistry tests were not easy at all! I met some of the hardest working and smartest students at Northwest Vista College. Each and every one of them has a reason why they started at Northwest Vista. There is nothing wrong with starting small and receiving little successful milestones that will one day lead up to your big goal in life.

My first semester at Northwest Vista was not anything near what I pictured. I was mentally prepared to transition into more difficult work knowing I was a deciding to be a STEM major. However, there was something missing. I would go to school, study, eat, sleep, and repeat. I decided to attend Northwest Vista because I could picture myself on campus, feeling like I belonged. Still, something was missing. I was disconnected and was not fulfilling the belonging part. How could I possibly feel a part of campus when I was there for a few hours a week?

Not only did I survive my first year in college, but I also thrived once I put the pieces together. Getting involved on campus, networking with my fellow peers, and giving back sparked my fire once more and reminded me of why I am here at Northwest Vista. I am not only here to get a paper that states I have a two-year degree but also to enter the lives of many and help others. This experience reminded me of why I decided to enter the STEM field and become a doctor: to help others. There was no stopping me. I became a student ambassador and joined multiple honor societies, such as becoming president of Phi Theta Kappa and a member of National Society of Leadership and Success. I became a peer mentor helping other incoming first-year students adjust to college life. I started volunteering at Methodist Stone Oak Hospital and got a great internship with the U.S. Department of Agriculture (USDA).

I experienced all this in a year in a half, and I would have never imagined the impact it made on my life. I survived college because I found out there was more to college life than the books. I found something I was passionate about, and that gave me the motivation to keep continuing my schooling to become a doctor. I was not able to help others in a medical aspect, but I was able to wrap my head around the idea of how my story, my actions, and my attitude could influence, help, and inspire others.

Attending Northwest Vista had challenges that anyone would expect. You have your homework, exams, and getting addicted to Starbucks refreshers so you can pull an all-nighter to get your work done. The hardest challenge I faced was making sure I did not lose track of my goal to major in biology. Many people change their major because they find their passion hidden in one they least expected. I got caught up wanting to major in everything because I wanted to be a doctor plus everything else. Someone would tell me about their major, and I would get interested and distracted thinking what my life would be like in that field. My parents always told me the sky is the limit, and as long as you are happy, go for it! Technically, I could be in school for my whole life majoring, but I would never excel and be great at one thing, so I had to bring myself back in and realize why I was there. I reminded myself, "Julissa, keep your eyes on the prize." My prize is helping other children, as I once was that child who needed help, and majoring in a STEM field would allow me to achieve that in the future.

The prize is helping children, right? It was something I decided to do probably after my second knee surgery. However, I also did not want to be close-minded. Back to the subject with the U.S. Department of Agriculture internship, which was another perk and one of the many great summer internships offered at Northwest Vista. This was one of those times where my curiosity took me to the big state of Wyoming, a state where the wildlife population was greater than the human population. There was this little pull inside of me wondering what the nature side of a biology degree would be like. I was 99 percent sure medical school was calling my name, but that 1 percent of doubt had me applying for this internship. I stepped out of my comfort zone and experienced the nature option of my STEM field. I packed my bags and stepped into a world completely unknown to me—a world I had pictured myself in but never knew what living this life would entail. To my colleagues, it was as simple as breathing, and for me, I struggled to stay afloat.

I envisioned glamorous, luxury camping, or glamping, as portrayed by the movies. Yes, I might have slept with a flashlight on and jumped at every crunch and snap, but with every minute in the frozen, isolated woods, something inside of me changed. It was my mindset. Often, our mindset leads us to our successes and our failures. I had to remind myself that I had signed up for this experience. It was my choice. I had to take a deep breath and remind myself that there was a greater meaning behind it all that plays a role in my purpose and why I am here.

I survived and concluded I would like to work in a hospital versus out in the woods. The moral to it all was if I had never stepped outside of my comfort zone, I would always wonder what if, or what if I fell in love with the woods and would have missed out? Find the balance of who you truly are, experience adventurous moments, and be open minded. A single experience in the STEM field can ultimately shape the rest of our lives. This was another one of those moments for me.

When I walked the stage earning my associate's degree in biology with a concentration in peace and conflict, I knew Northwest Vista offered me everything imaginable, and it was my time to share my story and what I learned. There was nothing left but to soak up what life kept throwing my way.

Maybe it was my knee injuries that started my passion to help others, or maybe it was my internship with the USDA that put me back on track, reminding me that entering the medical field and helping children was for me. Regardless, these moments all pointed to the STEM field, a place where I can see myself thriving. Taking risks, learning from others, and tackling what life threw at me ultimately made me understand why I am here and what my purpose is in life. Committing to a STEM field of study does take time and perseverance. Don't let anyone or any event stop you from reaching your maximum potential. If you get knocked down, get back up because you know someone else is getting back up just like you. It shouldn't matter if statistics show a small number of Latinxs enter careers in the STEM fields. If your passion and your purpose falls in the STEM spectrum, show everyone around you that you took what life threw at you to get you where you are today. You are worthy to aspire and dream beyond what you think is possible. At the end of the day, if you have the drive, your purpose will have no limitation, and it will only lead the way for a very rewarding life.

Here I am, a Latina who was able to attend a big four-year university. I am currently a proud junior at the University of Texas-Austin working on my bachelor of science in biology (Hook 'em!). I am so close to the end of this chapter in my life, and I cannot wait to see what medical school will throw my way. I am doing what I set out to do, and I am loving every moment. Being a STEM major is so rewarding, and majoring in biology prepared me to go through the next door as I apply to medical school.

I will continue my degree in the STEM field, but knowing the rigor to come will be a new challenge. Getting involved, feeling like I belong, and sharing what I have to offer at a new campus is another challenge I am facing. I am reminded that the mixture of my most profound moments experienced in life were the ones that brought the most challenges. Those are the moments I would not trade for the world because they have all led me to the STEM life. My advice to you is to run with those challenges and know that one day you will see the meaning behind it all, perhaps strengthening and pointing you further into a STEM field.

TESTIMONIO 5
Xiomara Elias Argote

Key Fields of Study: Biochemistry, Microbiology, Biotechnology
Quality Compliance Manager, Food Science Industry

What differentiates us from other cultures is that we have the support from our families. School will not be easy since it requires long hours of study, discipline, organization, and time management, especially for those who will be working, but it can be done. I have seen kids with the potential to be the next Einstein but just needed a push to believe in themselves.

Freedom is written with blood, and work is written with sweat. This was the motto I heard throughout my childhood, but I did not understand it completely until years later. Nevertheless, it guided me toward a career in science because I wanted to help others and alleviate suffering among my people. The first part of my life was lived during the civil war in El Salvador, and the second half has been a part of me since I can remember. It was in the decade of the 1970s when El Salvador was undergoing civil problems that originated from repression and many years of socioeconomic inequality. The most affected were peasants, who did not have a way to voice their rights. However, there was a priest named Monseñor Romero, who encouraged them to fight for justice. In the eyes of those in power, he was an extremist who needed to be silenced to avoid an upsurge among the peasants. In 1980, Monseñor Romero was killed by a single shot while he was giving mass in San Salvador. After this, many more activities followed that left our country in a battle that lasted 12 years before a peace treaty was signed. A year later, I was born in the middle of protests on the first anniversary after Monseñor Romero's death on March 24th. Since then, my life has been filled with experiences making me a strong person who fights for equality and opportunities for the less fortunate. My story is the one many immigrants share, a story filled with overcoming obstacles for a better life, and where dreams and our faith in God are the powerful forces that keep us going.

Experiences during the first few years of a person's life can leave indelible marks. A good education, diet, and the environment, among other factors, can determine how successful a person may be in adulthood. If we take these aspects into consideration, then all the odds would have been against me, and I would not have had the opportunity to write this essay, but family support and the will to make a difference inspired me to keep fighting. It was a difficult childhood to be born in a society that appreciates males, and being born female did not give me an advantage. My mother was a single parent in a peasant family who had to work very hard to bring bread to the table every day. We had the basics: a ceiling to protect us and a bed to keep dreaming. I was raised by my grandmother who had a very strong character, and I learned to be obedient not by love but by fear. We were a total of seven kids in a complex family of grandparents, aunts, and cousins. Being the youngest, I was pushed around but learned to fight for my rights. Despite our poverty, we had great moments and learned to share and care for those who had even less. We had a small patch of land to cultivate corn, spinach, and other vegetables that were sold at the local market. All of the grandchildren contributed from an early age in cleaning, cooking, harvesting, carrying water, doing laundry by hand, and in my case, to sewing as my mother was a seamstress. These early years taught me that hard work is the key to meet goals, and the results from such are the ones that bring satisfaction and pride to oneself.

Since 1970, there were civil conflicts and battles mainly in the rural areas of El Salvador. In 1989, Farabundo Marti para la Liberacion Nacional (FMLN) insurgents took areas surrounding the capital, San Salvador; this attack is now known as "ofensiva." In late October of that year, there were protests and closed roads that forced schools to shut their doors early. Every year schools would hold a closing ceremony, but that year, everybody just stopped going, and classes were terminated. I was in third grade and do not remember all the details that escalated to battles in which many civilians died, but I do remember the morning of November 12th when the news of the ofensiva had expanded, and the next 40 days that followed left scars in every Salvadoran. I grew up in Calle Real about 10 kilometers from San Salvador, which is located in the path to Guazapa volcano; one of the most affected areas during the insurgence. A triangle of helicopters traveled down that path to bombard the north of El Salvador, and to this day, the sound of a helicopter still brings memories back. Death, hunger, and pain filled the air in those days. Electric posts were bombarded, living in houses without electricity, and the nights were illuminated with fireballs to target "guerrilleros" (insurgents). The sight of the falling bullets towards the fields now reminds me of inverted fireworks, yet not in the sense of a celebration but of destruction. Mined roads and curfews kept many civilians inside their house, and little by little, the food supply was decreasing. The only times that war was off the mind of Salvadorians was during soccer games, especially when our national team was playing. Those moments taught me that union creates a powerful force, and together we are stronger.

Salvadorians learned to appreciate food, work hard, and give thanks for being alive and together as a family even if there was not enough food on the table. My grandfather had a weak heart, and all the civil problems aggravated his condition. Our economic status did not permit proper health care for him, and as a result, he died in front of my eyes in late January 1990. That was the highest price to pay in a civil war, and this single event, along with the daily suffering seen in many Salvadoran families, inspired me to pursue a career in medicine. Nobody in my family had a college education or experienced positive reinforcement. We learned to move forward through negative reinforcement and from trial and error. My mother has been the strongest motivator in my life. She was the first in her family to get a high school degree, but machismo did not allow her to put her education into practice. I learned to refine my work as she used to make me redo things over and over again until I would get them right, even for simple things like laundry. For sure, my socks were extra clean as she used to inspect carefully all the pieces I washed. Going back, simple acts like this shaped my views and my habits at an early age, which have been very useful in a science field where attention to detail and perseverance are highly appreciated.

Many of my classmates did not come back to school the next year. Some of them left the country, and others I do not know what happened to them. They probably emigrated, left for other cities, or their families were heavily affected during the *ofensiva*. Life needed to continue, and I was fortunate to capture information easily in the class. The death of my father (grandpa) and the difficult times motivated me to keep going. My teachers, however, played an important role in my development and influenced my life. One of them was my fourth-grade teacher, *Señorita* Fatima, who was caring and friendly, which was just what a kid needed after a difficult time. I started to participate in math, grammar, and contests. In fifth grade, I had the same teacher, and my development continued. However, my sixth-grade teacher had a different personality than *Señorita* Fatima. She was like a dictator and inculcated discipline in me. In the end, she was one of the best teachers I could have had. My primary schooling then continued at a private Catholic school where caring, discipline, and responsibility were prized. I was lucky to get half of a scholarship at the private school and completed my high school education there. All the support from my school teachers paid off, as I ended the school year with top honors as well as in high school.

From my early experiences, I had made up my mind to study medicine, so in high school, I chose the science field option. I was intrigued by the natural sciences and wanted to explore these areas. In my last year of high school, I applied to the school of medicine and got in. However, through my father, I was also presented with the opportunity to come to the United States and study English. He had supported me financially during my schooling through my high school years. Until I was 16 years old, I never lived with him and thought this will be a great opportunity to unify my family. Leaving El Salvador was one of the most difficult things I have ever done. The minute the airplane took off, my soul was left back in my country because I was leaving my mother, my 1-year-old sister, my relatives, and my friends. I was almost 17 when I came to California and started developing my English skills with good proficiency. My father offered me the opportunity to study in this country as an international student. Thus, I had to choose between going back to my country or staying in the United States. Since the civil war left El Salvador with socioeconomic problems, especially high delinquency, I wanted my younger sister to have a better life than the one I had in my childhood. Thus, I left my family and my studies in El Salvador to start a new life as an immigrant in the United States.

I finally unified with my mother and sister a little over a year after I left El Salvador, and we all moved to San Luis Obispo, California. Since I was an international student, I was limited with the colleges I could apply to, since my parents did not have enough money to pay for extra housing. I attended a community college named Cuesta in my local town where I continued my basic education to get units for a four-year university and also pursued an associate's degree in science.

My parents had to work very hard to pay for my college tuition, so I was responsible for my little sister and became a mother figure to her. I also worked part-time at the community college to help with the tuition. Upon completing my units, I then transferred to California Polytechnic State University (Cal Poly) in San Luis Obispo to pursue a degree in biochemistry. I was not aware of the ranking of this school but later found out that their program was in high demand due to their hands-on teaching style, which helps students process information easier and gets students exposed to current problems that can be solved with science, technology, and the work field. College years were hard because I had to help my family at home, work with my father who did gardening work on the weekends, and be a mother for my sister. In addition, my father had a very difficult temper, which made my life difficult. Nevertheless, I wanted to complete a degree to become independent and be able to stand by myself. As an English language learner, I had to study harder to get good grades. At the beginning, I had to literally translate every sentence, but later classes became easier. Getting hands-on experience was the best method to learning as one can show their work through projects and activities, learn from mistakes, and improve methods that are already established.

I put aside family issues and took advantage of all the opportunities I could have at the university. My family was the main financial support, but I also applied to any scholarship that was available for international students. I started Cal Poly in 2001 and later found an advertisement to do an internship abroad with a full scholarship. I got very excited and put my application together, which ended up being a microbiology internship in Mallorca, Spain, for the summer of 2002. This opened the doors to the world of research. I was part of a team that was isolating bacteria that degrades hydrocarbons, and I spent the whole summer with a group of scientists who propelled me into scientific investigation. As part of the internship program, we were required to present our project at a national conference, and even though I was extremely shy, I got first place with my poster in the field of environmental biology in the junior category. I wanted to explore more, and the next summer I did another internship through the University of California, Santa Barbara (UCSB) in the field of biotechnology, which exposed me to more research. I applied to medical school, but my choice of schools was limited due to my immigration status, so I was not successful.

In 2004, I graduated with a degree in biochemistry and microbiology with a minor in biotechnology. I wished I could I have continued my graduate school right after my bachelor's degree, but I could not afford school as an international student and did not want to be dependent on my parents, so I decided to look for a job in biotechnology with a one-year work permit and later with an extension. My goal was to get a sponsorship to continue working, but, unfortunately, limited employers want to hire international citizens with only a bachelor's degree in science. Then, the market crashed, and there were fewer job opportunities, so I decided to obtain a master's degree to increase the chances of getting a job and a sponsorship for a work visa. I applied to different majors, and at the end, I decided to pursue a degree at California Polytechnic State University, San Luis Obispo because my professor offered a full scholarship while I worked on research at the Dairy Product Technology Center (DPTC). In addition, I could still be together with mother and sister while I was getting a graduate a degree. The career was in agriculture, but I studied food science and chemistry and applied it to milk and its derivatives.

Graduate school was an amazing experience because I could develop my presentation and socials skills, which are very important in today's society. Up to that time, presentations were nightmares to me as I did not like standing in front of people, but graduate school makes students present their work so frequently that we are no longer afraid to discuss topics in front of an audience. In addition, students learn to think independently and organize their daily research/work schedule. There are challenges to be faced almost every single day. Besides going to school and working at the same time, many times we have to learn by trial and error, which prolongs the time in graduate school. It is frustrating to perform an experiment that lasts weeks just to find out at the end that it was not the right path to do an analysis. However, great ideas have emerged from experiments that have gone wrong, and I learned to take those trials and use them as the base for the next stage. For my thesis, I studied the changes of protein in milk during processing from cold storage to pasteurization, and I spent a lot of hours in the laboratory. I would often be the one working in the lab in the middle of the night, as well as the weekends. Nevertheless, every minute of that work was worth it. I did my research in three different departments: chemistry, food science, and biology while taking advantage of the latest technology in each area. Later, I submitted my work for the 2012 American Association of Hispanics in Higher Education (AAHHE) outstanding thesis competition, which was a partnership with the U.S. Department of Agriculture (USDA), the National Institute of Food and Agriculture (NIFA), and Texas A&M University-Corpus Christi (TAMUCC). To my surprise, I won first place! I could not have done it without all the collaboration from the different departments that involved my thesis, showing me that team work is very important for success.

My current career is different than the one I originally dreamed about. I currently work in the food science industry as a quality compliance manager where I apply my background. I did not become a doctor, but I do use my knowledge to help other people who require assistance in science, especially letting Latinxs know the consequences of overuse of antibiotics. Earlier, I used to tutor at primary schools, helping children understand basic science and math. Now, my work schedule makes this activity more difficult due to timing and traveling. I do my best to help others, as the most rewarding aspect of a career in science is to understand how systems work, how they are connected, and share that knowledge with other people. The person who has benefited the most has been my younger sister, whom I pushed so much to study hard and be involved in sports, as the latter helps to balance education and take away stress. She has been my motivation to keep working hard, and now she is my pride. Her hard work paid off, and she was accepted into a prestigious university, Johns Hopkins, for chemical engineering. She wants to study medicine later, and even if she changes her major or final goal, I am sure she will be successful because a career in STEM provides the basics to succeed in any field.

Latinx Americans have innovation, courage, and determination to get things done, which can make a positive impact on this country. Immigration status may diminish us from getting any further, but we have the heart to fight and accomplish our goals. Latinx children have the mind to explore and the will to accomplish goals, and this is what is needed to be successful in science, technology, engineering, or mathematics. I enjoy seeing the energy in Latinx children who show their enthusiasm in their eyes because they want a better life for their family and themselves. However, some prospective college students may be scared to apply to college due to financial reasons. They should be aware that there are many scholarships that are available, and even if they are not, college can be planned to achieve goals even if it takes longer. It is never too late to study. I am still thinking of pursuing a doctorate degree in another science field. What differentiates us from other cultures is that we have the support from our families. School will not be easy since it requires long hours of study, discipline, organization, and time management, especially for those who will be working, but it can be done. I have seen kids with the potential to be the next Einstein who just needed a push to believe in themselves. Women have an even greater obstacle to fight in our Latinx community: machismo. But they have the heart to fight, and we need to believe in them. This country requires the energy of Latinx Americans and needs community leaders who can guide those who are less fortunate. Education can get us there, and if we all inculcate this value into our children, society will be better with more people using their knowledge and skills to invigorate others. We can make a difference in the United States by pursuing a career in any STEM field.

TESTIMONIO 6
Dana M. García

Key Fields of Study: Zoology, Physiology
Professor and Associate Chair of Biology
College of Science and Engineering
Texas State University-San Marcos

During the 1960s and early 1970s, the U.S. government made science and technology a national priority, and culturally, there seemed to be a consensus that science would solve all the world's problems. My parents strongly valued science and hoped that their children would pursue science-dependent careers such as medicine, engineering, or dentistry.

I was born during the height of the space race between the United States and the United Soviet Socialist Republic in 1964 in Waco, Texas, at Hillcrest Baptist Hospital to José Filiberto and Theda York García, the fourth of their children. My family lived in Waco at that time because my father, who had completed a college degree in chemistry at Texas A&I University (now known as Texas A&M University-Kingsville), worked for Ling-Temco-Vought (LTV), which in turn was contracted by the U.S. government to support its space, rocket, and missile programs. My father's particular efforts were oriented toward the research and development of rocket fuels. My mother had her college degree in home economics (family and consumer sciences in today's parlance) from the University of Maryland. My parents met in Maryland when my father worked for the Naval Research Laboratories. During the 1960s and early 1970s, the U.S. government made science and technology a national priority, and culturally, there seemed to be a consensus that science would solve all the world's problems. My parents strongly valued science and hoped that their children would pursue science-dependent careers such as medicine, engineering, or dentistry.

Although we moved around some in my early years as my father pursued advancement with LTV, by 1969, we had settled in Kingsville, Texas, my father's hometown, and he left chemistry to become a cattle rancher and businessman. My mother was a stay-at-home mom, who cultivated in us a love of reading and music. My entire K-12 education was accomplished in Kingsville, and with the exception of kindergarten, it was entirely public education. I was blessed with good teachers and was well prepared for college through my public-school experience with a sound foundation in English, math (although I slacked some there in that I opted out of taking high school calculus), and science. Additionally, my best friends in high school had very kind parents who believed I could do anything I wanted to and who taught me to believe the same. Furthermore, my parents instilled in me a sense of obligation to make the most of my God-given talents to serve society as best I could. For most of high school and about half of college, I understood that to mean I should prepare myself for a career in medicine.

Accordingly, I decided to attend Texas A&M University in College Station, where I started out as a pre-med student. Texas A&M had aggressively recruited me to come to their school by offering me a President's Endowed Scholarship and a National Merit Scholarship, which together pretty well paid all my college expenses. Prior to that, I had been leaning toward The University of Texas at Austin, where two of my older siblings had gone. As things turned out, Texas A&M was the only university for which I completed an application. The scholarships were definitely important, but Texas A&M was also well known for its veterinarian program, and I presumed that it was generally a good place to major in life sciences. Fortunately, I was right.

Eventually, I decided medical school was not the direction I wanted to go, and at about that time, I fell in love—with science. The awakening of a love of science, and especially of biological science, happened when I was taking biochemistry and psychology concurrently with physiology with Dr. Duncan McKenzie; the relatedness of the topics just clicked. My courses made a lot of sense, and everything fit together. Additionally, Dr. McKenzie was a very young professor, and his enthusiasm for physiology was contagious. I wanted to be just like him. I ended up completing a degree in zoology, which was the major with course requirements closest to my previous pre-med curriculum.

At Texas A&M, I joined the fledgling honor's program. Consequently, I received a booklet written by two of A&M's chemistry professors called *Toward Success in College*, which is out of print but available online at http://www.chem.tamu.edu /class/fyp/toward-success/toward-success.html. I highly recommend this book. I got my first explicit lessons in time management from this book. In addition, I learned important guidelines for how much studying was necessary to achieve the grades I desired, and how it was possible to do all that studying while still attending all the home football games and yell practices (i.e., pep rallies) along with other events.

One of the options in the honor's program at Texas A&M was to write an honor's thesis based on undergraduate research. My roommate suggested that I should approach Dr. Evelyn Tiffany-Castiglioni about the possibility of doing research in her lab. I met with her, and she accepted me into her laboratory, despite the fact that I kept dosing off during my interview. I am not sure whether she noticed or whether she just chalked it up to my being overwhelmed by the volume of information she was sharing. Either way, one thing she said stuck with me: In science, 90 percent of your experiments will fail. She was letting me know that success in science requires perseverance and resilience.

My senior year, I was so on fire for science that I was sorry to see my undergraduate years ending. Nevertheless, I thought it would be smart to take a year off to work and save up money for graduate school. Fortunately, Dr. Tiffany-Castiglioni had a grant and hired me as a technician in her lab. I spent the year after I graduated working on our manuscript, applying for graduate school, and applying for fellowships. My strategy for applying was to pick the universities with the best reputations and with PhD programs in physiology. My thought was that if I was denied admission, I would apply the following year to lower tier universities.

I applied to and was accepted at Harvard, Yale, Northwestern, and the University of California at Berkeley. I also applied to the University of Texas at Austin, but they declined me. Additionally, I was awarded a National Science Foundation Graduate Fellowship, which allowed me to choose a graduate school without being so concerned about how I would finance myself. This was good news because I thought graduate school was going to be very expensive, and I had been following my own austerity program in which I only buy food that cost less than $1 per pound, and I turned off the AC, heater, and water heater in my apartment.

After interviewing at the various campuses, I decided to go to UC Berkeley. A number of factors went into that decision, including the kindness of the graduate students—especially Deborah Bravo and Leticia Márquez—and the climate. That it was among the top programs in cell biology was a given based on my earlier decision to apply to top-rated programs, so I could let more personal factors influence my decision.

When I got to Berkeley, I learned that the physiology program was actually being discontinued. The eight or so students admitted to the program would be the second to the last class. At that time, physiology was seen as sort of passé or old school, and many programs were dropping it in favor of programs in molecular cell biology (MCB), on the one hand, and integrative biology on the other. That turn of events was fortunate for me because the new MCB program encouraged graduate students to test multiple labs before deciding where they would do their doctoral research. I spent my first rotation in Dr. John Forte's lab learning about how the stomach makes acid (and how his graduate students made coffee). Then, I moved to Dr. Beth Burnside's lab, and that is where I ended up staying.

In Beth's lab, we were interested primarily in understanding how the cells in the retina of fish eyes were able to adjust to changes in light conditions by changing their shapes (in the case of rods and cones) and by rearranging light-absorbing, shade-producing pigment granules (in the case of the retinal pigment epithelium, or RPE). We looked at everything from what the chemical signals that cued these transformations were to the molecular machinery that enabled them to be carried out. My particular interest was in the chemical signals that signaled the RPE when it was dark outside. My research touched on both the signals themselves and the mechanisms by which they were conveyed to the cells. My research led to a whole new way of looking at how cells communicate with one another.

After I completed my degree, I was fortunate to be invited to apply for a faculty position. I was asked to interview, and then I was offered the position. Being a faculty member was daunting and exciting. As a new faculty member, I was mentored primarily by Dr. Joseph Koke, who introduced me to the regulatory burdens associated with working with animals, which Beth Burnside had shielded us from in graduate school, and was very helpful in teaching me about writing grant proposals. I was fortunate to be well funded, thanks in part to programs developed at the National Science Foundation that were designed to help minority scientists get started and help primarily undergraduate institutions develop research programs.

ADVICE FOR HIGH SCHOOL STUDENTS ENTERING A STEM FIELD OF STUDY

Presuming you have made the decision to go to college and to major in a STEM discipline, here are some words of advice:

1. Make friends with people who will help you become the person you want to be in the long term. In the short term, you want to succeed in your classes, which means mastering the content and skills required. Normally good grades follow. Some universities offer students the opportunity to join living, learning communities (LLCs), which cluster students of similar majors or interests in residence halls. If you can get in a STEM LLC, then you should expect the students you are living with to understand that studying is required for success. You will still have opportunities to have fun (see my earlier reference to "Toward Success in College" and time management), but maybe not as much recreational time as some of your non-STEM major acquaintances. Additionally, studying

with other students can make the studying more fun and provides an opportunity to test your knowledge and challenge each other. "If you want to learn something, try teaching it." In the longer term, you and your friends may help one another find jobs and other opportunities like summer research programs, scholarships or fellowships.

2. Get to know your professors, and take advantage of their office hours or any study or review sessions they hold outside of class. In addition to helping with content mastery, out-of-class sessions and meetings help professors get to know you so that if you need a letter of recommendation to get into a summer program or a graduate program, they will have something more to say than "Tony was in my class. S/he made an A." The need to get to take extra steps to get to know your professor is increasing as more and more professors get away from essay exams (which help the professor understand how and what you think and how you express yourself), using multiple choice instead.

3. Take advantage of opportunities to work in laboratories or do field work. Sometimes students can use their work/study allocation to work in a lab; sometimes professors have grant funds that can support an undergraduate student work in the lab; sometimes the funds can support undergraduate research. Many universities have Research Experience for Undergraduate programs funded by the National Science Foundation or other summer research programs. Many of these programs pay students to participate.

4. Take time to rest and recreate but not too much time. As the saying goes, "All work and no play makes Jack a dull boy; all play and no work makes Jack a mere toy." Take care of your health and important relationships.

TESTIMONIO 7
Karla Gutierrez

Key Field of Study: Industrial Engineering
Research Associate and Doctoral Candidate in Environmental
Science and Engineering (Energy track)
The University of Texas at El Paso

*You, the reader, the youth of this generation, are the future of the world,
and we need your fresh and different ideas so we can build a better and
more efficient world. We just need a little more of a "push," and hopefully
this manuscript helps you to decide on an engineering or a science field.
The important part is that you pursue your goals and dreams.*

I am going to start by telling you my name, which is Karla Rocio Gutierrez Lucero. I was born in Ciudad Juarez, Chihuahua, Mexico. My mom and dad are both Mexicans, and so is my one and only brother, who is also younger than me. I consider myself to be part of a small family, which formerly consisted of four members. A few months ago, it grew because I married a wonderful engineer. It seems like I am surrounded by engineers in my life. I grew up in Ciudad Juarez. This remarkable city is located across the border from El Paso, Texas, and because of this fact, these two cities share a lot in common. "Border people" frequently travel between cities, and since I was 8 years old, I had dreamed of going to the University of Texas at El Paso (UTEP). This was the university my dad attended when he was young, and I wanted to attend this university as well. Just like he made it part of his life, I also wanted it to be part of mine. My dad was, and still is, my inspiration. He is an electrical engineer. He graduated from UTEP, and because of him and all his hard work, I have always wanted to be an engineer. He always had interesting work and experiences to share. He always had a challenge that he somehow managed to resolve. Still now, after so many years of manufacturing-related jobs, he talks about his work with so much passion that it gets you involved in the talk.

When I graduated from high school, The Preparatoria El Chamizal in Juarez, we moved to El Paso. When we moved to the United States, I started the paperwork and the exams required to enroll in UTEP, which to be honest, was an exciting time but also a little scary. I was going to start school in a different city and a different country. Even though we shared a lot of similarities, a huge difference would be the language. My first and hardest challenge was to start fluently speaking, writing, and simply thinking in English. Thanks to my ESL teachers and my determination, I excelled in those courses, and now I hold an industrial engineering degree as well as a master's degree in industrial engineering, and by the end of the year, I will have earned a doctoral degree in the field of environmental science and engineering with a track in energy. All of these achievements have been inspired by family, friends, and, of course, my professors.

Besides my dad, several Mexican Latina women have inspired me throughout my life. The first Latina who inspires me is my mom, who has always tried to reach her goals. When we moved to the United States, more specifically El Paso Texas, she did not know any English, but that did not stop her. She went to several English courses and succeeded in learning the language. Now she orders food without hesitation or difficulty. She goes grocery shopping and even tells the cashiers to match their ad prices. She is my heroine. She has always encouraged me to keep studying and to pursue my goals. My second inspiration has been my adviser, counselor, and academic guidance counselor Dr. Heidi Taboada. She is the reason I am almost done with my PhD today. She has always encouraged her students to learn about new things and challenge themselves. My first research experience was in one of her classes, where we needed to present a poster in a local conference. That was a big challenge for me because not only was I barely exposed to the research field, but the topic was also totally cutting edge. On top of that, I was an ESL student talking in front of experts in the field of engineering and science for the first time in my college career. However, that experience made me a lot more confident in regard to my English-speaking abilities and also with my own knowledge in the field.

I chose the University of Texas at El Paso to be my alma mater, first of all, because my dad graduated from there. Second of all, it was because I did not have to leave my home or my family. As Mexicans, we are so used to our families that it is hard to leave them behind. Since I did not want to go out of town, I stayed in El Paso, and I do not regret it at all. I made a lot of friends, and I got to work with awesome professors such as my mentor Dr. Taboada, Dr. Espiritu, and Dr. Contreras. I learned so many things about engineering in general, but also about life, that I really cannot imagine learning in a different place. It was hard to pay for college because at the beginning coming from a foreign country with no knowledge about scholarships or how to apply to them I could not take advantage of any financial help. On the other hand, being a U.S. permanent resident did not give a lot of choices for scholarships, so I had to borrow money from federal funding. I was never able to get financial aid because supposedly my dad was earning enough money to pay for my college. Of course, it was not true, so the loans helped me to finance my five years as an undergraduate student.

As soon as I graduated, my first thought was to find a job and pay off my loans as well as to help my family with the expenses. I also wanted to help my little brother with his college tuition because he was going to start college soon. When I started looking for positions, Dr. Taboada asked me if I wanted to do an internship for the summer doing research. I did not hesitate and agreed to the project. It was such an exciting summer that I just could not say no to staying in school and starting my master's program.

The following two years of my master's program, Dr. Taboada offered me a job as a teaching assistant for her industrial layout course, where I had to prepare lesson plans for several layout software programs such as: AutoCAD, FactoryCAD, Bloc plan among others. Later on, I was also research assistant where I had to research several artificial intelligence algorithms such as genetic algorithms, ant colony, and bee algorithms. From these techniques, I developed my master's thesis, creating a new searching technique based on echolocation. As you can imagine, it was extensive work, but the sense of discovery and learning new things every day was so encouraging. With these two positions, I learned how to prepare and teach classes. Most importantly, I learned how to conduct investigations, prepare formal presentations for international conferences, and how to write a thesis.

The most important aspect of having the opportunity to work on campus doing research was, and still is, having money to pay for my graduate school. Without the opportunity that Dr. Taboada gave me, I would not be where I am now, and I would not have the money to pay for my schooling. In addition to the economic reasons, I have grown as a professional in the engineering field by taking advantage of national and international conferences where I have presented and published my research. Furthermore, the experiences go beyond the professional aspect because the places I have visited are so beautiful: Florida, Puerto Rico, California, Canada, and others. The social experiences are also part of the learning experience and are important to grow as a qualified engineer. These experiences have been one of the most rewarding throughout my career.

Now that I am going for my doctorate, I still perform investigations as a research associate and still teach some classes when my adviser is out of town. These experiences have helped me develop a passion for academia and research. I am definitely thinking of working in a research laboratory or a government agency where I can help develop new algorithms to facilitate logistics operations. Also, I want to educate people about the importance of sustainability in every field of industry.

I would love to see more women in the science, technology, and engineering fields. Every time I would go to one of my engineering classes at the university, I would notice that the majority of students enrolled in the classes were male. I have noticed that not a lot of females take the route of teaching science, technology, engineering, and mathematics (STEM) courses. It is important to encourage our equals to pursue this discipline. We need the female side to be part of this isolated field along with the Latina side. We as Latinxs have so many different backgrounds, cultures, and ways to do things that can be helpful in solving problems, whether it is designing the car of the future or finding emission-free combustibles.

The idea of a multicultural or diverse STEM field should complement our ideas and experiences to make our world a better place to live in and make our life easier. Sometimes when we get stuck with only one type of culture in the workplace, we tend to end with just one type of idea. We get stuck with only one way of thinking, and everything ends up being one-sided. Ideas do not flow as we would like, and we cannot seem to find the obvious. This is why we need to have more diversity in the workplace. We need more Latinx who are interested in the fields of science and engineering so that we can help make a better future.

Women in general need to get involved more in STEM fields. We are brave, strong, and courageous, and Latinas excel in all of these disciplines. This should push us to become leaders of the society in which we reside. Also, we multitask by focusing on several things at the same time. If we do all of these, then anything we dream of can be done. We just need determination to finish what we have started. Sometimes we tend to blame everything that is wrong in the world and on the country to other people, but we do not try to help. Sometimes we just go with it, and we do not try to do anything to help others. We need to start seeing that we are the solution. You are the solution. You, the reader, the youth of this generation, are the future of the world, and we need your fresh and different ideas so we can build a better and more efficient world. We just need a little more of a "push," and hopefully this manuscript helps you to decide on an engineering or a science field. The important part is that you pursue your goals and dreams.

The advice I can give to any Latinx student thinking of a career related to the STEM field is to go ahead and believe in themselves. We have the courage to finish what we start. Yes, it is going to be hard, but any field of study has its complications. Nothing comes with an easy button, because if it did, we would not be engineers or scientists. We like to explore things and experiment. Do not be afraid of pursuing your goals because every effort has its reward. In any field of STEM, the reward is bigger because we help in the creation or enhancement of products and services for the common good.

TESTIMONIO 8
Rodolfo Jimenez

Key Fields of Study: Cellular and Molecular Biology, Biochemistry
STEM Coordinator and Data Analyst, Longhorn Center for
Academic Excellence
The University of Texas at Austin

If this were 20 years ago, I would say my journey through STEM had not been very typical, but I have heard many others tell of similar stories. That is why I am grateful for all the mentors I have had in my life, from family to professors. I feel it is their guidance that has helped me get to where I am today, and I will never forget this. That is why I take it upon myself to make sure that I give back to my community, as well as the world, in any way that I can.

The term scientist was never really used when I was growing up. That's not to say science was not talked about, but it was more in relation to medicine. The idea of curing cancer was seen as something you would do as a physician. The concept of being a scientist was there, but the career path to achieve such a title was lost because of lack of information. This is not the fault of my family, friends, or the local schools. The term scientist was never used in South Texas because no one had witnessed anyone living his or her life as a scientist, but even with the lack of knowledge of what it entailed to be a scientist, I feel my upbringing in a Latinx family prepared me to become a scientist.

I was born in Edinburg, Texas, a town in South Texas, to Anna and Rodolfo Jimenez, Sr. My mother's parents are originally from Dolores, Guanajuato, Mexico, and of the 15 children they brought into this world, six were born in Mexico. My grandparents knew that for their children and their grandchildren to have a better life, they would have to move to the United States. In order to bring his family over to the states legally, my grandfather would cross the border illegally to work. Once my grandfather had enough money to pay for the immigration process, he brought the family to the States. With such a large family, my grandparents would not be able to provide for their family by themselves, so once the children became old enough, they would join my grandparents and work in the fields. This way of life continued until all the children were out of high school, and some of the older siblings continued this way of life even after they had started their own families.

My father's family has a different origin. Both of my father's parents were born just near the U.S.-Mexico border, on the U.S. side. This does not mean their life was any easier. As my mother's parents were field workers, so too were my father's parents, but instead of traveling to other states to work in the fields, my father's parents mainly worked in the fields in Texas. My grandmother did start school as a child but eventually had to drop out in the fifth grade to help provide for her family. My grandfather did finish high school but not in the traditional way. When my grandfather was 17, he was drafted into the Army and spent three years in the service, which included a tour during the Korean War. Post-graduation, my grandfather mainly worked manual labor jobs. In his early 30s he was able to obtain a job working for the Texas Employment Commission (TEC). Not to be held back by his limited schooling, my grandfather was able to make a career at TEC and spent 31 years employed as a job placement specialist.

Being that my parents were so young when they had me, both 20 at the time, they both had to put school on hold in order to provide for their new family. My father worked night shifts as an orderly in the local hospital, and my mother worked as a teacher's aide. Because of my father's varying schedule, my Grandma Lupita (paternal grandmother) had a big role in raising me. My father's parents lived outside of town on about 3 acres of land and not the best TV reception, so my forms of entertainment were either playing outside or watching PBS. This lack of television entertainment helped me to develop my curiosity for how things worked. This curiosity developed from watching a show on PBS called *Newton's Apple*. The curiosity developed from watching this show led me to explore what I was surrounded by at my grandparent's house. I was constantly digging up the dirt and wondering what it was made of, mixing certain liquids together to see what the mixture would make, and also trying to see what I could create from loose materials around my grandfather's garage. Luckily, any mixture I created never caused me, or anything around me, any harm.

That curiosity continued when I started school. I was not just interested in learning what was taught, I wanted to go into further detail as to why it was that way. Between the ages of 5 and 10, I was definitely the "why" child of my family. Most of the time my family understood it was because I was actually curious and not trying to be annoying, but, trust me, there were plenty of times they wished I would stop asking why. Around this time, I was introduced to school science fairs. Whenever it was time to start my project, I was always trying to do a project that would ensure a victory.

Something else that happened around this time was my ability to play sports well. Though I was a rather large child in elementary, my size never really stopped me from excelling in sports, but my size did bring about teasing and bullying from my classmates. I think the combination of my size and intellectual curiosity in elementary caused me to be an easy target for others to pick on, more so because I was never really an outgoing child. Thankfully my parents took notice to my problems at school and helped me in every way they could. They first reassured me that I was an intelligent and good person, and though I was a bit overweight, this is not what defined me. They saw it as their fault I was overweight and took responsibility to make sure that I was a healthy child. To encourage me to lose weight, my mother came home one summer day and showed me jean shorts she had bought me. When I tried them on, I was saddened because none of them fit me. My mother looked at me and said she had 30 days to return the shorts, so if I wanted to keep them, I had 30 days to lose weight and make them fit. I accepted her challenge, and with both my parents' help, we figured out how to make the weight loss a reality.

With it being summer, my parents enrolled me in golf lessons for the morning and a sports camp for the afternoon. After all this was done, my father took the extra step and would jog with me for a least a quarter of a mile. All the physical activity, as well as better eating habits, allowed me to fit into the shorts in 20 days. Losing this weight allowed me to think positively about myself and not put myself down all the time. This is just one of the many examples of how my parents have helped to pick me up and encourage me to work hard for what I want.

My first exposure to a scientific laboratory was the summer after my fifth-grade year. There was a summer science camp held by our school district that exposed students to various STEM fields. Some of the activities we performed were dissecting a frog and a customized paper airplane designed to fly farther than a normal paper airplane. This camp truly amazed me at what could be done with science. From that point forward, I decided that I would pursue a career involving science, which to me meant I would pursue a career in the health field. I decided I would become an optometrist, due to the fact that I wore glasses and was fascinated with the machinery in the office. Also around this time I, like any Texas boy, was becoming more fascinated with sports. I think it was around this time I started to put more effort into sports than into my schoolwork, not that I did not enjoy and do well in school as I was still a straight A student and was reading constantly. The sport that became my primary focus was football. I had a bit more pressure on me when it came to playing football because my father exceled in the sport at the same high school. I knew the importance of having to do as well as my father when he sat me down before the start of the seventh grade and asked if I was ready to commit to being the best I could be. Though this maybe a strange thing to hear a father ask his son, I completely understood why he did it. I now understand this was his way of telling me, for the next six years, I was going to be compared to him, and he was just preparing me for what was to come. There was never a time when my parents told me sports was more important than school. In fact, throughout my athletic career, if I missed school, my parents would not allow me to participate in whatever sport I was in at the time. They were never sure if I would compete in sports at the college level, but they did know I needed to have good grades in order to get to the college of my choice. It was actually my participation in sports that led me to change my choice in career from optometry to physical therapy.

As time went on, it was clear I had the ability to play college sports, and with me being in the top 35 of my class, it was clear I would continue onto college even if I did not play collegiate sports. Throughout this time, I continued to have a fascination with science, but I could tell it was not my main focus at the time. There was a point in high school when I knew my level of commitment to science was not as strong as it used to be. My sophomore year I wanted to compete in a regional crystal competition for my chemistry class. As the competition neared, I became nervous I was not going to be selected as the one to represent my school, as the lack of attention to my crystals resulted in a less than stellar product, and as I had feared, I was not selected. This came as a bit of a shocker to me because up until this point I was always a student referred to as a science guy. The anger that came from this incident was used as fuel to do better in sports, when it should have been a wake-up call that I needed to put even more effort into my studies, but it was also around this time I had my first life-changing experience. My sophomore year I was moved up to the varsity football squad for our playoff run. Though we ultimately lost in the semifinals, my performance led everyone to believe my junior year would be a breakout year for me. As the fall came and practices began, it seemed the anticipation of my level of play was what everyone was expecting. It was around the second week of the season when I was beginning to feel short of breath during my playing time. As the weeks went on, my ability to play a whole game became less and less possible. For some reason, I was never able to catch my breath after three or four plays. It was not until after our seventh game I was advised to go see a doctor.

Now I know it is maybe unusual to wait so long for me to go see a doctor, but for those weeks, many thought I was just out of shape and nothing more. Initially I saw the team doctor at his office where he took an EKG. He saw there was a bit of an abnormality in the results, so he scheduled an appointment for me with a cardiologist for the next day. At this point, I was not sure what to think as I never thought I would be seeing a cardiologist at the age of 16. Walking into the office of the cardiologist was a bit shocking to me since there did not seem to be anyone under the age of 70 there. The doctor examined my initial tests from the team doctor and told me he would do another EKG as well as an echocardiogram. After the tests were done and he reviewed them, he came into the room and said I had a heart murmur and needed to be checked into a hospital immediately. I initially thought he was kidding, and I even asked him if he was joking. He looked me in the face and said that he was not kidding, and it was necessary to get me into the hospital so I could be under constant observation. As I checked into the hospital later that day, I told myself I would not let this hold me back from doing whatever I was put on this earth to do. The doctor ran multiple tests to see if he could pinpoint why I had this irregular heartbeat, but he was never able to come up with a solid reason. He gave me some medication and told me he would monitor me for six months. Glad to be alive, I was constantly asking why did this happen to me? Would I be able to live a normal life? For the time being, it limited me only in sports. The time off from sports allowed me to reflect on what it meant to be alive and what I wanted to do with my life. This scare cemented that I would not let anything stop me from going to college and pursuing a career as a physical therapist, but during this time, I was also determined to get back onto the football field. As time went on, I was allowed to increase the amount of physical activity little by little, and when track season started, I was allowed to compete in the discus and shot put, which gave me hope I would be able to play football in the fall. In early August, I went to see my cardiologist to get clearance to play my senior year of football. When he looked over the results of all the tests that were run, it was clear my heartbeat was back to normal. I was allowed to enjoy my senior year both athletically and academically. I performed well enough in football and track to garner interest from colleges, and academically, I was in the top 10 percent of my class, which meant I had automatic admission to any public university in the state of Texas.

In the end, I chose to attend Texas State University in San Marcos because of the possibility to play collegiate sports there, as well as try to earn a spot in their physical therapy school after completing my bachelor's degree. When I arrived to try out for the football team, I was shocked to learn that the coach who had wanted me to walk onto the football team had left the university. With this disappointing news, my football career was over. Still eager to play collegiate sports, I was able to walk onto the track team as a discus and shot put thrower.

At the same time I was concerned about my athletic career, I was equally concerned about my academic career. In my first biology class, I finally felt what it was like to be a minority. For someone who came from a part of the state that was predominantly Hispanic, it was easy for me to notice I was one of the few students of color in the class. At first it did not seem too uncomfortable in the new setting, but as I conversed with some of my classmates, I started to feel uncomfortable. This unease was not due to outright racism but to the surprise of my valley accent. When I speak in English, I use the proper pronunciation of Spanish words such as tortillas and San Marcos, but when my classmates, as well as those who were not my classmates, heard me use proper Spanish pronunciation, they would give me a curious look. When I asked them why they gave me a curious look, they would reply that they had never conversed with someone in English who would pronounce Spanish words correctly and wondered why I would need to do so. Never in my life had I been looked at funny or questioned for speaking in a certain way. During many of these instances, I was not sure how to act. Do I get mad? Do I explain why I speak this way? Should I have to explain my pronunciation? At this point in my life, I was not very outgoing, so I was insecure as to how I should respond, and because of this insecurity, I began to watch how I spoke and acted around certain people. On top of this newly added pressure to act a certain way, I was finding my undergraduate courses were more challenging than any of my high school or dual enrollment courses. Struggling in a class was something I had never really had to deal with before, and I really did not know who I could reach out to. I remember there were office hours offered by the professor, but I felt if I went and asked for help I would be seen as a failure and did not belong in the class. Having this mindset comes from, I believe, the culture I grew up in. In the Latinx culture, it is looked down upon to ask for help. I believe this mindset prevented me, as well as others, from asking for help. Because of this unwillingness to ask for help, my grades in my STEM classes were not very impressive, but it was another life-changing event in the middle of my first semester that led to my decision to dedicate my life to become a scientist.

At the beginning of every track practice, the throwers warmed up by doing a combination of running and jump rope. One day, as I was doing my jump rope drills, I became lightheaded and collapsed. When I awoke, the trainers were around me asking me how my head felt and if I had any difficulty breathing. I told them no and figured I collapsed due to not breathing correctly. I continued with the workout, but as soon as I started to do the high repetition weight workout, I started to get tunnel vision and became lightheaded again, so I stopped and was taken to the trainer's room to be observed for the rest of the day. The next day I took it a bit easy during my workout and seemed to be fine. As it seemed to be an isolated incident, I continued to do the intense workouts for the next couple of weeks until I had another incident where I collapsed during a workout. After the second incident, the trainers advised me to visit with my cardiologist over Thanksgiving break to see if he could diagnose the problem Until then, I was not allowed to do any kind of physical activity. Accordingly, I complied and made an appointment with my cardiologist for the day after Thanksgiving.

About a week before the break, I experienced a major health scare. As I was returning to my residence hall after dinner one day, I went up some stairs and started to feel short of breath. The feeling was similar to what I had felt during the times I collapsed during track practice, except this time I did not get lightheaded. I was able to make my way back to my residence hall and thought maybe I just needed to sit down and relax, but after about 30 minutes, my heart rate did not seem to slow down. My roommate took me to the emergency room, and I was immediately admitted because my heart rate was at 256 beats per minute. A normal heart rate is about 60 beats per minute. All the staff who helped me were amazed that I was functioning normally and alive. Doctors initially tried to put me back into a regular rhythm through medication but were unsuccessful. They decided to use a defibrillator. While all of this is happening in San Marcos, my parents had just started a four-hour drive to come be with me. Fortunately, I had a tio (uncle) who lived in San Antonio, which was only 30 minutes away, who could be with me at the hospital. The defibrillator was successful in putting me into a more normal rhythm, and when I woke up, my heart rate was at 80 beats per minute. I spent the night in ICU for further observation, and my tio informed me that my parents would be stopping in San Antonio for the night and would make their way up to San Marcos the next morning. The next day I met with a cardiologist in Austin. When I arrived, the doctor looked at my EKG and was surprised I was alive. Looking at my test results and consulting with her colleagues, it was determined that I had a hypertrophic cardiomyopathy and would require an internal defibrillator to be implanted. This event did not cause me to become mad at the world, God, or anyone for that matter. What it did do was make me curious as to what physiologically happened that led to me developing a hypertrophic cardiomyopathy. This major medical event in my life is what led me to devote my career to science.

By the end of the first semester, I had finished with C's in my STEM lecture courses, but I had achieved an A and B in my chemistry and biology labs, respectively. Though I was disappointed with my overall performance, I was glad my grades in the lab courses were much better. It was also around this time that I went to talk to my chemistry professor, Dr. Debra Feakes, about how I would be able to explore what happened to me physiologically. After asking that question, she steered me towards changing my major from biology to biochemistry, which was in its second year of existence in the department. She told me this major would give me more hands-on experience and preparation for a PhD route. My face must have informed her I had never thought about getting a PhD degree. It was something that had never really crossed my mind, and to be honest, I did not really know what getting a PhD required or what I could do with that degree. She was great at breaking it down for me, but the main thing I came away with was that if I wanted to dive deep into my condition, I would need to get a PhD From there on out, I made it a goal of mine to get a PhD. During my sophomore year, I almost scratched my goal of getting a PhD because of organic chemistry. I struggled in both sections of organic chemistry, getting C's in both, but my lab grades were much better. During my struggles, my parents became worried about me. They knew how much pressure I put on myself to do the best I could and how much this one class was causing me to stress, and their way of helping me was suggesting other majors that did not seem to be as challenging as biochemistry. It was not that they did not believe in me. It was because they were worried as to what the stress could do to my already damaged health. I told them I would continue on in biochemistry, and if it did not click, or if I did not enjoy it anymore, I would consider changing majors.

During the fall semester of my junior year, I was able to take my first biochemistry course: introductory biochemistry. I am not sure if it was the material, the professor (Dr. Watkins), or the fact that I had better study habits, but everything just started to make sense. I started doing better in all my courses and even started doing research in Dr. Feakes's lab. It was my first exposure to actual scientific research, and I was hooked. The freedom I had over the decision making of my project was invigorating. From this point on, I was always involved in independent research. I even joined Dr. Watkins' lab the following year in a collaborative project. It was around this time that I felt the need to give back to the Latinx community. I felt lucky to have so many great people in my life who had helped me, and I wanted to make sure that those who were not as blessed as me had someone to reach out to. As an undergraduate, I got involved with the Society of Mexican American Engineers and Scientists (MAES). Little did I know that as soon as I joined, I would be launched into a leadership role. As I became involved with the organization, I discovered the current president was in her last semester at the university and needed help, especially with MAES's annual science extravaganza (SE). The SE is a day-long program that show cases various fields of STEM to 250 local fourth and fifth graders, most of whom are from underrepresented and low-income backgrounds. I saw this as an opportunity to contribute, not only to the organization, but to the Latinx community, so I volunteered to take responsibility of the SE. This was my first exposure to helping others out through STEM and my first real leadership opportunity since high school, and I loved every minute of the experience. I eventually became president of the organization, for which I held office until I graduated, and these experiences are what led me to want to help others.

Wanting to get greater exposure to research, I applied to multiple summer research programs the spring semester of my junior year. I ended up accepting an offer from the University of Georgia (UGA). At UGA, I got to work with Dr. R. Kelly Dawe in the department of plant biochemistry. This program allowed me to understand the amount of sacrifice and commitment it would take to be a successful scientist. This was the first time I had lived out of the state of Texas and the first time I had missed a family reunion. There were times where I asked myself if I did the right thing by leaving my family for the summer. As hard as it was to accept,

I knew I had made the right choice not only for myself but also for those of my community. With the Latinx community being so family driven, there is always a sense that leaving our family is something that we should not ever consider, but with me taking on this challenge, I knew I would be able to help others face that challenge when it presented itself. My mentor, Dr. Dawe, also helped to reassure me I had made the right decision in going to UGA for the summer when he told me, "You have what it takes to be a scientist." It was at that moment when I had no doubt that I would be getting my doctoral degree.

Graduating in four and a half years gave me the opportunity to do another summer program at the University of Texas Health Science Center in San Antonio (UTHSCSA). There I worked under the direction of Dr. Lily Dong in the cellular and structural biology program. Her research was focused on diabetes, the topic to which I wanted to dedicate my life. My time spent in her lab was useful to understand the complexity of diabetes as a disease. Dr. Dong was a completely different personality than what I was used to; she was faster paced and stricter than my previous research mentors. It is not as though this prevented me from getting along with Dr. Dong, but it just brought to my attention that I would have to work with many different personalities throughout my career. I am very thankful for Dr. Dong in helping me realize that, as well as how to handle those transitions accordingly.

Going into my last semester at Texas State, I started to prepare my applications for graduate schools. Because of my struggles in my first year and second year of college, I was not sure how many programs would actually accept me. Of the 10 colleges I applied to, I got interviews with three programs: Texas A&M University, University of Texas at San Antonio (UTSA), and UTHSCSA. I assumed I would get an interview with UGA, but my application was lost, and by the time that was figured out, it was too late to resubmit my application. After interviewing with all the programs, I chose to pursue my PhD at UTSA in their cellular and molecular biology program. It was, and still is, a relatively new program, but I imagined myself helping to establish the program with my research.

It was not until my first biochemistry test that I realized graduate school was a totally different animal compared to the undergraduate level. With my undergraduate degree being in biochemistry, I became overconfident even before the first test was given and did not put in as much time studying as I should have. At that time, I also had a few family events taking place back home, and with my overconfidence, I felt it was fine for me to travel back home for a few weekends to take part in those events. However, as soon as the first test was handed to me, I began to panic. The material was familiar, but I knew I could not answer the questions with the amount of detail that it would take to get full credit for the question. I ended up getting a C on that test, which in graduate school, is failing. This caused me to realize I was going to have to put even more work into making sure I was successful for the rest of the semester. In other words, I was going to have to possibly triple my studying time, and I learned that my choice to pursue a PhD was going to come with some personal sacrifices. This was not easy to accept, as I felt that I might be abandoning my family for selfish reasons. I changed up my schedule and had set times for everything: eating, research, reading, studying, talking with my family, and sleeping. This is what I needed to do to guarantee my success, and thankfully, my family and friends were extremely supportive. When my next test came around, I made sure I was prepared. I ended up getting a 97 on the test, second best in the class. From that point on, I knew that most of my life was going to have to be planned out in order to guarantee my success.

As I mentioned, sacrifices are something one makes when getting a PhD. Not everyone's sacrifice will be the same. For me, my sacrifice was missing out on family events. A few years into my graduate program, during our weekly phone call, my grandfather reassured me that my family was accepting of the sacrifices I had to make when he said, "Don't worry about us. We are doing just fine. You keep working hard and do what you were meant to do." That was the last time I spoke to my grandfather. Later that week, he had a seizure and hit his head on the corner of the table. The blow he suffered caused him to pass a month later. This was most certainly one of the most challenging times, not just in graduate school but my life. Just a month earlier, I lost my cousin to a stage 4 glioblastoma multiform. As a scientist, I took it very personal that I could not directly help or find a way to help my loved ones, but it was at this time I realized I would not be able to solve the world's problems on my own. I think this is something all young leaders, whether in STEM or not, have to realize.

During my graduate career, I was able to continue my outreach with the Latinx community. My graduate adviser, Dr. G. Jilani Chaudry, was very encouraging of diversifying my academic/personal portfolio. He knew we needed to be well-rounded scientists, but he also knew we needed to be involved with activities outside of the lab to stay sane. This mentorship allowed me to continue with the UTSA chapter of MAES as a graduate adviser and SE director. As a graduate student, I was introduced to the Society for the Advancement of Chicanos and Native Americans in the Sciences (SACNAS). As a member of SACNAS, I was able to gain great mentorship and life lessons specifically as it related to being a person of color in the sciences. As a graduate student, I would have thought well-educated people would not hold the same perceptions for people of color that less educated people had, but sadly, this wasn't true at all.

As a graduate student, you are encouraged to go to conferences to make your presence known in the scientific community. It was at these national scientific conferences where I experienced some of the harshest racism. There have been times at these conferences where I was confused for the service staff and not a fellow scientist. It was confusing to me as to how such educated minds could not see me as an equal. As I learned from my mentors early on, this is just something to expect. They also said I did not have to stand for it, and it was my responsibility to help drive out that type of thinking. I did take it as my responsibility, and I knew that I would continue to fight to change this way of thinking until the day I die.

It was SACNAS that exposed me to scientific careers that have more impact on diversifying the science world. Through SACNAS, I gained exposure to what it took to be on the administrative side of a national organization as a member of the national board of directors. As a student board member, I was able to see the work that takes place to create high-impact policy. To be around people who had been scientists for longer than I was alive was truly an honor, but it was equally amazing to see how such large personalities, who would not always agree with one another on certain topics, could come together for the good of the organization and the cause. My experiences from my time on the board guided me towards choosing a career other than a tenure track professor. I knew I wanted to have a successful career in some type of administrative role, whether it was for a nonprofit or in academia. Making the decision to not go into academia was not well taken by some of my mentors. One of my mentors told me that by choosing to pursue a nontenure career, she had failed at her life mission. At the same time, I also had mentors who came to my defense regarding my decision. They understood that the job environment in science did not allow for everyone to pursue a tenure track position. Additionally, had it not been for me deciding to not pursue a tenure track position early on, I would have never been prepared for what happened after I successfully defended my PhD.

Even before I was told I could start preparing for my dissertation, I had started to look for postdoctoral positions. As I was looking for positions, the government was also implementing the required sequester to help balance the budget. During a time when laboratories were experiencing funding cuts across the nation, I obtained interviews with three labs. One of those positions was in Dr. George Church's lab at Harvard Medical School. Dr. Church is a member of the prestigious National Academy of Sciences and the National Academy of Engineering, sits on the board for eight biotech companies, and has a 100-member lab. It was truly an honor to interview with such a prestigious lab, and though I have no doubt I would have been successful in his lab, I knew this lab was not for me. The lab I ended up choosing was at The University of Texas at Austin in the pharmacology and toxicology department under the direction of Dr. Ted Mills. Ted's lab was doing good work in diabetes and only had seven members at the time. I felt comfortable with Ted and the rest of his lab. That's not to say that I was not comfortable with George Church and his lab, but it just felt as though my connection with Ted was much stronger right away. Additionally, it was when Ted and I were discussing life that he told me he understood that post doctorates have a life outside the lab, and he was fine with that, as long as they got their work done. This was something he said of his own volition and not something that I had to dig for. That was important to me because at the same time that I was looking to finish with graduate school, I was preparing to start my life with the love of my life. I met Jessika, my wife, at Texas State, and we dated during my sophomore year. Though our relationship did not last at the time, we were able to keep a friendship over the years, and we eventually came back together during my fifth year in graduate school. After sticking with me during the preparation of my dissertation, which can kill relationships, I knew that she was the one I would eventually call my wife. Jessika is from Austin and at the time of our reconnection was still living in Austin. Therefore, finding a position at UT-Austin was something that I took as a sign.

My plan was to do research in Ted's lab for three to four years and build up my resume with experience to help me get an administrative position afterwards. I defended my PhD in December and planned to wrap up my work before I started my post doc at UT-Austin in July. It was around May that my plans would be completely changed for me. Between December and May, I periodically checked with Ted to make sure the government sequester would not affect the grant I was going to be funded by, and he assured me it should not be a problem. One day, I got an email from him saying he needed to speak with me immediately. He told me the government sequester had affected the grant after all, and because my position was not funded yet, the money was taken away. At the same time, he made me aware of a position for a STEM coordinator in the Longhorn Center for Academic Excellence (LCAE) at UT-Austin. It involved mentoring students, who were predominantly minorities and first-generation college students, in STEM. He figured with my background in outreach programs that this position would interest me. I immediately reached out to another contact I had at UT-Austin to inquire if he knew anybody in that center, and he did. He gave me that person's email, and I was able to setup a phone call to get more of an idea about the position. After speaking with this person, I automatically knew this position could be the start of my administrative career. The person I spoke to was also impressed with what I had done and encouraged me to apply. I eventually obtained the position and could not be happier with my decision to not pursue another post doctorate. By taking this position, I have been able to meet people, create connections, and gain experience that I would have never been able to as a post doctorate.

If this were 20 years ago, I would say my journey through STEM had not been very typical, but I have heard many others tell of similar stories. That is why I am grateful for all the mentors I have had in my life, from family to professors. I feel it is their guidance that has helped me get to where I am today, and I will never forget this. That is why I take it upon myself to make sure that I give back to my community, as well as the world, in any way that I can.

TESTIMONIO 9

Ricardo Martinez

Key Fields of Study: Mathematics, Curriculum and Instructional
Technology, and Mathematics Education
Doctoral Student
Iowa State University

In my first year of doctoral study, I was able to teach and impact the training of more than 200 future math teachers. With my research, I am establishing my own theory of how people learn to make math more equitable. Now this one kid who did not think he mattered has the opportunity to influence people across the country, if not the world. As you read my story, realize that you are one person who can grow to influence others.

When I was a kid in school and even as a young adult in my first years of college, I would say "why does it matter—I am just one person—I do not matter." Now I have a bachelor of science (four-year degree) in mathematics, a master of education degree (two years after bachelor's) in curriculum and instructional technology, and I am working on a doctoral degree (four years after a master's) in mathematics education. I was a high school mathematics teacher for six years, and now I do research and teach courses at the university level. I help train future math teachers. In my first year of doctoral study I was able to teach and impact the training of more than 200 future math teachers. With my research, I am establishing my own theory of how people learn to make math more equitable. The work I do will help train future math teachers how to incorporate the rich cultural knowledge of their students in the classroom while understanding that teachers can and need to support all students to pursue their dreams. As a Latino, I am proud to contribute to the rich STEM history that is associated with the Latinx culture—from all the great pyramids built in Mexico and Latin America to the science behind sun dials and lunar calendars to modern inventions such as the AcceleGlove. Latinxs are powerful problem solvers. The AcceleGlove, for example, was created by Jose Hernandez-Rebollar. It is a glove that turns sign language into audio. Now this one kid who did not think he mattered has the opportunity to influence people across the country, if not the world. As you read my story, realize that you are one person who can grow to influence others.

I was born in a small town of about 60,000 people in Delano, California. I have two brothers, one eight years older, and the other is 12 years older. My sister, the oldest, is 15 years older than me. My mother worked in the fields, mostly picking grapes. Growing up, my family was poor. We lived in six different houses, and this was normal for many families in my community. My father left my mother before I was born, and still to this day, I only remember talking to him once. It was the time my older brother was arrested. The police knocked down our front door and arrested him, my mother, my sister, and me. We were all handcuffed, thrown on the floor, and had guns pointed at us. We were in jail for two days; everyone but my brother was released. I was 19 and had finished my first year of college when this happened. My father heard what had happened, so he came from Mexico to see how he could help. When he knocked on our door, I answered and all I could say is "Hello, can I help you?" because I had no idea who he was. My brother, who was born in Mexico, is no longer allowed into the United States.

My biggest influence growing up was my sister, who attended college and became an elementary teacher. She is the one who taught me the value of reading at a young age. My oldest brother joined the Army when I was in the first grade, making my home me, my older brother, and my mother. My older brother was one of my main parental figures growing up. Many of my friends and cousins who I grew up with were gang members. I remember trying my first cigarette in the third grade, and I know that I had already tried beer and liquor way before that. The town I grew up in was not a safe community. Shootings, stabbings, and fights were common. I remember my first week of high school where every day during lunch there was a fight, and the police and/or ambulance had to come to school. During high school, we would have the police dogs on campus at least twice a week checking random classrooms for drugs. My older brother, who is no longer allowed in the country, told me to remember this: "You had it rough, but you were not alone. Many people and kids deal with tough times and tougher times than you did." I write these words in hopes that you realize that it does not matter how tough your life has been. You still have the ability and deserve the opportunity to do whatever you want to do.

My first year of high school was difficult. I would skip class anywhere from three to five times each week, and because of that, I earned a D in my first semester of algebra I. I got into a lot of trouble at school but not at home. My second semester I actually had to show up every day to class, and I ended up earning an A in the second half of algebra I. When summer came around, I talked to other students, and they said that I should just try to take the least amount of math classes. I decided to take geometry over the summer with the plan of taking general math as a sophomore. We only needed six semesters of math to graduate, and a D is passing, so I was on the easy path. When I showed up for my first day of geometry over the summer, my algebra teacher told me that I needed to just re-take the first half of algebra I and then I could be in the honors program. He believed in me, and because of him, I stayed with math all through high school and even passed both AP physics and AP calculus exams as a senior. My high school teacher knew that it does not matter who you are or where you come from because anyone and everyone is capable of learning. I graduated high school with a 2.56 GPA, and now I will graduate with a doctorate. People will call me Dr. Ricardo Martinez when I am done.

After high school, I applied to the local college because I noticed everyone else was. I was accepted and given financial aid to go to college, plus I got a job working in the library. I did not even know financial aid and scholarships were an option, nor did I know that the university could help find a job through the work study program. Now I know that if you apply early and to multiple schools you can compare which schools will provide the best financial aid. I learned that work study is something you should ask the counselors before the semester begins and the information is online. I even learned that the higher you score on the ACT or SAT the more opportunities you have to get some scholarships. All I had heard from TV was that college is expensive, and you must be really smart to go. The truth is that college is expensive, but there are programs, scholarships, and grants that can help you pay for part of it. Even if you have to take out a loan, it can pay for itself in the future. People with college degrees do, on average, make more money, especially in STEM careers. The truth is you do have to be smart to be successful in college, but being smart is not knowing a bunch of facts. People who are truly smart know that being great at things comes from not being afraid to fail. You have to expect to fail and realize that you do not have all the answers. Just be prepared to not give up and learn from that failure. Learning from practice and experience is how you can become smart.

In college, I was pushed into engineering because I was good at math and science. Even though I was pushed into engineering, I think it was the best start for me. When you start in general engineering, you are required to take a math class, a physics class, a chemistry class, and an introduction to engineering class during your first year in college. This allowed me to see what I really enjoyed about math and science. My first semester I took an introduction to engineering class and realized that engineering is more than just being good at math. I learned there are many different types of engineers. One thing I was not told is that you can be creative in engineering, and you have to know how to communicate with others and work as a team because it is okay to not have all the answers. For example, I thought I was a big shot in my engineering class. I was one of the few students who had started in calculus II, and others were in "lower" math classes. This is where I learned that engineering and problem solving are more than just knowing a lot of math. Some of my classmates who came from community colleges and/or started in remedial math were creating projects that were better than mine. This motivated me not only to try harder but also to learn from others.

My third semester in college I took two math classes (ordinary differential equations and linear algebra) that made me switch my major from engineering to mathematics. That is why I recommend that students start in engineering because it allows you to easily switch STEM majors without delaying your graduation. I could have switched to chemistry, biology, math, physics, or computer science without being behind, but I changed my major to pure math. Here I learned that my university had three different paths in mathematics. One track was to be a math teacher, the other was to do applied math, and the third was pure or theoretical math. Applied math would lead to getting a job doing math, such as being an engineer, an economist, or working for a company to solve problems. People who do theoretical math are the people who make and develop new math ideas. When I made the switch, I also had the opportunity to become a math tutor for the university. It was not until my final year as a math major that I realized I wanted to teach. I ran into my old high school algebra teacher and realized I enjoyed math tutoring and helping people more than working on math problems, so I made the change and became a high school math teacher because I wanted to help students the way my algebra teacher changed my life.

I taught high school math for a total of six years, and in my last three years of teaching, I earned a master of education degree in curriculum and instructional technology. That just means I know how to use technology to help people learn. While working on my master's, I did a good job on one assignment, and I was able to work with two university professors to create a lesson that uses augmented reality to help students learn. At that moment, I knew I wanted to continue to get my PhD because I want to teach future teachers to be like my algebra teacher. Now my job is to be a student. I did not know that in many majors when you attempt to get a PhD the school pays you to study and work. Right now, my doctoral education is being paid for by Iowa State University, and the university pays me money every month to work 20 hours a week. This opportunity is not a special scholarship or a rare prize. Many students working on a PhD get the same benefits that I do.

The most rewarding aspect of my STEM career is that I have the chance to change how people learn and teach mathematics. One part of what I do, that is fun, is I get to play with random technologies, and I get to call it research. One day I played in a virtual world for half a day because we were exploring how games and other technologies could be used to teach math. Other days I will play with robots such as the Sphere/BB-8 and find ways to use it to teach math or science. When I was a kid, more so when I was 25 (a big kid!), I would have never imaged that I could be going to college where I am playing with toys and saying how people should learn math. Knowing that Latinx students do have the power to change the world is something that not all Latinx students know. If it was not for my algebra teacher, I would not have known that I was smart. Based on my high school GPA, I was not a smart student, yet now my university GPA is 3.84, and I am presenting my research at national and international conferences.

Now for advice to future STEM professionals (yes that is you!). Did you know getting a PhD does not mean that you are the smartest person? It just means that you put in the time and the effort to learn, and that effort comes from your passion to do. Latinxs are a growing population, so naturally there should be more of us in STEM careers. I want every Latinx student to be educated to the point where they can make and have the choice to be what they want to be. Creativity and problem solving is a huge part of STEM. Latinx have a rich culture and history that need to be seen in the world. This culture has not been seen and fully accepted in STEM fields. Such a culture can inspire new ways of solving real problems, so in many ways, to have a healthy society, we need more Latinx students in STEM fields because there are many problems waiting to be solved.

My advice to you is this: realize that one person can make a difference. As early as the first year of high school, do not be afraid to send emails to adults who are in careers that you are interested in pursuing. Have the confidence to send emails to professors at universities to get more information. Use the Internet to research careers that interest you. Above all else, know that your voice is just as powerful as mine. I know my voice will continue to grow, and I know every young Latinx student has the ability to grow greater than me.

TESTIMONIO 10
Olivia Moreno

Key Fields of Study: Environmental Science and
Engineering, Industrial Engineering
PhD Candidate in Environmental Science and Engineering (Energy Track)
Program Specialist with U.S. Department of Agriculture-Institute of
Bioenergy, Climate and Environment

Knowing that I am serving my government and serving the people of this country is very gratifying. I feel empowered that I am using my expertise to get a role in processing government funds to better serve and educate our Latinx communities. The range of funded research from the USDA ranges from determining how to provide healthier school lunches for kids to defining how to make cleaner energy to leave a better planet for future generations.

If someone had asked me a couple of years ago, after I finished my bachelor's degree, if I thought I would be where I am today, I would have said not at all. My name is Olivia Carolina Moreno, and I am about to finish my doctoral degree in environmental science and engineering from the University of Texas at El Paso (UTEP). I was born and raised in the small border town of El Paso, Texas, next to the Mexican city of Juarez, Chihuahua.

I am the first in my family to attend and graduate college. Both of my parents completed high school. As a result, I knew I wanted to go to college because I saw the many hardships that my parents went through while we were growing. Sometimes they worked two jobs and, as a result, would not see us very often. Although we did not see one another much, we always had food on the table. I remember how hard both of my parents worked so that my two brothers, my sister, and I had new clothes, shoes, and school supplies every school year.

Throughout my early school years, I became aware of how much I loved math and science. Even if it was not cool to be smart, I was good at it. When I got to high school, I started not to care if they labeled me as a nerd, and on career day in my calculus class, my life changed. Throughout my four years in high school, I was in the magnet school for future teachers and coaches, but I decided to change my plans completely and to major in electrical engineering after high school. I remember precisely the day this happened. A group of engineers from The University of Texas at El Paso (UTEP) came to present to my math class on career day about their cool and fun jobs. They worked for the company Texas Instruments while finishing up their electrical engineering degrees. I thought to myself, how cool of a job is that? I could be writing and coding the programs that go into computers and games. I spoke to them after they presented, and my mind was convinced that I should major in engineering. They persuaded me by telling me how math is applied to everyday problems and that their jobs were extremely fun.

In May of that year, I graduated with honors from Riverside High School. I was ranked number eight in a class of 311 students, so I felt I had a real chance to make it if I majored in engineering. Even though I had full scholarships to attend the University of Texas at Austin (UT Austin) and Our Lady of The Lake University in San Antonio, I decided to take advantage of my Presidential Excellence scholarship at my home university of UTEP. But I am not going to lie. I was scared of leaving my family and my hometown at the age of 18 to start college in a brandnew city. Most of my good friends left for UT Austin to start college, and I did not join them. I said that I would transfer after I completed my basics at UTEP. I decided to start classes in the summer through the College Assistant Migrant Program (CAMP) at UTEP. I was not aware that I had qualified for this program until they called me and told me that I could start early at UTEP by attending summer school and stay at the school dorms to better transition into college life. I ended up getting free room and board, a small summer stipend, tutoring sessions, and, best of all, that college transition experience all because my father had worked in the field for a couple of months.

That first year of college was the most challenging for me since I had to struggle with time management. I was very glad to know where to ask for help and where to go for tutoring sessions. I had a part-time job, and my parents dropped me off and picked me up from school because I did not have a car yet. I developed this bad habit of procrastination and doing my assigned work and studying at the last minute. Soon, my grades started to reflect that, and I was on the edge of losing my scholarship. I was on academic probation for the spring semester, and if my GPA was below a 2.80 by the end of the summer, my scholarship was going to be taken away. In order to try and save my scholarship, I enrolled in summer classes. Fortunately, I did great and kept my scholarship for the remaining three years. However, I did change my major from electrical engineering to industrial engineering. The classes and content of electrical engineering were too difficult for me to handle along with the other things going on in my personal life. I finished my bachelor's degree in industrial engineering in 2009, and during that last semester, I met my professor who would eventually be my adviser for my master's thesis and doctoral dissertation. She was not my favorite teacher because she was very demanding with homework and assignments. Her exams and quizzes were very challenging, and she was not very lenient when it came to grading. Now that I look back and reflect on how hard she was, I can honestly say that I appreciate her being like that because it made me try harder to be the successful woman I am today. She also exposed me to developing my oral presentation skills by attending a regional conference as an undergraduate where we had to make a poster about a project for her class. After my group won, she invited me to her office to talk about the kind of research she was doing and asked me if I wanted to join her team. I really liked the fact that she was working on cutting-edge research, and I decided to join her team and pursue a master's degree in industrial engineering too. Pursuing my doctoral degree was a lot easier since the research I had done for my master's thesis was expanded a bit more to be able to write and publish my doctoral dissertation. However, one of the most challenging things I had to overcome while in graduate school was to continue to develop my oral presentation skills and my writing skills for publishing scientific journals. Once you enter graduate school, it is very popular to attend research conferences to publish and present your work.

A semester before finishing my graduate degree, my adviser asked if I wanted to complete a summer internship in Washington, D.C. with the headquarter offices of the U.S. Department of Agriculture (USDA). This agency had previously funded my adviser's research under an educational grant, and one of the objectives was to expose students to careers within the government. Today, I can say that this is my fourth summer interning in Washington, D.C. with the USDA. Upon completion of my doctoral degree this upcoming 2016 spring semester, they will convert me into a full-time government employee. All the training and the experience I have been exposed to these summers have been one the most rewarding steps towards my STEM career. Knowing that I am serving my government and serving the people of this country is very gratifying. I feel empowered that I am using my expertise to get a role in processing government funds to better serve and educate our Latinx communities. The range of funded research from USDA ranges from determining how to provide healthier school lunches for kids to defining how to make cleaner energy to leave a better planet for future generations.

My time spent in our nation's capital has made me aware of how under-represented our Latinx community is. The way we can change that is by graduating with STEM degrees to better our chances of landing those leadership roles and jobs that can have a direct impact on the way our Latinx community is represented. A last piece of advice I can share with you is to pursue what you want to study because you will more than likely be doing that for the rest of your life. It is a great and rewarding feeling when you are getting paid to do what you really love and are passionate about. Also, keep in mind that it is okay to leave or move for college from your hometown. If I could have done one thing differently, it would have been to take advantage of the scholarships available at the other universities. I am not saying my home university was not great. I am saying, though, that it is good to have some diversity in experience and get that feeling of being independent and having responsibilities that come with relying only on yourself in order to grow and mature. Finally, when you graduate with your bachelor's degree, the best thing you can do is to pursue a master's degree. It's possibly the best two years of your life on which you can spend your money and time. You will not regret it.

TESTIMONIO 11
Elvia Elisa Niebla

Key Field of Study: Soil Chemistry
Former National Coordinator for Global Change Research
at the Forest Service—USDA

In fact, the most rewarding aspect of my work has been knowing that I contributed to the progress of humankind, improving the environment, and promoting significant research in the field. The cutting edge work I engaged in while at EPA and later as national coordinator of Global Change Research in the Forest Service moved the environmental agenda forward in significant ways. When the IPCC shared the Nobel Peace Prize with Al Gore, I felt that we, the scientists, who worked in the field were being recognized; we had made a difference.

As a young girl, I looked at the sky and wondered what made up clouds? Where did they come from? I was in awe to see that huge watermelons grew from the tiny seeds my father planted in our yard. How could that be? I was full of questions, and as I grew older, it seemed to me that science had the answers to my questions.

However, I never imagined that choosing to study science would lead me to such a significant and exciting life. I was born in the border town of Nogales, Sonora, and grew up in Nogales, Arizona, the fourth daughter of a tight-knit family with strong roots on both sides of the border. All I had to do was cross the street, and I would be in a different country visiting my relatives. We lived in Mexico, and my father came to the United States in the early 1940s wanting to volunteer to join the war effort, but his job in the food import industry was deemed essential, and he was not allowed to enlist. However, it was not until 1952 that the family moved to Nogales, Arizona, where my maternal grandmother, Bertha Rankin, resided. During the post-WWII era, when I was growing up, the border was a vibrant, joyful place full of possibility. My step-grandfather, Charles D. Rankin, was a contractor who built the elementary school I attended. On my father's side, my great-grandfather, Juan Gómez, was a teacher in Caborca, a small town in northern Sonora. Not surprisingly, my grand-aunts and grand-uncles, as well as my father's siblings, were educators in Mexico; my grandfather's sister, Manuela Niebla de Pedroza, was the principal of the high school. Two of aunts and an uncle, Aída Josefina, Emma, and Hector Manuel were educators, and Uncle Roberto was a lawyer. So, in some ways, I defied the family tradition by becoming a scientist.

Obviously, my family, especially my mother and my aunts, influenced my life. Tia Chuly (Aída Josefina) was a strong, opinionated woman who held her own in political debates and who read to me from literary and political works. She was my role model. My mother's advice and support no doubt influenced my decision to follow my passion for science. I was a curious child who incessantly asked how things worked; both my parents indulged my curiosity and nurtured the budding scientist.

Right after high school, I was fortunate to attend Fullerton Community College in California where I lived with my brother and his wife and young daughter. Their support was invaluable. My father died the semester I transferred to the University of Arizona in Tucson; that was one of my first challenges, as I was now on my own. I majored in zoology, mathematics, and physics and minored in chemistry. The most important factor in choosing the University of Arizona was proximity to my family, as my brother had moved away to Florida to work with NASA, and I had to return to Arizona. Upon graduation, I didn't have a job, so I stayed one more year and earned a master of education degree with a special education specialization. I taught for two years and then applied and was accepted into the PhD program at the University of Arizona. I had hopes of becoming an analytical chemist as I was intrigued with the process of analyzing various substances. However, as a graduate assistant, I began working in soil chemistry and found my passion. It was clear that the field was much more relevant to solving issues related to the environment.

When I was in high school, I prepared to study science in college by taking as many mathematics and science courses as possible; unfortunately, I attended a small high school with few resources. However, one high school teacher, Mr. Summers spent countless hours after school providing me with additional instruction. Once at the community college in California, I also took the college level mathematics and science classes, including organic and inorganic chemistry. This prepared me very well, and when I transferred to the University of Arizona, I was able to out-perform my classmates. I also made sure that all the classes I took at Fullerton Community College were transferable.

The first two years at Fullerton Community College I only paid $50 out-of-state tuition and lived with my brother, so the costs were minimal. I didn't have a car or many expenses. At the University of Arizona, however, I had to support myself entirely, so I worked in the ornithology department classifying and stuffing birds that were gathered from all over the world. I loved the work-study assignment. I remember going to the administrator in charge of work-study positions to ask for a job given what I considered my desperate situation. After hearing me out, he sent me immediately to the ornithology department. I asked how I would know if I had the job. He simply answered, "You already have a job." His generosity surprised and comforted me; I felt that I had allies out in the world who provided support even when I thought I was on my own.

I survived my college experience with the support of my family and the financial assistance that the work-study program provided. Aside from financial need, other obstacles were mostly cultural, as I had little experience in academia. Furthermore, I had very limited experience working in a fully equipped experimental laboratory, so when I went into my classes, I was at a disadvantage. In all my college career, I was usually the only person of color or one of no more than two or three females in science classes. I suppose those were obstacles, although at the time I didn't see these circumstances as obstacles and felt very lucky to be able to pursue my desire for a college education. I loved every minute of college.

I decided to earn a graduate degree because I wanted to work in a field that I loved and where I could control the variables. As a special education teacher, I had no control of many of the variables affecting my students. Just as I had as an under-graduate, I faced financial and cultural challenges in graduate school. However, they were of a different nature. One of the biggest challenges when I was starting my graduate program was when I was ready for a research fellowship. Since I was so good at teaching, the departmental committee that assigned the fellowships awarded me a teaching instead of research fellowship. Later in my program, I was helped by the fact that I was a full-time research associate, and, therefore, I had good salary and benefits. In addition, this position allowed me flexibility in my work schedule so I could attend classes. I was the first Chicana and the first female to earn a PhD in soil chemistry from the University of Arizona.

After graduation, I took a position with the National Park Service Western Arche-ological Center (NPSWA) working on the preservation of adobe structures in the Western region, which included several states. I traveled to sites seeking the soil that was originally used to make the adobes. Being in charge of the laboratory while at the NPSWA, I realized that I needed management training, so I applied to and was admitted to the University of Northern Colorado master of science in busi-ness administration program. The equivalent of the MBA allowed me to work towards making the laboratory self-supporting.

After five years working with the Park Service, I changed jobs. The Environmental Protection Agency (EPA) had seen my publications on sludge application to soil and offered me a job to write the regulations on the very same topic. Although unplanned, my doctoral research had led to my move to Washington, D.C. Most of my work at EPA focused on looking for solutions to treating the sludge that resulted from the Clean Water Act regulations. My job was to determine the safe levels of sludge that could be applied to soil. The main research question I was investigating was: Could soil clean out the toxins from the sludge through filtration? I was exhilarated to discover that indeed there were certain soils that were effective filters, although we also found great variation in the soil capacity.

After five years at EPA, I moved again. The United States was establishing the Global Change Program with representatives from various departments to coordinate the research. I applied and got hired to be the coordinator of global change research in the Forest Service within the Department of Agriculture. In that position, I coordinated the research efforts of over 200 scientists nationally who worked for the regional offices of the Forest Service. My work as a scientist led me to that position, and in that capacity, I worked nationally and internationally with top scientists in the field to find solutions to the challenges global change presents.

In my capacity as coordinator, I presented the research findings to the U.S. Global Change Program that in turn worked with the International Panel on Climate Change (IPCC). For me, global change, including climate change, is the biggest threat to the planet, and working in this field at the national and international levels has made my life's work worthwhile. In fact, the most rewarding aspect of my work has been knowing that I contributed to the progress of humankind, improving the environment and promoting significant research in the field. The cutting edge work I engaged in while at EPA and later as national coordinator of global change research in the Forest Service moved the environmental agenda forward in significant ways. When the IPCC shared the Nobel Peace Prize with Al Gore, I felt that we, the scientists, who worked in the field were being recognized; we had made a difference.

Moreover, I loved my life in Washington, D.C.—the travel, the people I met from all over the world whose goals aligned with mine, the excitement of helping shape policy that would affect our nation and our world. My assignments included various key positions. I was a Brookings fellow assigned to the staff to Congressman Pastor. In that position, I gleaned much valuable experience in the legislative process that helped me with my work. As a senior executive fellow at Harvard, I had many memorable and impactful experiences as I was there during the 1992 campaign, and I was privy to many political debates and had the privilege of meeting many of the candidates who came to Harvard to deliver lectures. Indeed, while in Washington, D.C. and as a research scientist working within the Department of Agriculture, I was fortunate to be involved in key discussions on global change in conjunction with other key personnel from the White House and Congress.

I can honestly say that as a student in Nogales High School, I never imagined that my life in science would result in such an exciting career. I was just taking the courses that I knew would prepare me for college, especially for being a science major. I would advise students who are aspiring to enter a STEM field of study to take as many mathematics and science courses as possible. I would urge them to make sure they have the basics down pat, because as they progress through their course of study, they will rely heavily on the courses that lay the groundwork for the more advanced courses and ultimately for their future research. I would also reinforce the need to take the time to learn the basics really well, not just for the test or for the grade but for life-changing opportunities that will come later. Of course, having mastery of the basics will also allow them to succeed in science courses. Another important factor or essential element is that they must choose a field that inspires passion because that is the driving force that will cause them to overcome any challenges they might encounter in their career path.

When I consider why Latinx students would want to enter the STEM fields, three main reasons emerge. Firstly, Latinx students should engage in STEM careers because they will be able to contribute to the betterment of their community in particular and to the greater society in general. Secondly, they will impact the future of the Latinx community insofar as their research or academic careers will improve the opportunities for access and for success of many who come after them. Finally, I believe that the self-satisfaction of being part of a STEM field cannot be greater. Aside from earning a very comfortable living, working in a STEM career brings the knowledge that one is making a contribution to society; that can be rewarding. Also, the self-satisfaction comes from the recognition of one's contributions. In my own life, I have garnered many rewards from having been a soil chemist and involved in global change.

Despite the obvious disadvantages of being a female in a male-dominated field and working with mostly male colleagues, I must say that I was never fazed by the inequities or the disparities; they were there to be sure, but I just proceeded to do my work and accomplish what needed to be done to the best of my ability. Invariably, the quality of my work was recognized, and the rewards in the form of promotions and job satisfaction followed. Challenges do not seem so overwhelming when you are accomplishing the goals you set for yourself and following one's passion.

Acknowledgements: I want to thank Dr. Norma Elia Cantú and Dr. Elsa C. Ruiz for their invaluable assistance in the preparation of this testimonio.

TESTIMONIO 12

Semarhy Quinones-Soto

Key Field of Study: Microbiology
Biology Lecturer and Academic Adviser
California State University, Sacramento

In 2011, I completed my graduate degree after many years of hard work. The first calls I made the day I received my PhD degree were to my abuelas to whom I

shouted "Ya soy Doctora." Those were heavy words! They recapped all the tears,
all my struggles in graduate school, and the time away from my family. They also
meant I had achieved a lifetime goal, and I had made my family proud.

The room full of students is silent. Everyone is quiet. Today, I find myself in the front of a classroom watching my students taking their final exam. I am a biology professor at Sacramento State, and I love my job! However, becoming a biology professor was not the career I originally envisioned for myself. Far from it. It would involve an unpredictable life journey with dedication to my schoolwork, the support of my family, exploration, and a bit of luck that brought me to my career.

I am from Humacao, a medium-size city on the southeast coast of the Spanish-speaking island of Puerto Rico. I lived in Humacao with my parents until I was 23 years old when I moved to California to pursue a graduate degree in biology. While I was growing up, both my parents had a huge influence on my development as a biologist, although they did in different ways.

My father loved exploring local marine life. From a very early age, he would take me snorkeling and taught me about the diverse and fragile marine ecology. This is where I learned about various life forms, such as sea urchins, tropical fish, and starfish and the habitats they call home. Through my father, I gained my deep respect and appreciation for zoology and biodiversity.

My mother worked at the University of Puerto Rico at Humacao (UPRH). She taught biology lectures and prepared materials for several microbiology lab courses. Preparing the materials for a microbiology lab took a lot of care. Since the labs used specific microbes, such as E. coli and Salmonella, she had to make certain everything was clean from contaminants (other bacteria and fungi). In addition, she must be cautious when handling bacteria to avoid contaminating herself and others. My mother taught me how to properly work in a microbiology lab. Every afternoon after school, I would help her prepare the media (food) used to grow bacteria. I would organize the tools the students would use in their courses, and I would help clean the materials. These lab experiences would contribute to my insight and skills that I would ultimately use while pursuing a bachelor's degree in biological sciences.

In 1998, I attended UPRH for my undergraduate education. Like other first-year students, I was filled with insecurities about the future and did not know what I wanted for a career. I knew it would be in biology, but doing what? There are so many fields and careers, and I did not want to make a mistake and choose the wrong one for me. Since I did not know what I wanted, I started identifying what I knew I did not want. I quickly found I did not like human biology or health sciences. Although I liked plants, I did not enjoy studying them. The only classes I enjoyed were zoology and microbiology, the two biology fields I learned from my parents. Although I found these courses exciting, they were not helping me make a decision between the two. My professors suggested that I get hands-on experience with undergraduate research. Undergraduate research would allow me to use what I learned in the classroom and determine how well I fit in a science field.

In 2000, I applied for a National Institutes of Health—Minorities Access to Research Careers (NIH-MARC) fellowship program. Since I had very good grades and excellent letters of recommendation from my professors, I was awarded two years' funding to work as an NIH-MARC undergraduate researcher on campus. While UPRH offered undergraduate research opportunities, it was not a research-intensive campus. The research topics and funding were limited. Participating in a research fellowship, such as the NIH-MARC program, provided me the opportunity to join a research lab and gain my first research experience. In addition to doing research on campus, earning the NIH-MARC fellowship allowed me to finance my last two years of college, and it facilitated travel during two summer breaks to the United States to work as an undergraduate researcher at research-intensive universities (Purdue University in the summer of 2001 and UC Berkeley in the summer of 2002). I used these research opportunities to decide between zoology and microbiology.

My first summer research experience abroad was at Purdue University, where I lived on campus for eight weeks and worked full-time as a researcher in the field of zoology studying a population of *Heliconius* butterflies. My research project required me to work inside a very hot and humid greenhouse surrounded with tropical plants and butterflies flying all around me. As part of my job, I had to count the butterflies every day, pay attention to where they laid their eggs, and follow the development of the caterpillars. While I enjoyed being surrounded by butterflies, I must admit I missed being in the lab, and I missed working with bacteria, so I started to think maybe zoology was not for me. My deciding moment came one morning when I went to the greenhouse to count my butterflies, and I could not find a single one. I had over 10 butterflies the day before, and that morning there were none. What happened to them? I looked all over the greenhouse. I searched every corner. Finally, I found a torn wing in one corner of the greenhouse. I felt my heart plunging into my stomach. Mice got to them overnight! I was devastated. My butterflies were gone, my research project was over, and I grieved their deaths. I thought to myself "this would not happen with bacteria."

I returned that fall to UPRH and added the microbiology concentration to my B.S. in biological sciences. I had picked a field! Now I had a new dilemma—what career would I pursue? I thought I had two choices: industry or academia. Those seemed to be the only choices available for anybody who was interested in pursuing a STEM career. I could either work as a researcher in a microbiology lab in the pharmaceutical industry or in a microbiology lab in a research-intensive university. Since I did not know what I wanted, industry or academia, I tested both choices.

First, I tried working as a researcher in academia by doing a second summer research program at University of California, Berkeley. My research project consisted of working in the area of bacterial genetics. I loved working in the area of bacterial genetics and worked on it for the next 12 years of my life. My experience at UC Berkeley allowed me to identify the field for me (bacterial genetics), but it also helped me identify a career I thought I did not want. I learned about the work professors do in academia and their commitment to working long hours. This knowledge led me to believe that academia was not for me. On top of working in the lab, professors have to teach different courses and perform several services for their schools. At that moment, I decided academia was not for me and wanted to try the industry aspect.

During my senior year of college, I participated in a co-op internship program hosted by UPRH, which allowed me to work full-time at Janssen, a *Johnson & Johnson* pharmaceutical company. I worked as part of the quality control team in the microbiology lab. My job was to prepare the materials the microbiologists required to perform quality checks on campus and on the company's products. I was great at my job! I loved the hours, and the money was great. However, I wanted to be one of the scientists not a lab technician. That position required a graduate degree.

Applying to graduate schools was time consuming. You must prepare for the Graduate Records Examinations (GRE), which is a standardized test used as an admissions requirement for graduate schools in the United States. If you do not know what school you want to attend, you must research several schools until you find the ones that best fit your interests. Then, you must prepare essays explaining how you are a good fit for your chosen schools. I knew I wanted to attend graduate school at UC Berkeley. I had already spent a summer on campus and knew they had a great program. I also loved living in California. I applied to UC Davis as a second choice. I knew their microbiology graduate program was good, and they offered the NIH-Initiative for Maximizing Student Development (IMSD) Program, a fellowship for underrepresented students who wished to complete a PhD degree.

I first heard back from UC Berkeley—I was not accepted! The news brought tears to my eyes, and I felt discouraged. Maybe a STEM career was not for me. I started questioning my decision and searching for job options. However, a few weeks later, I received an acceptance letter from UC Davis, and I had also obtained the NIH-IMSD fellowship. I was going to graduate school! Looking back, I know now that UC Davis was the best fit for me.

While I am not the first member of my family to attend college, I am the first (and only) member to pursue and receive a PhD degree. After completing my B.S. in biological sciences with a concentration in microbiology, I moved to California to pursue a PhD degree in the microbiology graduate group at UC Davis. Up to this point, my life had been relatively easy going. I had emotional and financial support of my parents and lots of friends in Puerto Rico. These were friends I had grown up with since I was 5 years old. However, in order to pursue my graduate degree, I had to leave behind everything I knew and go venture on my own in unknown territory.

For the first time in my life, I was facing difficult challenges with little support. I was homesick. I had never lived away from my family, and I missed their comfort. The culture shock, while expected, hit me hard. I could not find my favorite foods on the local stores. My mom mailed me care packages every month with some of my Puerto Rican favorites, such as coffee and cooking condiments, but most of the time I felt lonely. I did meet wonderful people throughout my graduate school years, but there were times where I would go several days without talking to another person. On top of my personal life changes, now I had to attend science classes taught in English. Although I was fluent in English, my entire education had always been in Spanish. Taking science classes in English was like learning a third language, and I still had to learn the course contents. I found myself taking blind notes in the classroom, translating my notes at home, and re-learning the terms in order to understand the lecture objectives. Luckily, I quickly learned the English scientific terms, and I was able to communicate my thoughts with ease by the end of my first year as a graduate student.

Graduate school was not easy. A week's lecture in graduate school seemed to cover the content learned over an entire semester of a similar course at the undergraduate level. This meant that classes were fast-paced, and I had to do a lot of self-teaching and learning at home. A big part of pursuing a doctorate degree is to work full-time as a researcher on an independent project directed to write a thesis at the end of your graduate education. I had numerous failed experiments, which made me question my career choice every day, but no matter how bad things were, I always said to myself "just give it one more day." This was my motto until my last day as a graduate student.

In 2011, I completed my graduate degree after many years of hard work. The first calls I made the day I received my PhD degree were to my *abuelas* to whom I shouted "*Ya soy Doctora.*" Those were heavy words! They recapped all the tears, all my struggles in graduate school, and the time away from my family. They also meant I had achieved a lifetime goal, and I had made my family proud. With a doctorate degree, I could look for a job and start my career as a researcher in a pharmaceutical company, or so I thought.

I started applying to several job openings in the pharmaceutical industry a year before I finished graduate school. I received a few interviews but no job offers. I was heartbroken and found it really hard to believe there were no jobs out there for me. Again, I started questioning myself. Did I choose the wrong career? What was I going to do next? After a year of trying to find a job, I (reluctantly) decided to try for a postdoctoral position in academia. I applied to several openings, received a few interviews, and got job offers. I accepted a position at UC Davis. While I was excited to have found a job, this position turned out to be the most challenging chapter of my life so far.

Most of my new lab mates were male—there was another female postdoctoral fellow, but she left the lab soon after I joined. I often felt judged and not taken seriously by some of my lab mates. One day at work, I was talking with some of the graduate (male) students from the lab, and they told me how they would never work for me as a senior scientist. I asked them, "Why not?" They replied they would not work for any researcher who was a female scientist. I am not sure if they were joking or not, but I felt belittled. They went on to say how female scientists were moody and could not be trusted to make difficult decisions. I had never felt so demeaned just because of my gender before that day, and I realized this might happen again.

My postdoctoral experience taught me how to be strong, resilient, and defend my thoughts. I learned I had to be outspoken and take charge of my career. Although this job environment was not the most suitable for me, I learned a lot about myself, and I developed a strong sense of self and respect. Throughout my postdoctoral position, I continued searching (unsuccessfully) for a job in the pharmaceutical industry. Tired of not hearing back with job offers, I took a chance and applied for a part-time teaching position at Sacramento State. I had gained some teaching experience during graduate school and thought the likelihood of getting a job offer was minimal. To my amazement, I got the job offer!

In 2013, I was hired to teach for the department of biological sciences at Sacramento State. My new job required me to only teach biology courses. However, I was not required to perform research work, which was the career I have been preparing for my whole life. To my surprise, I did not miss it. I taught lab courses, which allowed me to perform experiments with my students, and that was enough lab time for me. After my first semester at Sacramento State, I had become a teacher—a career I once thought was not for me. Every day, I get to work with students (inside and outside the classroom), and that is the most rewarding aspect of my job. I finally found *my* career.

Now, I wish to point out some concerns and solutions for anybody who aspires to pursue a STEM career based on my experiences. First, I want to say that it is okay to start college and not know exactly what you want. College is a time for exploration. That is why we take so many classes in so many different areas. We identify the subjects we like and the ones we dislike. Even if you start college thinking you already know what career you want to pursue, you may find out that the career you had chosen is not the best fit for you, and that is perfectly normal. During college, take advantage of the career centers, and visit your academic advisers as often as possible. Advisers have a wealth of knowledge about classes, majors, careers, and can help explore the best options for you. Luckily, we also start shaping who we are during our college years, and we develop interpersonal skills that will allow us to succeed no matter what career we choose.

Secondly, be ready to spend a lot of time studying. Majoring in a STEM field requires complete dedication to your schoolwork. In addition to good grades, succeeding in a STEM field requires hands-on research experience. Seek out research opportunities, and search for fellowships envisioned to promote underrepresented groups in the STEM fields. However, keep in mind that Latinxs (and women) are underrepresented in these careers. That is why we need to prepare ourselves for competitive research careers and strive for leadership positions in the STEM fields.

Lastly, I wish to tell you that every experience, such as your classes, failed experiments, rejection letters, and unlikely job opportunities, may lead to an unforeseen career perfectly fitted for you!

TESTIMONIO 13
Marina B. Suarez
Key Fields of Study: Geology, Geosciences
Assistant Professor, The University of Texas at San Antonio

It had been my dream since I was a kid, using my dad's tools to dig holes in the ground, to find a dinosaur . . . to be the first person to lay eyes on something that lived millions of years ago. I could have died a happy person that day. It turns out the site had many bones . . . probably at least two new species. One of them was named for my twin sister and me: Geminiraptor suarezarum.

As I begin writing this essay, I'm sitting in my stable isotope lab with an extra small lab coat on, and it's still too big! I am a mere 4 foot, 9¾ inches tall . . . and I think at the start it was my short stature that got me going in the field of geology.

I was born in San Antonio, Texas, and as my family tells it . . . I was the surprise. I have an identical twin sister, and back then, I guess they were not as good at telling when there were two! As identical twins, we sort of had to split the height. Since we were short, I think both of us just happened to notice things on the ground more because we were closer to the ground than most. I don't remember when I started collecting rocks, because I don't remember a time when I didn't collect rocks. I have never grown out of it. In second grade, we learned about dinosaurs, and I never grew out of loving dinosaurs either.

My curiosity was maintained by the fact that my parents were educators. During spring break, because my mother also had time off, we always planned our week around going to the zoo, the botanical gardens, hiking, the public library, and the museum. At the zoo and the botanical gardens, I was always fascinated by the diversity of the plants and the animals, while hiking the interaction between the Earth and life were on display, and, of course, I was always looking to collect a rock. At the library, I spent time in the rocks and fossils sections, checking out books so I could identify things in my collection. At the museum, staring at the *Triceratops* on display never got old.

Needless to say, I never questioned going to college. I knew that if I wanted to be a scientist, I would need to go to college and would need to get a graduate degree. The first step was deciding on a college. As a senior in high school, we had the opportunity to take an independent study course. Part of the study was to interview people who were professionals in our respective disciplines. This is how I met my first great mentor, Dr. Edward C. Roy, Jr. at Trinity University in San Antonio. He was so passionate about geology, paleontology, and teaching in general. I like to call him my geology grandfather. He had such a warm personality. I decided to apply to Trinity for my undergraduate degree, as did Celina, my twin sister. It seemed like a great fit for me. My mom had attended Trinity for her undergraduate degree after she was awarded a scholarship for local students from low-income areas. She said it was hard but that she never regretted going, and it opened many doors for her.

While she got a full scholarship for her degree, I had to get a mix of scholar-ships, loans, and grants. I fully believe that had I not made the financial investment to do my undergraduate degree at Trinity, I would not have come as far as I have so far. The faculty are truly interested in educating students. Most of my classes were very small (the largest being about 80), so getting help from professors was much easier than it would have been at a larger school, not that one could not be successful going to a larger school. It was just a better fit for me. In addition, Trinity had the requirement that students live on campus for three of their four years. This was perfect for me. I was always close to the library and to my professors' offices. Also, growing up in San Antonio, all of my immediate and most of my extended family live in San Antonio, so I had never really traveled. Leaving home was a pretty big step for me. Living on campus but still in San Antonio was a great baby step for me. It also helped a lot that Celina came with me. We were both interested in geology and paleontology, so we took many of the same classes. I think it was really vital that Celina and I were both interested in the same topic because I auto-matically had a study partner. If I had to give advice to college students, I'd say start trying to find a network of people who are passionate about your chosen field of study as you are so you can have a group of people to bounce ideas off and to help study.

In 2003, I earned my bachelor of science degree in geosciences from Trinity University. During the previous year, I started to apply to various programs for mas-ter's or PhD programs. As my last year at Trinity started to come to an end, I received letter after letter saying things like "We regret to inform you that we are not able to admit you to . . ." It was the first time that I thought maybe my dream of becoming a professor would not happen. One of the things I learned was that, many times, it's a bit of luck when it comes to going to grad school. Many universities won't accept students if they cannot at least partially support you financially. One of the pieces of advice my professors at Trinity gave me was to not go to a university if they don't pay your tuition. It was good advice. I think I only paid one semester's worth of tuition in the years that I was in grad school.

Another piece of advice I would give students is to try to get a summer intern-ship while you are an undergraduate. This gives you some valuable experience. For me, this proved vital. I had two internships while I was an undergrad, one with the National Park Service at Badlands National Park and one with the Bureau of Land Management. During my internship at Badlands National Park, I met the per-son who would be my next great mentor: Dr. Dennis Terry from Temple University in Philadelphia. After not getting accepted to the universities that I had originally applied to, I contacted Dennis. Both I and my twin sister were able to get teaching assistantships at Temple. This was the first time I would live away from San Anto-nio. It was pretty hard at first, but it was a good opportunity to grow. I made friends whom I still have to this day.

It was while I was a student at Temple University, during field work for my thesis, that I had one of the coolest days in my life. My research project was to describe and interpret the rocks in and around a dinosaur quarry in Utah. One day my twin sister and I were scouting for outcrops to describe when we saw a night gully with well-exposed rocks. As I scrambled down the steep side of the gully, I noticed a few bones sticking out of a sandstone. A few more were in the scree below me. "Jackpot," I yelled! Because we had a surface collecting permit, we collected a few and hurried back to the rest of the group to show them our find. On the way, we ran up to the top of a hill to get cell reception so I could call my mom. It had been my dream since I was a kid, using my dad's tools to dig holes in the ground, to find a dinosaur . . . to be the first person to lay eyes on something that lived millions of years ago. I could have died a happy person that day. It turns out the site had many bones . . . probably at least two new species. One of them was named for my twin sister and me: *Geminiraptor suarezarum*.

It was also while I was at Temple University that I experienced one of the worst days in my life. This was the evening when my father called to tell me that my youngest sister, an avid runner and one of the top runners on her team at Texas Lutheran University, was hit and killed by a car while training. No one can put into words the despair that is experienced when a sibling is killed. My friends and professors at Temple were extremely supportive of the time off I needed to return to San Antonio, and the patience they showed in the weeks afterward. After such a monumental loss, it becomes very hard to focus on the things that you need to do while in school. It was the first time I considered quitting. I did ask my mother soon after if she wanted me to stop being a student and come home. Actually, it probably wasn't a fair question because I knew she would want me to stay home, but she reminded me that being in San Antonio or being in Philadelphia wouldn't make a difference. My little sister, Elisa, was close to home when the accident occurred, but it still happened. It was my dream to be a scientist and professor, so I know even though part of her, and part of me, was ready to call it quits and move home, I know I had started this, and I wouldn't forgive myself if I quit. I'm pretty sure my little sister wouldn't want me to quit either.

Soon my time in Philadelphia was coming to an end, and since they didn't have a PhD program, I began looking for another school. I was accepted at three places: the University of Alaska at Fairbanks, Southern Methodist University in Dallas, and the University of Kansas. Alaska did not have the resources to offer me support, so I decided that would not work out. SMU could offer a teaching assistant (TA) position, and it was closer to San Antonio, so I gave it a lot of consideration. I was able to travel to both SMU and Kansas to visit the campuses. It was while at Kansas that I met the person who would be my next advisers, mentors, and friends. Dr. Luis González ran the stable isotope lab at Kansas, and if I were to come to Kansas, I would be working under an NSF grant that he and his colleague (Dr. Gregory Ludvigson, who would be my co-adviser) were awarded to better quantify the climate in the Cretaceous Period. During my visit, I brought some samples I had collected from Utah that were part of my master's research. Luis stayed up late one night with me working on the samples by analyzing them using a method known as cathodoluminescence. It was this experience that convinced me to go to Kansas. If someone were going to go to those lengths to help someone who wasn't a student, I knew this person would have my best interests in mind as a student. This was also the first time I had an adviser who was also Latino. It was an invaluable experience to have a professor who knew my background and could give career advice from the perspective of being a minority.

I finished my PhD in 2009. I applied to some post-doctoral positions and received a position in the department of Earth and planetary sciences at Johns Hopkins University. I remember one evening having dinner with my post-doctoral advisers Dr. Ben Passey and Dr. Naomi Levin and a visiting scientist from Africa, Dr. Zalalem Kubsa. I remember being struck by how interesting it was and how lucky we were to be united in our passion for understanding the Earth but from many different backgrounds, me a Latina from San Antonio, Naomi from Brooklyn, Ben from Utah, and Zalalem from Africa. This diversity in backgrounds brings different perspectives to our science, and as geoscientist, these different backgrounds and experiences are vital to understanding the Earth as a whole system.

Soon after starting at Johns Hopkins, I was offered a position at The University of Texas at San Antonio. Luckily, I was able to get my position delayed so I could finish my post-doctoral position. I was very excited to return to San Antonio. I had long given up hope of ever returning to San Antonio. Professorial positions are hard to come by, so you often have to go wherever there is a job. The opportunity to give back to the community that I grew up in has been one of the rewarding parts of my job. It has also been a lot harder work that anyone could expect. Being a professor is not just about teaching. There's research (multiple research projects at the same time), writing grants, writing papers, keeping up with the lab (essentially being a lab manager too), dealing with facilities, being an accountant, and paperwork . . . lots and lots and lots of paperwork, even for a simple field trip with students. Despite all this work, the best thing about being a scientist and a professor is that you get to learn something new every day. What more could one ask for?

To recap, here's advice for students who want to be a professor or a scientist in any field:

- Make sure you are passionate about your chosen field. This will be your life, especially in graduate school. Make sure you like what you are doing.

- Find good mentors. I would never have gotten to the point that I am were it not for the guidance and caring of my mentors. No matter what field you decide to go into, try to find out about people you will work with, especially advisers. Talk to their previous students, and ask if it would be okay with them to share their experiences (confidentially) with you. If you find that previous students would have no desire to work with their adviser again, no matter if they are the top person in that field, that might be a red flag that they are not a good mentor.

- Find good colleagues and classmates with which to work. I am lucky in that I had a twin sister who was interested in the same topic as me. If you can, find a network of classmates you can interact with for study groups, to challenge each other, and bounce ideas off each other.

- Stay focused. There are many things in life that can get between you and your field. It isn't easy sometimes to stay focused. Sometimes you do need a break. Find your limits and stay within them. I used to think that if I just worked harder or stayed up a little later, I could do anything; however, there is a point in which working harder just means you are working more but without better results.

- Get involved and look for opportunities. Find internships, scholarships, and grants. Get involved with clubs or societies in your chosen field. Professional societies often have various programs for students such as internships. This will allow you to meet other professionals from around the country and maybe around the world and help you begin your professional network.

- Be open minded. I always thought I would be a vertebrate paleontologist. While I still work with many vertebrate paleontologists, I'm actually an isotope geochemist. I never thought I would be because chemistry, even though I liked it, never came naturally to me. Once I learned that I could apply it to understanding past environments, it became much more approachable.

TESTIMONIO 14
Simon Trevino

Key Fields of Study: Biological and Biomedical Sciences
Postdoctoral Scientist III
Texas Biomedical Research Institute, San Antonio, Texas

As an undergraduate, I also got to do a summer internship at Harvard. Many schools with major research programs offer this opportunity. In the span of something like 10 weeks, I learned a new topic, new skills, and expanded my network. This offered a way to not only get introduced to people there who were connected to people on the admissions committee, but it also got me acquainted with a new city and culture, which helped ease my transition a year or so later. Some of the other students in my summer program ended up going to Harvard as well, so I began the year already having some friends, rather than starting the school year alone. This was a huge benefit.

What do you think you want to do? For many students pursuing a PhD in biomedical sciences, the ultimate goal is to run a university lab. This is based on the idea that if you work hard enough, you might be able to direct other scientists and students towards some question that is interesting to you. This plan, however, unfolds in only a slim number of cases—fewer than 1 in 8 PhDs will end up working a tenured professor, and it's not necessarily a bad thing.

Instead of answering your career question with a position, I think it's worthwhile to scale back and look at the bigger picture. Since you're reading this, you might say, "I want to study and discover something new in biology." With this as your motivation, I can absolutely recommend that you consider going to graduate school.

Once you've grappled with what it is you want to do, it's worthwhile to understand why you, as a Latinx student, are needed in STEM. When I was in high school, I didn't really understand why it was important. Science is the determination of objective truth—how could it matter whose hands and brains are doing it? In reality, this is a very simplified view. Science is a deeply creative pursuit. The more cultural diversity we have in the laboratory, the more ways we have at viewing and tackling problems. More importantly, science is political and steeped in a history of racism. As such, the scientific community researches problems that may not be important to your community simply because nobody with the power to do so really cares about your community. Latinxs with advanced degrees in the sciences can help to balance the interests of education, government, and industry, bringing such overlooked problems to light. Finally, the institutional structures that run the United States are not geared to help minorities, much less minorities who are not wealthy. This imperfect framework has kept many bright students who would flourish and find meaning from scientific work away from it; a right that should be yours to explore.

Throughout the process of getting your degree(s), you may, like many others, experience firsthand that some people can be racist. A lot of people you meet will not think you are as smart as you are or that you deserve to be where you are, and even when they do accept your legitimacy, they might attribute your accomplishments to affirmative action or leniency.

With the deck stacked against you, what kinds of things can I tell you that fell into place for me? Well, I'm a Chicano from South Texas, from a lower-middle class, single-income family, with parents who were not able to seek college degrees—a kid who knew not a single scientist (or anybody older with any college degree) in my extended family.

The path that led me to do my PhD at Harvard and now postdoctoral work (the most common position one takes after finishing the doctorate) started when I was an undergraduate student with:

1. An exceptional research mentor.
2. Programs that were willing to provide financial support.

Those two factors were essential. As an undergrad, you want to get in a lab under good guidance as early as possible and hopefully with some kind of financial support. After college, your progress largely depends on the people you've encountered on the way, more mentors who go out of their way to help, and any friends and collaborators who push you in their own unique ways.

Understanding the money side of paying for college is straightforward. If you demonstrate strong interest in science, you might be able to get sponsored by programs such as Minority Biomedical Research Support (MBRS), Maximizing Access to Research Careers (MARC), or another similar program, which are designed to help transition undergrads into scientific research. If you're completely lost, find the head of the program, and send them an email or meet in person.

Usually, you'll get paid to work on an independent research project of your choosing in a lab and hone your skills by adding helpful courses in literature analysis, writing, grad school application, and career workshops. Alternatively, you can approach professors who run research labs directly and find out about any independent studies they might know about.

How did I find out about this process? I don't remember exactly, but I am pretty sure I saw a flyer, posted somewhere in the biology building at UTSA, advertising what looked kind of like a work-study opening. For me, a steady paycheck was key to getting through college. Before I entered the Minority Biomedical Research Support program (MBRS), school costs were covered by a federal Pell grant, a private student loan, and working full-time at Wal-Mart and telemarketing. Getting out of retail was important, as it was physically and mentally draining, cut into class time, and did not contribute to what (I guessed) were my long-term goals.

I applied to MBRS in my first year, and Gail Taylor was great about helping me find a lab that fit my interests and personality, the lab of Andrew Tsin. Soon I was working in a real lab doing things that really engaged me and benefited my career, and, of course, benefited science on the whole.

At this stage, I still wasn't sure I wanted to commit a big chunk of my life to research. When I had just started college, I thought I was going to end up in medicine and maybe go to optometry school, but the idea of learning a set amount of information and then just applying that over and over to different patients wasn't super enticing.

Still, I wanted to stay in that general area, so to learn more about the eye, and to "try out" research, I joined a lab that was figuring out how the color-sensing cells in the retina detect light differently than the cells that detect only the dimness of light. Just that question alone felt like I was opening the door to Narnia. To understand how that happens, you have to understand what enzymes are and how they work, how cells specialize, the relationship between cells in a tissue, and you have to have an understanding of neurobiology as well, not to mention learning about the history of how people came to know what they know about these cells, the old and new methods they used to experiment, and how each method falls a little short of telling you the whole story. After dissecting a cow retina and discovering, really unexpectedly, this rainbow-oil colored *tapetum lucidum* behind it, I was hooked! I knew deep down I wanted to tear stuff apart and mess with things.

Before research, I had only really equated work with, well, work. Getting paid to do something you might tolerate but not something you actually want to do. In contrast to clocking in and mentally checking out, science is not a 9-to-5 job. You will absolutely have to be a self-starter and driven by your own curiosity to an extreme because the technical work is often long, repetitive, and not supervised. Like cashiering, lab work was physically and mentally draining, and it cut into classes as well, but it was *fulfilling*.

There I was, a no-nothing teenager, pipetting alongside people that had been doing science their whole lives, and with each passing day more and more of my own ideas about what could be explored next. Being an undergrad member of a lab helped me in many ways. Doing actual research helped classwork indirectly and kept me interested in science, far more than any classroom lab course. Lab work also kept me on campus morning to night, which was immensely better than driving around town, and I was able to do homework while longer experiments were running.

Most importantly, it connected me with an immediate mentor. My mentor had graduated many students before and laid a very important, basic understanding about what science is and how, while I may never do it perfectly, I could, on a string of good days, do it well. In addition to introducing me to the framework of science, he introduced me to a lot of other people who lent their own ideas about science and the industry of academic science and how they got to their career levels. This kind of encouragement is really important no matter what you find yourself doing in life. I also met undergraduates and other professors who shared related but not identical research goals and ideas. Maybe these different interactions will inspire you to change your research a little bit or entirely.

I also learned what the day-to-day was like for scientists:

1. Read about a topic until you are an expert. You will know where knowledge about something ends.
2. Carry on a research project someone has abandoned/will share with you or one of your own.
3. Pipette like you work in a factory. Learn the quirks of many different kinds of analytical machines. Make many mistakes.
4. Attend seminars to broaden your understanding of what kinds of questions people are asking and what kinds of ways there are to solve them.
5. From your findings, write abstracts and papers, and communicate them to other scientists and the public.

One of the first roadblocks I hit as a Chicano in science was my own learned insecurity. As I said before, we're underrepresented in academics, especially the sciences, so I simply hadn't grown up around professors and scientists—there was no immediate way to feel comfortable around people I didn't know much about. The blunt, critical academic way was also new to me. I was raised to defer to adults, not ask too many questions, and to be overly polite. This is something I broke out of quickly and probably overcompensated for during college. This academic culture would've been a good thing to know about going in.

As an undergraduate, I also got to do a summer internship at Harvard. Many schools with major research programs offer this opportunity. In the span of something like 10 weeks, I learned a new topic, new skills, and expanded my network. This offered a way to not only get introduced to people there who were connected to people on the admissions committee, but it also got me acquainted with a new city and culture, which helped ease my transition a year or so later. Some of the other students in my summer program ended up going to Harvard as well, so I began the year already having some friends, rather than starting the school year alone. This was a huge benefit.

College research is what motivated me to apply to graduate school. At this point, I really didn't have a plan B and didn't care to. I knew I wanted to do at least a few more years of science and move out of my comfort zone even more. I only applied to UC Berkeley, Harvard, and MIT. This probably wasn't the wisest decision—most people apply to about 10 schools. At the time, I was just really sold on what I had seen going on in Boston, not only at Harvard during my summer program, but at MIT. MIT and Harvard have a lot of crosstalk and collaboration and even share graduate students sometimes.

It is nearly impossible to get into a PhD program without prior lab experience. Admissions offices want to know that you have a sense about what the course and workload is like, and that you are going to be a good bet in finishing the program, since their funding is linked to this metric. In other words, if you've worked in a lab, maybe got a paper or two out as an undergrad, and have not been discouraged from science completely (it is not for everyone), you're a safer bet. There are always exceptions—when I interviewed at MIT, one candidate had a political science degree and had spent only a summer in a lab but was very motivated to continue on doing science, so he got the interview.

Graduate school echoed a lot of what I had learned in undergrad, but the emphasis of attention was flipped. In college, grades and classes are what determine your degree completion, with research filling more of an extracurricular role. In graduate school, classes take a backseat to the completion of your research project, and exams are more critical-thinking and analysis-based than rote memorization. While everyone has about three semesters of classes, differences in research projects and expectations from your mentor and dissertation committee will make the time required to completion variable between students.

The second major roadblock I hit was a result of having been raised around a different language—a fusion between English and Spanish. Having a strong command of American English is critical for science communication. Many might argue against my next point, but promoting your science clearly is more important than the actual significance of the science when you are applying for grants. If I could give one nugget of advice to my younger self, it would simply be to read a lot more literature and to take as many science writing courses as possible.

Probably the biggest hurdle I had to overcome was retaking what's called the qualifying exam. This is judged in two parts: a written and an oral defense of a research project outside of your field. After I didn't get a clear pass the first time, it felt like the sky had imploded—and my situation crystallized as I called home to say I hadn't passed. It dawned on me that I was the only person in my extended family to be in an Ivy League school, and I felt that pressure for the first time—not really from my parents but from myself. The idea of going back to Texas without a degree, after all the long nights I had spent in a lab and after so many people had invested in me, really hit me much harder than I anticipated, not to mention being in Boston and doing science is really exactly where I wanted to be; leaving so soon was the last thing I wanted to happen. And those ridiculous racist ideas *did* swirl in my head—maybe there *are* reasons people like me don't make it in science so often.

Going through that was important because it is where I began to see the absence of privilege we as Latinxs have. One of my best friends, a native East Coaster, whose parents were professors, with siblings all in Ivy League schools, reassured me that repeating the assignment was not a big deal at all. It wasn't until later that I realized how much easier it is for him to say that because he's seen it happen over and over in his life. I'm sure he knows college dropouts who had really excellent career prospects after leaving their degree programs through personal connections. For many people, everything is not on the line. I realized just how foreign academics were to me, even after excelling in it for so long, and it's something I won't forget. He was absolutely right about an exam not being the end of world, and I was lucky to have his opinion as a friend.

Harvard was extraordinarily good at downplaying what might seem crushingly critical into something that is part of the process of becoming a scientist. That's another bit of advice—I recommend you look into programs that are known to include international students and diversity, because they "get it." After a few writing exercises with an adviser outside of my committee (thanks to Josh Kaplan), I came out of it a better writer. For what it's worth, when I defended my actual PhD, the first thing one of my committee members said was "Before we get started, I just want to say I really enjoyed reading your introduction."

As an undergrad, choosing a lab and your mentor is key—they will be your greatest advocate and door to understanding how science is done professionally. Most lab heads have reputations that other students will tell you about, and you will get to rotate (usually in two or three labs) for a short amount of time before choosing who you'll be working with for the next three to five years.

It was also critical to really flesh out what was my working style. There are positives and negatives for each kind of working style and working environment. I had friends who were in labs where their bosses would call at 7 a.m. on Sunday mornings to find out who was and who was not in attendance. That would never have worked for me. I will put in long hours, but I am useless before 10 a.m. At the other extreme, I knew one student who had his boss physically run his experiments for him because he felt it was essential they get the data collected the first time without any mistakes. This lab would not have worked for me either. I don't respond well to micromanagement, and I learn best by making mistakes. Figure out what your style is.

I personally liked independence and knew I had a lot to learn, so I chose a mentor (Jack Szostak) who was known to be more "hands off" in terms of mentorship and who ran a very large lab with experts in different disciplines. This experience helped me learn to seek others for collaboration and helped me to become very independent in both my interests and approaches to problems. Getting into a lab that had organic chemists working alongside biochemists working alongside molecular biologists was transformative. Every one-on-one meeting with Jack, or group meetings with everyone else, was like getting dunked upside-down into a new way of tackling a problem. Graduate school on the whole is crazy—you are better at what you do, and that lets you appreciate people who are even better at what they do.

The culture I was born into was in many ways at odds with the culture required to succeed in academics. To get multiple degrees, I had to geographically move around, and I still feel guilty about leaving my family behind. I was absent for many milestones (babies, graduations, and weddings) and couldn't provide the kind of daily support to my family that is so often taken for granted. Success for many first- and second-generation immigrants is tied to economic wealth more than the achievement of personal goals and interests. "Why are you working so often and moving everywhere for a job that doesn't pay much and isn't (physician/lawyer)?" That's a question I've gotten from more than one family member on more than one occasion. Finally, I've had to adapt on a personal level. I'm more a combination of where I've lived than where I was born, able to accommodate different types of people with wildly different backgrounds and motivations. Is this ongoing identity crisis fundamentally bad? I don't think so. I think mine is a very American story, and yours can be, too.

What comes after all of the education is up to you. You can do more bench work, teach, work with patents, start a company, or work in policy or public communication. Really anything. Remember, going through undergrad plus a PhD can take up about 10 to 11 years of your life. Your professional interests will likely change, but your motivation to further science will likely not.

PART V

College and University Directories for STEM Programs

CHAPTER NINE

Listing of the Best STEM Colleges and Universities for Latinx Students

Demeturie Toso-Lafaele Gogue and Sarah Maria Childs

Latinx communities have long existed in the United States. While various populations of Latinx communities continue to grow in size, there is still an underrepresentation of Latinx students pursuing degrees and careers in science, technology, engineering, and mathematics (STEM). Capturing this reality, Litow (2008) described the lack of Latinx participation in STEM as "worrisome" because Latinx students represent a rapidly growing segment of the labor force and exhorted that this "silent crisis" needed to be reframed as an opportunity to ensure that American ingenuity did not suffer. Such a reality leaves students in a precarious position because in some cases students may not be seeking educational opportunities to engage in STEM-related courses or programs due to factors in their educational and community settings that are beyond their control and through no fault of their own.

Generally speaking, a support network of family and friends, advising, mentoring, career planning, practical experiences related to academics, and student engagement opportunities are significant to the success of any college student. There are, however, even more specific and nuanced factors that are critical to the persistence and degree attainment of Latinx students. Academic preparation plays a key role in the professional preparation of college students post-undergraduate tenure. Academic rigor and research skills developed in college foster professional confidence necessary to facilitate entrance into fields of study that all require astuteness and creativity not only within singular fields but also across disciplines.

In efforts to attract more students of color and women into STEM fields and careers, colleges and universities across the United States have developed STEM programs for these underrepresented and often underserved communities. These programs are often created and function on-campus or through partnerships with external organizations (companies and nonprofit organizations). These programs are vital because of the enormous impact they have on a student's academic and professional aspirations. There are numerous examples of programs that have a specific focus on the recruitment, retention, persistence, and success of Latinx youth via K-12 pipelines through undergraduate STEM programs. Each of these programs has a variety of features, characteristics, and institutional strengths that ultimately aids and promotes the ability of every Latinx student to participate, thrive, persist, and graduate from college with a STEM degree. In aiding such an outcome, these programs play a key role in ensuring that more and more Latinx students pursue STEM careers.

This chapter is written with you—the student—in mind. Whether your interest in a STEM field is purely our own interest, that of your family, or perhaps from the encouragement of a teacher, there is a lot to consider in preparing for undergraduate studies in science, technology, engineering, and mathematics. Previous chapters discussed the many factors you ought to consider to inform your decision to pursue a STEM degree or career. You were asked to consider questions during the different stages of your life—as a high school student or as a first-year college student. These questions included: What schools should I apply to? How will I pay for college? What should I consider when making a decision about where to go to college? How do I apply to college? While these more general questions are essential to consider in the grand scheme of things, there are several other questions you were encouraged to consider as well. These questions are specifically related to the needs of Latinx students and are more culturally responsive. For example, does the college/university I am applying to have an identity/cultural center (like a multicultural student center or Latinx cultural center)? Are there existing programs at the college to engage my family in the recruitment and orientation process? Are these programs offered in English *and* Spanish? Do programs and services exist to encourage Latinx student involvement in STEM fields, and do they provide financial aid? Asking these questions will aid you in narrowing down your list of potential colleges and desired majors based on characteristics that are important to you.

STEM PROGRAMS FOCUSED ON LATINX STUDENT SUCCESS

Within each state in the United States, there exist several colleges and universities which are bastions for higher learning and brilliant homes for budding, emerging, and established scholars. As the student, it is within your sphere of control and within reasonable expectation to play an active role in creating the experience that you wish to have as a student. Recognize what you need. Identify what you want. Ask lots of questions and own your experience as a student. It is highly unlikely that you will have many other opportunities in life to be a student in the way you can be a student in college. You have constant access to educational opportunities, networking with a community of students, staff, and faculty from around the country and world, and the support of educators who want to ensure that you are successful. You have more time and a perfect space to explore anything and everything that catches your interest academically and personally.

Table 9.1   List of Institutions and STEM Programs

State	Institution	Type of Institution	Institution Description	Program	Program Description/Website
Alabama	The University of Alabama	4-Yr. Public	At the University of Alabama, there are a total of 37,100 enrolled students with a freshman class of 7,211 (Quick Facts, The University of Alabama, 2015). The university has a total of 1,260 undergraduates who are Hispanic (2015 At a Glance: Total Enrollment, 2015). Within the College of Engineering, 3 percent of the 5,300 undergraduates in the college are Hispanic (College of Engineering: By the Numbers, 2015).	Multicultural Engineering Program	The multicultural engineering program aims to increase the number of underrepresented populations who apply and are accepted to university's engineering program, provide resources to retain students and ensure their success, and foster a diverse community for underrepresented populations to thrive. The program provides opportunities for students at the pre-college (K–12) and the undergraduate level. Website: http://students.eng.ua.edu /programs/mep/.
Alaska	The University of Alaska Anchorage	4-Yr. Public	In 2014, the University of Alaska Anchorage (UAA) had an enrollment of 18,649 students. Of the total student population, 6.2 percent were of Hispanic origin. During this time, UAA saw an increase in diversity among faculty and staff. UAA employed 83 staff members and 38 faculty members who were of Hispanic origin (Diversity at UAA, University of Alaska Anchorage, 2014).	EXITO Scholars	The goal of EXITO Scholars is to increase the number of underrepresented students who pursue a career in biomedical research. Once accepted into the program, EXITO Scholars receive funding, mentoring, and research experience that will prepare them for higher education and for the biomedical research field. Website: http://greenandgold.uaa.alaska .edu/blog/32902/now-recruiting-for-exito -scholars/.

(continued)

205

Table 9.1 *(Continued)*

State	Institution	Type of Institution	Institution Description	Program	Program Description/Website
Arizona	Arizona State University	4-Yr. Public	Arizona State University (ASU) has four different campuses with a total enrollment of 83,301 students (81 percent are undergraduate students and 19 percent graduate students). At ASU, 20.2 percent of the undergraduate population is Hispanic/Latino. Of the 67,507 undergraduates, 50.8 percent are men, and 49.2 percent are women (Quick Facts, Arizona State University, 2014).	Society of Hispanic Professional Engineers (SHPE de ASU)	SHPE de ASU aims to empower the Hispanic community to create change by providing access to and an awareness of the STEM field. Through various programs that cater to professional development as well as community outreach, SHPE hopes to provide a network of STEM scholars and researchers that can impact how Hispanics are viewed within the STEM field. Website: http://www.shpedeasu.org/.
Arizona	University of Arizona	4-Yr. Public	The University of Arizona exemplifies the definition of a large campus with a total undergraduate enrollment of 33,732 students. Of this total, 8,544 are Hispanic. In 2015, the university enrolled a total of 1,008 new students. A total of 1,967 Hispanic students entered as freshmen, and 656 Hispanic students transferred to the institution (Fact Book, University of Arizona, 2015),	Center for the Mathematics Education of Latinos/as (CEMELA)	Bridging mathematics education with cultural and language, CEMELA hopes to advance the way mathematics is taught to best serve low-income Latino students. Through the collaboration of experts in math and those in language and culture, CEMELA hopes to create teaching practices and strategies that best support the Latino community in the classroom. Website: http://math.arizona.edu/~cemela/english/.

State	Institution	Type		Program	
Arizona	Phoenix College	2-Yr. Public	Phoenix College was established in 1920, serving as the flagship institution among the Maricopa Community Colleges. Although the institution caters to a total of 28,000 students each year, Phoenix College still enrolls more than 10 percent Hispanic students, designating its campus as a Hispanic-serving institution (Discover Phoenix College, Phoenix College).	Primer Abrazo	Primer Abrazo is a course that new high school graduates can enroll in to master their math skills. This course is aimed at underrepresented populations, including Hispanics/Latinos/as, and provides students with college credit, academic support, and financial support for books and meals. This course aims to help students interested in STEM advance their skills. Website: http://www.phoenixcollege.edu/build-your-skills-summer-2016.
Arkansas	Northwest Arkansas Community College	2-Yr. Public	Northwest Arkansas Community College (NWACC) is gradually becoming the largest two-year college in Arkansas with a total enrollment of 7,744 students. 16.5 percent of the total population is Hispanic, which is the second largest racial/ethnic group behind White students (Fact Book, NWACC, 2015).	Latino Student Support Scholarship	"Recipients must be Hispanic or Latino; enrolled in a minimum of six credit hours; not eligible to receive federal grants, loans, or work study; have a minimum 2.75 GPA; be willing to participate in Latin Culture Club, DREAMers of NWACC, PASS Mentor Program, and/or other student activities" (NWACC Scholarships, Northwest Arkansas Community College). Website: http://www.nwacc.edu/web/scholarships/nwacc_scholarships.

(*continued*)

Table 9.1 *(Continued)*

State	Institution	Type of Institution	Institution Description	Program	Program Description/Website
California	California State University— Fullerton	4-Yr. Public	California State University, Fullerton (CSUF) is a Hispanic-serving institution, catering to a student population with 40.5 percent who are Hispanic. Of the 38,948 students enrolled, 56 percent of this population is female (Fast Facts, CSUF, 2015). CSUF offers a bachelor's, master's, and doctoral degree in a variety of majors, such as nursing and education.	Mathematics Intensive Summer Session (Proj- ect M.I.S.S.)	Project M.I.S.S. is an intensive summer mathematic program enhances the skills of young women, especially those from underrepresented communities. The goal is to increase the number of women in STEM majors and those who pursue a career in that field. Website: http://www.fullerton.edu/miss/.
California	University of California, Davis	4-Yr. Public	The University of California, Davis has an undergraduate population of 28,384 and a graduate population of 6,802. Of the undergraduate population, 19 percent are Hispanic. Moreover, 59 percent of the undergraduate population are women (Student Profile, UC Davis, 2015). With over 104 undergraduate majors, students are able to find a course of study they enjoy (Facts, UC Davis).	Chicano and Latino Engineers and Scientists Society (CALESS)	CALESS was formed to provide support for members through employment opportunities and scholarships, tutor high school students to increase representation of Chicanos and Latinos in STEM, and create a community across various chapters at other institutions. Website: http://caless.engineering .ucdavis.edu/.

| California | East Los Angeles College | 2-Yr. Public | East Los Angeles College (ELAC) is located in one of the most diverse cities in the Los Angeles region. With an enrollment of 38,983 students, ELAC helps a little over 1,000 students transfer to a four-year institution. Of the total population enrolled at ELAC, 78.4 percent are Hispanic/Latino. Moreover, 58.3 percent of the total enrollment is female (Annual Report 2014–2015, East Los Angeles College). | Mathematics, Engineering, and Science Achievement (MESA) | ELAC MESA aims to address the underrepresentation of Hispanics in the STEM field by providing internship opportunities in STEM careers, resources (i.e., access to computers and STEM advisers), and the possibility of working with tutors and faculty who are well-versed in the STEM field. Website: https://www.elac.edu/academics /programs/mesa/about.htm. |
| California | California Institute of Technology | 4-Yr. Private | The California Institute of Technology is a small, private institution with a total enrollment of 2,255. This small student population allows students to have more contact with faculty, which is represented in the 3:1 student to faculty ratio (Caltech at a Glance, California Institute of Technology, 2015). Of the 1,001 undergraduates, 61 percent are men, and 16 percent identify as an underrepresented minority (American Indian or Alaskan Native, Black or African American, Hispanic or Latino, Native Hawaiian, or other Pacific Islander) (Fall Enrollment 2015–16, California Institute of Technology). | Freshman Summer Research Institute (FSRI) | The FSRI program helps incoming underrepresented and/or underserved students acclimate to Caltech's campus and academic rigor by allowing students to take part in a full-funded opportunity to conduct research, prepare for Caltech's first year math course, and live on campus while being able to take part in activities on and off campus. The goal is to support these students in their transition to college. Website:https://diversitycenter.caltech .edu/academics/fsri. |

(*continued*)

Table 9.1 (*Continued*)

State	Institution	Type of Institution	Institution Description	Program	Program Description/Website
Colorado	Metropolitan State University of Denver	4-Yr. Public	Metropolitan State University of Denver (MSU Denver) has a diverse undergraduate population, with 37.1 percent of the student population who are students of color and 31.6 percent who are first-generation college students. Hispanic students are a large portion of the students of color (22.1 percent) who are at MSU Denver (University Fact Sheet, MSU Denver, 2015).	Louis Stokes Colorado Alliance for Minority Participation (LS-COAMP)	The Center provides academic tutoring, faculty mentoring, and personal support for African American, Hispanic American, Pacific Islanders, and Native Americans who are interested in pursuing a field in STEM. The goal of the center is to serve as a resource for underrepresented students to ensure their success in the STEM field in higher education. Website: https://www.msudenver.edu/case/ls-coamp/.
Connecticut	University of Connecticut	4-Yr. Public	The University of Connecticut, with its main campus located in Storrs, CT, and four other regional campuses, boasts a total of 108 majors. This gives students the ability to choose a major that fits for them. The total enrollment of 23,407 undergraduate students, with 50 percent who are female and 30 percent who are minority (2016 Fact Sheet, University of Connecticut, 2015).	Louis Stokes Alliance for Minority Participation (LSAMP) Leadership and Academic Enhancement Program	This scholars program fosters a community, offers academic support, and provides access to resources for underrepresented students (i.e., African American, Latino/a, and Native American) who are pursuing a major in the STEM field. The goal of the program is to increase the number of minority students earning a degree in STEM as well as pursuing a career in that field. Website: http://lsamp.uconn.edu/about/.

| Delaware | University of Delaware | 4-Yr. Public | The University of Delaware is a public research institution that was founded in 1743. Although the institution is located in Newark, Delaware, it has satellite campuses in Wilmington, Dover, Georgetown, and Lewes. The university also has a total undergraduate population of 18,353 students. Of the 17,575 undergraduate students at the Newark campus, 7.4 percent are Hispanic (Facts & Figures 2015–2016, University of Delaware, 2015). | Society of Hispanic Professional Engineers (SHPE) at University of Delaware | The SHPE organization is a group of undergraduate and graduate Hispanic engineers who promote the STEM field through outreaching events and who foster a sense of community through social activities. The organization also provides various resources for current students to assist in their success. Website: https://studentcentral.udel.edu /organization/shpe/about. |
| District of Columbia | Georgetown University | 4-Yr. Private | Georgetown University was established in 1789 and is the nation's oldest Catholic and Jesuit institution. This private institution has nine schools within the university, which includes a law and medical program. Georgetown University has a total undergraduate enrollment of 7,562 students (Georgetown Key Facts, Georgetown University, 2015). In 2016, Georgetown University's undergraduate enrollment for the class of 2020 had a 9 percent Hispanic population (Georgetown 2016, Georgetown University). | Community Scholars Program (CSP) | The Community Scholars Program (CSP) at Georgetown University is devoted to enrolling a more racially and socioeconomically diverse student population. CSP offers a five-week academic summer program that allows students to acclimate to the college environment and to take courses to help students familiarize themselves with the academic rigor of higher education. Throughout the year, the program supports students through academic advising, mentoring, and study groups. Website: https://cmea.georgetown.edu /community-scholars. |

(continued)

Table 9.1 *(Continued)*

State	Institution	Type of Institution	Institution Description	Program	Program Description/Website
Florida	Miami Dade College	4-Yr. Public	In 2013, Miami Dade College (MDC) had the largest undergraduate enrollment than any other higher education institution in the country. Designated as a Hispanic-serving institution, MDC's total enrollment is 71 percent Hispanic, and 17 percent is black non-Hispanics. Adding to its diverse population, MDC found that 72 percent of its total enrollment were U.S. citizens in 2014, and those who were noncitizens represented a variety of countries. About 32 percent of MDC's incoming students test as college ready; therefore, MDC serves as an excellent starting point for those who may feel unprepared (Highlights and Facts, Miami Dade College).	STEM Summer Bridge Program	The STEM Summer Bridge Program allows incoming first-year students to take part in a seven-week program that includes taking a college level course, attending orientation, participating in workshops, completing a STEM project, and having access to resources such as faculty, staff, and second year students who serve as mentors. The goal of the program is to ease the transition from high school to college and provide STEM students with an understanding of the types of resources available to them. Website: http://www.mdc.edu/stemfye/summer-bridge.aspx.
Florida	University of Central Florida	4-Yr. Public	The University of Central Florida (UCF) is the second largest university in the nation with a total enrollment of 60,810. With its 13 colleges, UCF is able to operate with an undergraduate population of 52,532. Of the total student population, 21.6 percent is Hispanic. UCF's most popular majors include psychology, health sciences,	Society of Hispanic Professional Engineers (SHPE)	The members of SHPE at UCF have access to workshops and resources that prepare students for the job search, such as resume building and networking with various companies in the engineering field. SHPE at UCF also works with their community through outreach events catered to high school students; their goal is to bring awareness to the community

Georgia	University of Georgia	4-Yr. Public	The University of Georgia (UGA) is Georgia's oldest and most diversified institution (The Mission of the University of Georgia, University of Georgia, 2014). With 17 schools and colleges, students are able take a variety of courses from the school of social work to those offered in the college of agricultural and environmental sciences. This large public institution has an undergraduate total of 27,547 students. Of this total, 1,544 are Hispanic (Fact Book 2015, University of Georgia, 2015). In addition to their wide array of academic programs, UGA also has more than 600 registered student organizations that students can join (UGA By the Numbers, University of Georgia, 2015).	The Peach State Louis Stokes Alliance for Minority Participation (Peach States LSAMP) Summer Bridge Institute

regarding the importance of STEM. SHPE also participates in a variety of conferences, which allow members to connect with other Hispanics in STEM and engage in professional development. Website: http://www.shpeucf.com/about-us/.

The Peach State LSAMP Summer Bridge Program hosts 14 incoming minority STEM first-year students for a three-week residential program. Students take part in professional development opportunities, academic and social activities, and gain more awareness of the different resources on campus. The goal of the program is to foster students transition from high school to college and to increase the number of minority students completing their degree in the STEM field. While UGA is the leading institution for the Peach State LSAMP alliance, six other institutions are also involved: Fort Valley State University, Georgia Institute of Technology, Georgia State University-Perimeter College, Kennesaw campus, Kennesaw State University-Marietta campus, and Savanna State University (all offer similar programs to UGA). Website: http://diversity.uga.edu/index .php/pro.grams/article/the-peach-state -lsamp-summer-bridge-institute

and biomedical sciences (UCF Facts 2014-2015, University of Central Florida, 2014).

(continued)

Table 9.1 (*Continued*)

State	Institution	Type of Institution	Institution Description	Program	Program Description/Website
Hawaii	University of Hawaii at Manoa	4 Yr Public	As the flagship campus of the University of Hawaii system, the University of Hawaii at Manoa (UH Manoa) welcome diversity of both students and staff who come from a variety of countries across the world. Although the majority of its students are in-state, UH Manoa does have a 28 percent out-of-state student population and a 6 percent international student population (Manoa Institutional Research Office, University of Hawaii at Manoa, 2015). UH Manoa has a total undergraduate population of 13,689, with 1.9 percent of the total population identifying as Hispanic (About UH Manoa, University of Hawaii at Manoa, 2015).	Society for the Advancement of Chicanos/ Hispanics and Native Americans in Science (SACNAS—'Ilima Chapter)	The 'Ilima SACNAS Chapter at the University of Hawaii at Manoa is open to all STEM students in Oahu, Hawaii, and aims to foster the success of minorities in STEM. Their goal is to increase the representation of these minority communities in STEM careers and leadership positions. The chapter allows members to engage in outreach opportunities, foster connections with professionals in the field, and have access to resources such as internships and scholarships. Website: http://www.sacnashawaii.org/.
Idaho	Boise State University	4-Yr. Public	Boise State University is public research institution located in Boise, Idaho. Of the 22,113 total student population, 2,991 are graduate students. About 41 percent of the total enrollment are part-time students. The institution also has a larger female	Louis Stokes Alliance for Minority Participation (LSAMP)	The goal of the Louis Stokes Alliance for Minority Participation (LSAMP) is to increase the recruitment, retention, and graduation rates of minority students in the STEM field. In addition to Boise State University, students at the College of Western Idaho benefit from the

			population (54 percent) in comparison to males. Boise State University's largest minority group is Hispanics, with 10 percent of the total enrollment identifying as such. While Boise State University offers a variety of majors and programs for students to choose from, most undergraduates are pursuing a degree in nursing, psychology, and community (Boise State University Facts and Figures 2015–2016, Boise State University, 2015).		resources of LSAMP, which include access to internship and research opportunities and other resources to help students in the STEM field be successful. Website: https://stem.boisestate.edu /lsamp/.
Illinois	City Colleges of Chicago— Richard J. Daley College	2-Yr. Public	Richard J. Daley College, a Hispanic-serving institution, is a two-year public institution that offers associate's degrees, short-term certificate programs, free adult education classes, and special interest courses. The total enrollment at Richard J. Daley College is 17,125 students (this includes those in credit career, adult education, and continuing education). 71 percent of the total enrollment is Hispanic. Moreover, 59 percent of the total population is female (Fiscal Year 2015: Statistical Digest, Richard J. Daley College, 2016).	Society of Hispanic Professional Engineers (SHPE)	The Society of Hispanic Professional Engineers (SHPE) aims to promote diversity within STEM and encourage more students to pursue a career in a related field. SHPE at Richard J. Daley College provide both educational and professional development opportunities. Website: http://www.ccc.edu/colleges /daley/services/Pages/Society-of -Hispanic-Professional-Engineers.aspx.

(*continued*)

Table 9.1 *(Continued)*

State	Institution	Type of Institution	Institution Description	Program	Program Description/Website
Indiana	Indiana University Bloomington	4-Yr. Public	Indiana University Bloomington was founded in 1820 and serves as the flagship campus of Indiana University's eight campuses (About, Indiana University Bloomington, 2016). The university had a total undergraduate enrollment of 38,364, but in addition with graduate, doctoral research, and doctoral practice students, the total enrollment is 48,514 students. Focusing specifically on undergraduate students, there ae 1,685 Hispanic/Latino students. With the 18 colleges, school, and divisions, students are able to take courses within a variety of subject areas, which include Jacobs School of Music and the School of Global and International Studies (University Institutional Research and Reporting, Indiana University Bloomington, 2015).	Society for the Advancement of Chicanos/Latinos and Native Americans in Science (SACNAS)	The goal of SACNAS at Indiana University Bloomington is to support minority students who are interested in STEM and to foster a diverse community by encouraging more students to pursue a major and career in the field. SACNAS supports Chicanos/Latinos and Native Americans by preparing students for the national conference, which allows students from across the country to connect and share their research. In addition, SACNAS outreaches to local high schools to encourage more students of color to pursue a degree in STEM. SACNAS acts as a support group for undergrads, grads, and professionals in STEM. Website: http://www.indiana.edu/~sacnas/index.htm.
Iowa	Iowa State University	4-Yr. Public	Iowa State University has a total undergraduate population of 30,034 students. Although Iowa State	Society for Advancement of Hispanics/	The goal of the Society for Advancement of Hispanics/Chicanos and Native Americans in Science (SACNAS)

State	University	Type		Organization	
			University is a predominantly white institution, the institution has 1,393 Hispanic/Latino undergraduates enrolled (Enrollment by Race/Ethnicity, Iowa State University, 2015). With 100 majors offered at the university, students are able to choose a major that suits their interest. Moreover, with more than 800 student organizations, students are able to find communities with similar interests and hobbies (About Iowa State, Iowa State University, 2016).	Chicanos and Native Americans in Science (SACNAS) at Iowa State University	chapter at Iowa State University is to increase the recruitment and retention of Hispanics, Chicanos, Native Americans, and other minority groups within the field of STEM. The chapter offers resources such as professional development workshops with STEM professionals and networking opportunities with other chapters and STEM scholars across the country. Website:https://www.stuorg.iastate.edu/site/2127/information.
Kansas	Kansas State University	4-Yr. Public	Since its founding in 1863, Kansas State University has been dedicated to serving its community and catering to the needs of its students. By 2025, Kansas State aims to be a top 50 public research institution. The university offers over 250 majors within its nine colleges, which allows students to have a variety of options to pursue their interest (About K-State, Kansas State University, 2016). While the university has a total enrollment of 24,146 students, 1,520 of these students are Hispanic, the second largest minority group (Enrollment Summary by Ethnicity, Kansas State University, 2015).	Kansas Louis Stokes Alliance for Minority Participation (KS-LAMP)	The Kansas Louis Stokes Alliance for Minority Participation (KS-LAMP) fosters a community of minority students who are interested in STEM, provides resources for students to improve persistence, and opportunities for students to take part in STEM internships and research to encourage professional development. Website: http://www.k-state.edu/lsamp/.

Table 9.1 (*Continued*)

State	Institution	Type of Institution	Institution Description	Program	Program Description/Website
Kentucky	University of Louisville	4-Yr. Public	The University of Louisville, which was established in 1798, is one of Kentucky's premier research universities. The total enrollment at the university is 22,367 students. About 72 percent of the incoming freshmen live on campus, which allows easier accessibility to more than 400 recognized student organizations on campus. While Kentucky has a large enrollment total, only 3.82 percent is Hispanic/Latino (Just the Facts 2015–16, University of Louisville, 2016).	Brown-Forman INSPIRE Summer Enrichment Program	The Brown-Forman INSPIRE (Increasing Student Preparedness and Interest in the Requisites for Engineering) summer enrichment program introduces underrepresented students (i.e., African American, Hispanic, Native American, and female students) to the field of engineering. In addition to participating in laboratory-oriented studies, students will also visit large technological and engineering industries in the area. While there is no cost to attend the program, students must find their own transportation to campus for this two-week program. Website: https://louisville.edu/speed /inspire/brown-forman-inspire-summer -enrichment-program.
Louisiana	Louisiana State University	4-Yr. Public	Louisiana State University (LSU) is Louisiana's flagship university with opportunities for students to not only pursue a major that fits their interest (over 235 academic fields of study) but also engage in research (About Us, Louisiana State University, 2016). LSU	Society of Hispanic Professional Engineers— Louisiana State University	The Louisiana State University's Society of Hispanic Professional Engineers is part of the national Hispanic engineering society which allows students and professionals in the STEM field to come together to promote more Hispanic students to pursue a career in STEM,

			and graduate students. 3.5 percent of the total student enrollment is Hispanic/Latino (Fall 2015 Enrollment, The University of Mississippi, 2015).		activities, academic training, and research experience with STEM faculty. Some participants also receive financial support for the events within LSMAMP. Website: https://www.usm.edu/science-technology/lsmamp.
Missouri	University of Missouri	4-Yr. Public	The University of Missouri (Mizzou) was founded in 1839 in Columbia, Missouri. Mizzou has a total enrollment that exceeds 35,000 students, 13,000 full-time employees, and 300,000 alumni. Mizzou also welcomes a student population that represents every county in Missouri, all 50 states, and 120 countries. The university offers more than 300 degree programs, which allows students to have a variety of options to choose from when thinking about a major (About Mizzou, University of Missouri, 2016). Although Mizzou's total enrollment is 35,448 students, 1,214 students are Hispanic and less than half of the total population (16,730) are female (Enrollment Summary, University of Missouri—Columbia, 2015).	Diversity Scholarships	The College of Engineering at the University of Missouri is offering scholarships of up to $3,000 for new students in engineering who are a member of an underrepresented minority group. The scholarships will help fund students to help recruit and retain a diverse student population within the STEM field. Scholarships are also renewable each year for a total of eight semesters. In addition to funding, students are also required to be involved in a student organization and become a member of the Diversity Scholars Program. Website: http://engineering.missouri.edu/diversity/scholarships/.

(continued)

Table 9.1 *(Continued)*

State	Institution	Type of Institution	Institution Description	Program	Program Description/Website
Montana	Montana State University	4-Yr. Public	Montana State University, the state's land-grant institution, was established in 1893 in Bozeman, Montana. In the fall of 2015, Montana State University reached its largest enrollment at 15,688 students. While most of the students who enroll at Montana State University are in-state, the university also receives a large number of students from Washington, California, and Colorado (MSU Quick Facts, Montana State University, 2015). Of the total enrollment, 543 of these students are Hispanic/Latino (Ethnic Distribution of Majors by College, Montana State University, 2015).	EMPower	EMPower aims to promote the success of underrepresented minorities and women in engineering and other STEM fields by providing these students with access to tutoring, professional and academic advising, scholarships, and other opportunities that foster students' success. Website: http://www.montana.edu/empower/.
Nebraska	University of Nebraska—Lincoln	4-Yr. Public	The University of Nebraska—Lincoln (UNL) was established in 1869 as a land-grant institution. The university has three primary missions: teaching, research, and service. UNL has a total enrollment of 25,260 students, with 79.9 percent undergraduates, 18.1 percent graduate, and 2 percent professional. The total number of Hispanic/Latino students at UNL is	Latinos in Science and Engineering (MAES/SHPE)	The Latinos in Science and Engineering organization aims to increase the number of Latino students who pursue a degree in STEM by creating a network with schools and youth organizations to encourage more interests and awareness within the community. Current Latino students in STEM have access to professional development opportunities with professionals in the field. The

			1,256, or 5 percent of the total enrollment. UNL also offers over 182 undergraduate majors, 70 master's programs, and 43 doctoral programs (2015–2016 Just the Facts, University of Nebraska—Lincoln, 2015).		organization provides academic resources to help retain Latino students in STEM and financial resources to aid students who want to take part in regional and national events coordinated by MAES and SHPE. Website: http://engineering.unl.edu /current-students/latinos-science-and -engineering-maesshpe/.
Nevada	University of Nevada—Reno	4-Yr. Public	The University of Nevada, Reno was founded in 1874 in Elko, Nevada. In 1885, the university relocated to Reno, Nevada, where more of the state's residents lived at the time. The university offers a variety of majors within the various colleges and schools, which range from agriculture to engineering (History, Stats & Highlights, University of Nevada, Reno). The university has a total student population of 20,898, with a total undergraduate population of 17,295 (Demographic, Population & Proximity Data, University of Nevada, Reno, 2015). 17.11 percent of the total student population is Hispanic/Latino, which is the largest underrepresented community at the university (The Center for Student Cultural Diversity Annual Report 2015, University of Nevada, Reno, 2015).	Mathematics, Engineering, Science Achievement (MESA)	The Mathematics, Engineering, Science Achievement (MESA) is a college-preparation program that strives to increase the college enrollment of minority, low-income, and first-generation students. The program offers a First-Generation Summer Camp where students are able to participate in science and engineering activities as well as learn more about the college experience. MESA also accepts volunteers who are interested in the STEM field to help local middle and high schools develop a foundational understanding of math and science. Website:http://www.unr.edu/engineering /research-and-outreach/k-12-outreach /mesa.

(continued)

Table 9.1 *(Continued)*

State	Institution	Type of Institution	Institution Description	Program	Program Description/Website
New Hampshire	University of New Hampshire	4-Yr. Public	The University of New Hampshire (UNH) is the flagship institution of New Hampshire and has three campuses: the main campus in Durham, NH; the UNH Manchester campus; and the UNH School of Law located in Concord, NH. UNH is a public research university that was founded in 1866. The main campus offers 200 degree programs (About, University of New Hampshire). The university has a total undergraduate enrollment of 12,494 students. The total number of Hispanic/Latino undergraduates is 417, which is the largest ethnic minority at UNH (Ethnicity by Degree Level, Residency & Gender, University of New Hampshire, 2015).	Connect STEM	The Connect program assists in first-generation and multicultural students' transition from high school to college. The program offers resources that foster growth and academic support throughout students' time at the university. The Connect STEM program, which is a unit of the Connect program, focuses primarily on students who have an interest in STEM. Students participate in a year-long mentoring partnership and form a living and learning community in one of the residence halls. This program takes place two weeks prior to move-in and throughout the academic year. Website: https://www.unh.edu/orientation/connect/connect-stem.
New Jersey	Hudson County Community College	2-Yr. Public	The Hudson County Community College (HCCC) was founded in 1974. The two-year public institution offers 49 degrees and 14 certificate programs. The college operates from two urban college campuses within the county, although the primary campus is located in Jersey City (the other campus is	Northern New Jersey Bridges to Baccalaureate (NNJ-B2B)	The Northern New Jersey Bridges to Baccalaureate (NNJ-B2B) is a partnership of five public associate's-degree granting, Hispanic-serving institutions in northern New Jersey (Hudson County Community College, Passaic County Community College, Bergen Community College, Middlesex County College, and Union

County College). The aim of this partnership is to assist underrepresented minority students in transferring to a baccalaureate STEM program. By engaging students in high-impact practices such as research, peer-led team learning, math bridge program, peer mentoring, career seminars, and transfer activities, the NNJ-BSB partnership hopes to increase the number of students pursuing a degree in STEM.
Website: http://www.hccc.edu/stem/b2b/.

located in Union City). In the fall of 2013, HCCC enrolled a total of 9,036 students. 55.38 percent of the total population at the time was Hispanic, which grants HCCC the title of being a Hispanic-serving institution (Fact Book 2013–2014, Hudson County Community College, 2013).

State	Institution	Type	Description	Program	Program Description
New Mexico	The University of New Mexico	4-Yr. Public	The University of New Mexico was founded in 1889 and serves as the flagship institution of New Mexico (About The University of New Mexico, The University of New Mexico). While the main campus is located in Albuquerque, there are branch campuses in Gallup, Los Alamos, Taos, and Valencia (Campuses and Special Programs, The University of New Mexico). The university's main campus has a total enrollment of 25,299, with 10,258 students who are Hispanic (Spring 2016 Official Enrollment Report, The University of New Mexico, 2016).	STEM Gateway	The mission of the STEM Gateway program is to increase the number of Hispanic and low-income students obtaining a degree within the STEM field. The program offers a reformed teaching model that provides better instruction and intentional curriculum that serves minority students. The program also fosters peer learning and offers a seminar course that helps students understand the connection between various STEM disciplines. By focusing resources on undergraduate courses in math and science, the program hopes to retain more Hispanic and low-income students within the field. Website: http://stemgateway.unm.edu/index.html.

(continued)

Table 9.1 (*Continued*)

State	Institution	Type of Institution	Institution Description	Program	Program Description/Website
New York	The City College of New York	4-Yr. Public	The City College of New York (CCNY) was founded in 1847. Since its inception, it has served as a place for diversity of thought and a place for its student population to flourish, especially with its prime location in New York, NY. The total undergraduate population surmounts to a total of 13,340 students. CCNY also offers master's and doctoral degrees, which places its total student population at 15,931. About 34 percent of the total student population is Hispanic. CCNY also offers a variety of majors that cater to students' passions, such as engineering, architecture, and education (City College of New York Fast Facts Fall 2015, City College of New York, 2015).	STEM Institute	The STEM institute was initiated in 1992 to increase the support for Hispanics and other underrepresented communities and to ensure their success in the STEM field. The STEM Institute at CCNY offers high school students the opportunity to take college level courses to acclimate them to the college experience. This free program also provides resources, such as advising and tutoring, for the students to ensure that they are successful during their time in and out of the classroom. Website: https://stem.ccny.cuny.edu/index .html.
New York	New York University	4-Yr. Private	New York University (NYU) is the largest private institution in the country, offering a diverse array of programs such as medicine, business, and global public health. The institution also operates on an international level with degree-granting campuses in Abu Dhabi and Shanghai. NYU has a total	Science and Technology Entry Program (STEP)	The Science and Technology Entry Program (STEP) is a pre-college program for middle and high school students in New York. The goal of the program is to encourage more underrepresented communities to pursue a major, as well as a career, within a STEM field. Students are able to take courses, access

State	Institution	Type	Description	Program	Program Description
			enrollment of 57,245, with 9 percent of the population who are Hispanic/Latino. NYU also has a large international population (25 percent), which adds to the diversity that the institution fosters (NYU at a Glance, New York University, 2014).		various resources (i.e., tutoring and counseling), and explore various careers within STEM. Some students will also have the opportunity to engage in research during their time in the program. Website:https://www.nyu.edu/admissions /undergraduate-admissions/how-to-apply /all-freshmen-applicants/opportunity -programs/middle-and-high-school -program.html.
North Dakota	North Dakota State University	4-Yr. Public	North Dakota State University (NDSU) is a land-grant research university that is located in Fargo, North Dakota. The university has a diverse student population, representing 47 states and 79 countries. NDSU promotes a more focused learning environment, especially since more than 70 percent of the courses offered have fewer than 40 students (Office of Admissions, North Dakota State University). In the fall of 2015, NDSU had a total enrollment of 14,516 students, which includes undergraduates, graduate students, and professional students. Of the total enrollment, 243 are Hispanic. With more than 11,000 white students, NDSU is a predominantly white institution (Compliance Report Enrollment, North Dakota State University, 2015).	All Nations Louis Stokes Alliance for Minorities Program (ANLSAMP)	The All Nations Louis Stokes Alliance for Minorities Program (ANLSAMP) provides undergraduate multicultural students who are in STEM with a stipend to help students offset financial costs while in college. Moreover, students accepted to the program are in a residential pre-college program to help students acclimate to their new environment. Scholars are also able to attend the ANLSAMP Conference or any other professional development opportunities in STEM with expenses paid. Website:https://www.ndsu.edu /multicultural/scholarships_tuition _assistance/.

(continued)

Table 9.1 (*Continued*)

State	Institution	Type of Institution	Institution Description	Program	Program Description/Website
Ohio	The Ohio State University	4-Yr. Public	The Ohio State University (OSU) was founded in 1870. While the main campus is located in Columbus, the university is present throughout the state of Ohio through its five other campuses, which are located in Lima, Mansfield, Marion, Newark, and Wooster (Ohio Agricultural Technical Institute). The Ohio State University also has 18 colleges and schools and offers more than 12,000 courses (Quick Facts, The Ohio State University). The entire university has an enrollment of 65,184 students, but the Columbus campus has a total enrollment of 58,663 students. The Columbus campus has a 3.79 percent Hispanic population, which is smaller than the percentage of African American and Asian American students on campus (Statistical Summary, The Ohio State University, 2015).	Society of Hispanic Professional Engineers (SHPE) at The Ohio State University	The mission of the Society of Hispanic Professional Engineers at The Ohio State University is to recruit and retain Hispanic students in engineering and other STEM disciplines. SHPE also works with local high schools to build awareness of the STEM field and assist high school students gain more interest in STEM-related majors. SPHE also offers academic support and professional development opportunities to help current students become successful and prepare for a career in the field. Website: http://shpe.org.ohio-state.edu/index.html.
Oklahoma	Oklahoma State University	4-Yr. Public	Oklahoma State University (OSU) is a public land-grant university that was established in 1890. With a five-	Oklahoma Louis Stokes Alliance for	The Oklahoma Louis Stokes Alliance for Minority Participation (OK-LSAMP) is a consortium of 11 institutions, including

(continued)

State	Institution	Type	Description	Program	Program Description
			campus system, OSU enrolls more than 35,000 students. The students at OSU are from all 50 states and represent about 120 nations (About OSU, Oklahoma State University, 2016). OSU also has a Latino/Hispanic undergraduate population of 1,315 students, which is 23.5 percent of the total undergraduate population (Undergraduate Enrollment by Ethnicity 2009–2015, Oklahoma State University, 2015).	Minority Participation (OK-LSAMP)	Southeastern Oklahoma State, University of Oklahoma, University of Tulsa, and even Oklahoma State University (lead institution). The goal of OK-LSAMP is to create programs that increase the number of students from underserved communities who receive a degree in a STEM field. Website: https://ok-lsamp.okstate.edu/.
Oregon	Portland Community College	2-Yr. Public	Portland Community College (PCC) is the largest postsecondary institution in Oregon and serves about 900,000 full-time and part-time students. PCC has four locations: Cascade, Rock Creek, Sylvania, and Southeast (About PCC, Portland Community College, 2016). According to the student enrollment 2015–17 data, 11 percent of the total student population is Hispanic, which is the largest minority group at PCC (Portland Community College, 2015).	Louis Stokes Alliance for Minority Participation (LSAMP)	The LSAMP program, which is comprised of Portland State University and Portland Community College, aims to increase the number of underrepresented students in STEM. Students who are accepted to the program have access to social events, campus STEM tours, networking sessions, and seminars and conferences. Given the partnership between PCC and Portland State University, students who want to transfer from PCC to Portland State experience an easier transition. Website:https://www.pcc.edu/resources/culture/cascade/lsamp.html.

Table 9.1 (*Continued*)

State	Institution	Type of Institution	Institution Description	Program	Program Description/Website
Pennsylvania	Pennsylvania State University	4-Yr. Public	Pennsylvania State University (Penn State) is a public research institution whose mission is teaching, research, and service. There are 24 campuses, 17,000 faculty and staff, and 100,000 students within the Penn State system. Penn State also serves as Pennsylvania's only land-grant institution (This is Penn State, Pennsylvania State University, 2015). The main campus in University Park has a total undergraduate enrollment of 40,742 students, which is the largest student population among all of Penn State's other locations, but combined with the other locations, it has a total enrollment of 70,680. 6.2 percent of the total enrollment are Hispanic students (Admission and University Statistics, Pennsylvania State University, 2015).	Society of Hispanic Professional Engineers (SHPE)	The purpose of the Society of Hispanic Professional Engineers (SHPE) at Penn State is to empower more students from the Hispanic community to pursue a career in STEM and to retain current undergraduate students who are pursuing a degree in a STEM-related field. SHPE provides networking events to prepare undergraduate students for their future careers and to meet other Hispanic STEM scholars from across the country. SHPE also has a high school program aimed at bringing Latin American high school students to Penn State to experience the campus culture through workshops and events. Website: http://www.shpepennstate.org /about-us.html.
Puerto Rico	University of Puerto Rico	4-Yr. Public	The University of Puerto Rico (UPR) was founded in 1903 (History of the UPR, University of Puerto Rico). With	Puerto Rico Louis Stokes Alliance for	The Puerto Rico Louis Stokes Alliance for Minority Participation (PR-LSAMP) aims to increase the quantity and quality

State	Institution	Type	Description	Program/Organization	Program Description
			11 campuses spread throughout Puerto Rico, students are able to find an area of study, whether it be philosophy or athletic therapy (Admissions Office, University of Puerto Rico).	Minority Participation (PR-LSAMP)	of minority students who are pursuing and completing a degree in the STEM field. The alliance is comprised of 11 higher education institutions in Puerto Rico that are known for their commitment to retaining and graduating a large number of undergraduates who then pursue a career in STEM. Website: https://prlsamp.rcse.upr.edu/.
Rhode Island	University of Rhode Island	4-Yr. Public	The University of Rhode Island (URI) was chartered as the state's agricultural school in 1888 and since then has changed to be a public research university. URI has a total of nine major academic units, which in total hosts more than 80 majors for students to choose from. The university's student population represents 62 nations and 44 U.S. states and territories (About the University, University of Rhode Island, 2015). URI has a total enrollment of 13,641 undergraduates. Of the total undergraduate population, 1,289 students are Hispanic (Final Enrollment Report, University of Rhode Island, 2015).	Society of Hispanic Professional Engineers	Society of Hispanic Professional Engineers aims to support Hispanic students who are in STEM by offering scholarships, internship opportunities, access to the SHPE Career Center to receive professional development opportunities to prepare for a future career in STEM, and providing a community of Hispanic STEM scholars. Website: http://egr.uri.edu/shpe/.

(continued)

Table 9.1 *(Continued)*

State	Institution	Type of Institution	Institution Description	Program	Program Description/Website
South Carolina	Clemson University	4-Yr. Public	Clemson University was founded in 1889 and currently serves as a science- and engineering-oriented institution. The university offers over 80 majors and more than 75 minors for students to choose from. These majors and minors span the seven colleges that exist within Clemson University. The university also has more than 400 student clubs and organizations (About Clemson University, Clemson University). Clemson University has a total enrollment of 22,698 undergraduates and graduate students. Of the total enrollment, 687 students are Hispanic (Clemson University Fact Book, Clemson University, 2015).	PEER & WISE	The PEER & WISE program is dedicated to increasing the number of women and underrepresented minorities in engineering and science. The center offers a variety of resources for students to ensure their success in their academics as well as their professional trajectory. Students receive mentoring, counseling, tutoring, and opportunities to form a community with other scholars in the STEM field. Website:http://www.clemson.edu/cecas/departments/peer-wise/index.html.
South Dakota	University of South Dakota	4-Yr. Public	The University of South Dakota (USD) was founded in 1862 in Vermillion, South Dakota. USD has nine colleges and schools, including an online program. Although USD offers a variety of majors for students to choose from, some of the more popular undergraduate fields of study include	Center for Diversity and Community (CDC)	The Center for Diversity and Community (CDC) strives to provide support to communities who have been historically marginalized. CDC welcomes diversity in many forms, which includes disability, gender identity, sexual orientation, religion, and race/ethnicity. CDC provides a variety of cultural and social

retention support programs to ensure students are excelling inside and out of the classroom. CDC also engages in recruitment activities, advising and support for student organizations, and student leadership development.
Website: http://www.usd.edu/student -life/diversity-and-community.

nursing, biology/medical biology, and elementary teacher education (USD at a Glance, University of South Dakota, 2015). USD also has a total enrollment of 7,435 undergraduate students. 245 of these undergraduate students are Hispanic (Statistical Highlights, University of South Dakota, 2015).

| Tennessee | Vanderbilt University | 4-Yr. Private | Vanderbilt University is a private university that was founded in 1873. The university has a total enrollment of 12,605 students; 6,883 are undergraduate students. Vanderbilt also has more than 500 clubs and organizations in which students to get involved. The university has 10 schools and colleges that offer a range of majors from which students can select. In order to provide support for students both in and out of the classroom, Vanderbilt has a staff of 19,997 individuals and 4,179 faculty (Quick Facts, Vanderbilt University, 2015). 8.4 percent of the undergraduate student population at Vanderbilt University is Hispanic (The Vanderbilt Profile, Vanderbilt University, 2015). | Tennessee Louis Stokes Alliance for Minority Participation (TLSAMP) | The Tennessee Louis Stokes Alliance for Minority Participation's (TLSAMP) mission is to increase the number of underrepresented minority students who receive a degree in a stem related field. The goal of the program is to recruit underrepresented Vanderbilt students, provide a better learning environment for these students in STEM, and ensure that many of these undergraduate students are prepared for graduate programs. The TLSAMP program offers tutoring services, a summer bridge program, and opportunities for internships and to conduct research. Website:http://engineering.vanderbilt.edu /tlsamp/about.php. |

(continued)

Table 9.1 (*Continued*)

State	Institution	Type of Institution	Institution Description	Program	Program Description/Website
Texas	The University of Texas at El Paso	4-Yr. Public	The University of Texas at El Paso (UTEP) was founded in 1914. With its location near the U.S.-Mexico border, UTEP prides itself as being an institution that caters to one of "the largest binational communities in the world" (The University of Texas at El Paso Facts 2015–2016, The University of Texas at El Paso, 2015). UTEP has a total enrollment of 23,397 students. In addition, more than half of the student population (80 percent) is Hispanic. With 72 bachelor's, 73 master's, and 21 doctoral degrees offered at UTEP, students are able to find a major that is right for them (The University of Texas at El Paso Facts 2015–2016, The University of Texas at El Paso, 2015).	STEM Talent Expansion Program (STEP)	The STEM Talent Expansion Program (STEP) at UTEP aims to foster the success for students in STEM majors by intervening early in students' undergraduate experience. Not only does the program hope to support students, but it also wants to ensure students in the STEM field graduate as well. Moreover, the STEP program allows undergraduates who have excelled in the STEM field to serve as peer tutors to those students seeking help. Not only does this cultivate collaboration between students, but it also encourages tutors to consider STEM education as a pathway for a future career. Website: http://academics.utep.edu /Default.aspx?alias=academics.utep.edu /step.
Texas	The University of Texas at San Antonio	4-Yr. Public	The University of Texas at San Antonio (UTSA) was established in 1968. Since then, it has grown to be an institution with over 28,700 students enrolled. More than half of the student population at UTSA is Hispanic. The students are geographically diverse,	Prefreshman Engineering Program (PREP)	The Prefreshman Engineering Program (PREP) at UTSA is a mathematics-based summer program that is hosted at a variety of colleges and universities in San Antonio, such as South Texas College. The program is geared towards middle and high school students with the

			representing 94 countries. UTSA also provides students the opportunity to select from 162 degree programs. The most popular programs are business, liberal and fine arts, science, education and human development, and engineering. In addition to an undergraduate degree, UTSA also offers a master's, doctoral, and post-baccalaureate degree (UTSA Fast Facts, The University of Texas at San Antonio, 2015).		intention of motivating and preparing students to pursue a career within the STEM field. By taking a college course, being exposed to various careers in the field, and working with faculty and staff who want these students to be successful, PREP hopes to increase the number of women and other minority communities who decide to enter the STEM field. Website: http://p20.utsa.edu/programs/prep/.
Utah	University of Utah	4-Yr. Public	The University of Utah was founded in 1850 and serves as the flagship institution of the state. About 100 different majors are offered at the undergraduate level, and more than 90 major fields are offered at the graduate level (About the University of Utah, University of Utah, 2016). The University of Utah has a total undergraduate and graduate enrollment of 31,673 students. Of this total, 3,012 students are Hispanic (Headcount Enrollment by Academic Level, Gender, and Ethnicity, University of Utah, 2015).	Society for Advancement of Chicanos/ Hispanics and Native Americans in Science (SACNAS)	The Society for Advancement of Chicanos/Hispanics and Native Americans in Science (SACNAS) aims to foster the success of underrepresented minority students at the University of Utah by encouraging these students to pursue a degree in STEM while also helping more middle school and high school students pursue a degree in the field. SACNAS provides a supportive network for students while providing networking and mentorship opportunities with professionals in the field. Website:http://biochem.web.utah.edu/sacnas/?page_id=2.

(continued)

237

Table 9.1 (*Continued*)

State	Institution	Type of Institution	Institution Description	Program	Program Description/Website
Vermont	The University of Vermont	4-Yr. Public	The University of Vermont (UVM) was chartered in 1791 as a private institution. It was not until 1862 that the university obtained public institution status (History and Traditions, The University of Vermont). UVM offers 100 majors in seven undergraduate schools and colleges; moreover, the university has 50 master's degree programs, 24 doctoral programs, and a medical program (UVM Facts, The University of Vermont. 2015). In 2015, the total undergraduate enrollment was 10,081 students. Of the total undergraduate enrollment, only 422 students are Hispanic/Latino (Headcount Multicultural and International Student Enrollment by College/School/Unit by Ethnic Origin, The University of Vermont, 2015).	Summer Enrichment Scholars Program (SESP)	The Summer Enrichment Scholars Program is a free summer bridge program hosted by the African, Latina/o, Asian, and Native American (ALANA) Student Center that invites incoming first-year students of color and bi/multiracial students to earn college credit by taking courses in science and English, build community with students who identify similarly, earn money through part-time on campus jobs, and explore the greater Burlington community. Website:https://www.uvm.edu/~asc/?Page=sesp.html&SM=eventsmenu.html.
Virginia	George Mason University	4-Yr. Public	George Mason University (GMU) was founded in 1957. Despite its recent establishment, GMU is the largest public university in Virginia with four campuses within the state and one in Korea. With more than 34,000 students on campus, the student population	Society of Hispanic Professional Engineers (SHPE) at GMU	The Society of Hispanic Professional Engineers (SHPE) at GMU works to empower the Hispanic community to impact the STEM field. By offering retention programs and opportunities for networking and professional development, SHPE hopes to foster

| Washington | University of Washington | 4-Yr. Public | The University of Washington (UW) was founded in 1861. Because 2,311 undergraduate courses are offered, the class sizes are often fewer than 100 students. The total undergraduate population at UW is 29,468 students. Of this total, 7.1 percent is Hispanic (About UW, University of Washington, 2015). UW also offers 165 majors across 79 departments; this allows students to have access to a variety of options when thinking about a program of study (Academics, University of Washington). | | |

brings a wealth of diversity and represents more than 130 countries. In addition, 80 percent of the students who graduate from GMU are able to find a job within the first six months (About Mason, George Mason University). GMU's U.S. campus has a total enrollment of 33,925 students. The second largest minority population at GMU are Hispanics, with 3,626 students (Facts and Figures, George Mason University, 2015).

Society of Hispanic Professional Engineers (SHPE)

The University of Washington Chapter of the Society of Hispanic Professional Engineers (SPHE) aims to pave the way to a STEM career for underrepresented students by offering support and opportunities for networking. SHPE also works with local middle schools and high schools to bring awareness of the STEM field and to encourage more students to pursue a career in a related field. Website:http://students.washington.edu /shpe/drupal/.

academic success for Hispanic students in the classroom and prepare these students to be leaders in the STEM field. SHPE also works with local high schools to spread awareness of the STEM field and to encourage more students to pursue a career in STEM. Website: http://www.gmu.edu/org/shpe/.

(continued)

239

Table 9.1 *(Continued)*

State	Institution	Type of Institution	Institution Description	Program	Program Description/Website
West Virginia	Marshall University	4-Yr. Public	Marshall University is a public university that was founded in 1837. The campus has 230 recognized student organizations in which students may be involved. The university also offers a variety of student services, such as the Center for African American Students and the Women's Center. Marshall University has 59 baccalaureate degree programs and offers associate's degrees, master's degrees, education specialist degrees, doctoral degrees, and professional degrees. The total student population at Marshall university is 13,631 students. 11 percent are minority students, and 4 percent are international students. The students are also diverse geographically, representing 49 states and 56 countries. (Quick Facts, Marshall University, 2015).	Louis Stokes Alliance for Minority Participation (LSAMP)	The purpose of the Louis Stokes Alliance for Minority Participation (LSAMP) program is to increase the number of underrepresented minority students pursue a degree in STEM. Marshall University is one of the schools in the Kentucky-West Virginia Alliance. The program provides students the opportunities to connect with other underrepresented minorities interested in STEM, receive tutoring and other academic support services, engage in research, and network with professionals in the field. Website:http://www.marshall.edu/intercultural/lsamp/.
Wisconsin	University of Wisconsin—Milwaukee	4-Yr. Public	The University of Wisconsin—Milwaukee (UWM) is a public research university that educates more than 27,000 students with a budget of $667 million. UWM offers 191 programs: 94	STEM-Inspire Program	The goal of STEM-Inspire is to recruit, retain, and graduate more underrepresented minorities in the STEM field. It offers opportunities for mentorship by both peers and faculty,

State	Institution	Type	Institution Description	Program	Program Description
			bachelor's degrees, 64 master's degrees, and 33 doctoral degrees. These 191 programs operate through the 14 different schools and colleges at UWM. The university has a total undergraduate enrollment of 22,321 students. The majority of those who attend UWM are in-state residents. Regardless, all 50 states are represented by the student population, and the international student population at UWM represents 81 countries (Facts and Impact 2015–2016, University of Wisconsin—Milwaukee, 2015)		engagement with research, and academic resources to help students be successful in the classroom. Students are paired with a peer mentor, peer tutor, and a faculty to help navigate the STEM field both academically and professionally. Not only are students being supported as undergraduates, but they are also preparing for a career in the field and graduate/professional school. Website: http://uwm.edu/steminspire/.
Wyoming	University of Wyoming	4-Yr. Public	The University of Wyoming was founded in 1886 in Laramie, Wyoming. The university offers about 200 programs of study across eight different colleges (UW Quick Facts, University of Wyoming). The University of Wyoming has a total on-campus undergraduate population of 8,650. 10 percent of the student enrollment are minority students, and there are more female students (53 percent) than male students (47 percent). With more than 250 student organizations and clubs, as well as 21 sports clubs, students are able to get involved in a variety of ways (UW 2015 Quick Facts, University of Wyoming, 2015).	Multicultural Resource Center	The Multicultural Resource Center (MRC) serves as a hub for students to provide academic support, encourages student leadership and advocacy, and builds upon intercultural awareness and diversity. The Multicultural Affairs Tutoring Program is an academic support program within the MRC that pairs students with tutors who can provide support and guidance to foster academic success in and out of the classroom. Other workshops and resources are offered, such as the time management worksheet, to provide students with the tools and strategies necessary to be successful. Website:http://www.uwyo.edu/oma /multicultural-resource-center/.

241

The list of factors you ought to consider in exploring STEM related majors and careers could be extensive. With innumerable options of two-year and four-year colleges and universities to attend in the United States, it is also likely that you can be overwhelmed when it is time to decide which final five, 10, or 15 schools you will apply to ultimately. With a goal to aid your selection process and make the information readily available to you, in this chapter we highlight select institutions and programs in all 50 states and Puerto Rico. A short description of the institution and the featured program is also provided. This list is not exhaustive by any means, but it is a representation of stellar programs that have catered and continue to cater to the needs of students of color, and in some instances specifically Latinx students, in a variety of geographic locations and institutional types. Many of these programs and institutions are highlighted because of their nationally known high-impact practices and known track record of mentoring students of color, especially Latinx students. Some of these institutions are Hispanic-serving institutions, while others are emerging or aspiring Hispanic-serving institutions. Some are located in states that are home to the largest Latinx communities in the United States. According to a Pew Research Center- Hispanic Trends report (Stepler and Lopez, 2016), the top 10 states with the largest Latinx populous are: California, Texas, Florida, New York, Illinois, Arizona, New Jersey, Colorado, New Mexico, and Georgia. This is important to note because these states could be leaders in K-20 educational initiatives and high-impact practices leading to greater degree attainment among Latinx students across a spectrum of fields. As you peruse the examples, we urge you to take careful notes to identify special characteristics of each program that likely resonate with you and your needs.

REFERENCES

Litow, S. (2008). A silent crisis: The underrepresentation of Latinos in STEM careers. *Education Week*. Retrieved from http://www.edweek.org/ew/articles /2008/07/18/44litow-com_web.h27.html

Stepler, R., & Lopez, M. H. (2016). U.S. Latino population growth and dispersion has slowed since onset of the great recession. *Pew Research Center (Hispanic Trends)*. Retrieved from http://www.pewhispanic.org/2016/09/08/latino -population-growth-and-dispersion-has-slowed-since-the-onset-of-the -great-recession/

PART VI

Resources

CHAPTER TEN

Resources for Latinx Students Interested in STEM Careers

Cynthia Diana Villarreal and Sarah Price

This chapter lists some basic resources to assist students, parents, and teachers in their quest toward gaining information on science, technology, engineering, and mathematics (STEM) careers, including information on scholarships, internships, and professional associations. Just like the career fields that provide the letters of the STEM acronym, the STEM field is ever-changing and evolving. To assist with the quest for resources on STEM careers, this chapter provides an overview of helpful websites, books, movies, articles, and social media profiles of Latinxs in STEM fields.

WEBSITES

STEM Connector

http://www.stemconnector.org/

The Stem Connector website is a resource and service created to inform the public about national, state, and local STEM entities, including companies, nonprofit associations, and professional societies. Sign up for their newsletter, STEMdaily, to be provided with that latest STEM innovations.

STEM-Up

www.STEMup.org

STEM-Up is a California-based initiative providing resources to surrounding communities that creates awareness, cultivates inspiration and motivation, and strengthens skills for students interested in pursuing a career in STEM. There are plenty of resources for students and parents regardless of the state in which they live.

NASA Education for Students

http://www.nasa.gov/audience/forstudents/index.html#.VRnMhvzF-5I

NASA Education for Students provides information for educators and students at varying levels in their education. The website lists NASA internships and other opportunities in addition to related STEM news and video clips.

NASA Hispanic Astronauts

http://oeop.larc.nasa.gov/hep/hep-astronauts.html

NASA Hispanic Astronauts showcases biographies of 14 Hispanic men and women participants of the NASA career astronauts program. Included are helpful tips on how to become an astronaut.

The Science Channel

http://www.sciencechannel.com/

Science Channel is a compilation of video clips on various science-related questions, theories, and research. These videos can awaken your scientific curiosity and provide understandable explanations to challenging concepts.

MAES Latinos in Science and Engineering

www.mymaes.org

MAES strives for the development of STEM leaders in the academic, executive, and technical communities. Offers scholarships, events, grants, symposia, conferences, and information for families.

Center for Advancement of Hispanics in Science and Engineering Education

http://www.cahsee.org/

The Center for Advancement of Hispanics in Science and Engineering Education aims to prepare talented Latino and other underrepresented minority students in science and engineering for STEM careers. This NASA-funded center for academic and professional excellence has been awarded for excellence in mentoring and pre-college preparation resulting in increased admission and retention of Latinos in STEM programs.

SCHOLARSHIP OPPORTUNITIES/FINANCIAL AID

TRiO Programs

A resource for students looking for Pell grants, loan services, and FAFSA guidelines. TRiO is a program designed to assist low-income, first-generation college students, and students with disabilities in obtaining financial resources to enter and continue higher education.

HENAAC Scholarship Program

http://www.greatmindsinstem.org/college/henaac-scholarship-program

The HENAAC Scholarship Program is designed to inspire more college students to pursue engineering and science careers. This program aims to promote leadership and STEM role models in Hispanic communities.

Gates Millennium Scholars Program

http://www.gmsp.org/

One thousand African American, American Indian/Native Alaskan, Asian Pacific Islander, and Hispanic American students pursuing a degree in the STEM or public health fields are recognized every year for academic achievement and leadership.

Hispanic Dental Association

http://www.hdassoc.org/hda-foundation/scholarship-program/

This scholarship awards grants to students while connecting them to corporate partners and individual donors.

League of United Latin American Citizens

http://lulac.org/programs/education/scholarships/index.html

LULAC councils partner with local and national businesses to boost participation in STEM fields for Latino students.

National Action Council for Minorities in Engineering

http://www.nacme.org/scholarships

NACME strives to support 1,200 underrepresented students in engineering programs. Each scholarship winner receives $2,500 to be used toward tuition.

NAMEPA

http://www.namepa.org

NAMEPA offers both national and regional scholarships for African American, Latino, and American Indian students interested in pursuing an undergraduate degree in engineering.

Hispanic Scholarship Fund

https://hsf.net/en/scholarships/

A resource for Hispanic students looking for scholarships in STEM programs. Students must have at least a 3.0 GPA in high school or a 2.5 GPA in college or university and plan to attend college full-time.

HACU Scholarship Program

http://www.hacu.net/hacu/Scholarships.asp

This program is for students who are enrolled at HACU membership colleges or universities in the United States or Puerto Rico.

National Association of Hispanic Nurses

http://nahnnet.org/NAHNScholarships.html

Full-time LVN/LPN, associate's, diploma, baccalaureate, and graduate nursing students are eligible to receive scholarships awarding between $2,000 to $5,000.

"Scholarships for Hispanic and Latino Students"

https://colleges.niche.com/scholarships/race/hispanic-and-latino/

A large list of scholarships available for Hispanic and Latino students interested in pursuing STEM degrees.

National Hispanic Health Foundation Scholarship Galas

http://www.nhmafoundation.org/index.php/scholarship-program

Students who attend the NHHF Scholarship Gala are eligible to receive scholarships.

American Chemical Society Scholars Program

http://www.acs.org/content/acs/en/funding-and-awards/scholarships/acsscholars.html

The ACSSP provides scholarships for African American, Hispanic, and American Indian students pursuing research in chemical sciences. Awards granted are up to $5,000 given to high school seniors or college freshmen, sophomores, or juniors enrolled in a college degree in the sciences or chemical technology programs.

MAGAZINES

S.T.E.M. Magazine

S.T.E.M. Magazine provides teachers, students, parents, and administrators with resources on careers in STEM, innovations, and helpful tips for a path toward success. The digital version of this monthly education publication is available at: http://www.stemmagazine.com/

Minority Engineer

Minority Engineer magazine in print is free to engineering students or minority professionals. The latest digital edition of the magazine is available on the website for free at: http://www.eop.com/mags-ME.php

MAES Magazine

MAES Magazine is a resource for Latinos STEM. The magazine provides information about the MAES symposium and other opportunities for students and professionals. The digital magazine, available at http://mymaes.org/magazine/, offers names of partnering institutions for Latinos interested in STEM.

SOCIAL MEDIA APPS AND ACCOUNTS

Twitter

Some notable Twitter feeds to follow are: @LatinasinSTEM; Minorities in STEM @MinSciTech; @STEMconnector; @PR_ADVANCE; @NSF; @GreatMindsSTEM; @HSFNews; @ChevronStemZone; @VEXRobotics; @HispanicEd; and Popular Mechanics @PopMech.

Facebook

Facebook profiles to like: Latino STEM Alliance; NASA Students; Society of Hispanic Professional Engineers; SACNAS; TED; Science Fact; Science Verse; MinutePhysics; Science Alert; Veritasium; and Cosmos Magazine.

NETWORKING, PROGRAMS, ORGANIZATIONS, AND LEADERSHIP OPPORTUNITIES

Technovation

http://www.technovationchallenge.org

Technovation is a technology entrepreneurship program and competition for young women ages 10 to 18. It takes place over the course of three months and teaches young girls how to work together, design, create mobile apps, and pitch their entrepreneurial ideas to judges. This program is free for all who are accepted.

STEM Explorers—Through LULAC National Educational Service Centers, Inc.

http://www.lnesc.org/#!stem-explorers/c20ea

This afterschool program for high school students aims to increase interest in the STEM fields through real-world practice that provide hands-on experience in the lab and in the field. LNESC currently operates in the following cities: Bronx, NY; Colorado Springs, CO; Corpus Christi, TX; Philadelphia, PA; San Antonio, TX; and Washington, D.C.

College Tours—Through LNESC

http://www.lnesc.org/#!college-tours/c16w8

With support from the U.S. Army and Nissan, College Tours gives high school students the opportunity to tour college campuses in New Mexico, Missouri, Texas, Florida, Colorado, New York, Illinois, and California. Underneath LULAC National Education Service Centers, the aim is to create lifelong learners and leaders in the Hispanic community.

HACU Latino STEM Summit

http://www.hacu.net/hacu/stem_summit.asp

The annual HACU Latino STEM Summit provides students the opportunity to learn about, network for, and prepare for internships and jobs in STEM fields.

Leaders on the Fast Track (LOFT) Institute

http://members.loftinstitute.org/

This is an online networking site for emerging Latino leaders that provides a platform to create connections and find resources for those researching in finance, public policy, foreign affairs, communications, education, entrepreneurship, and many fields.

National Society of Hispanic Physicists

http://www.hispanicphysicists.org/

NSHP seeks to celebrate the accomplishments of Hispanic physicists and promote their research, development, and well-being in the field. They encourage Hispanic students to enter the field of physics and join their community of high achieving professionals.

Society for Advancement of Chicanos and Native Americans in Science

http://sacnas.org/

SACNAS is dedicated to helping Hispanic, Chicano, and Native Americans meet their dreams of entering the STEM fields through higher numbers of degree holders, increase leadership in these fields, and increase governmental commitment increase resources, eliminate barriers, and create greater equity for students and professionals.

Society of Hispanic Professional Engineers

http://www.shpe.org/

This national organization strives to create networking opportunities for professional and student engineers. SHPE's goal is to create a world where Hispanic innovators, scientists, mathematicians, and engineers are highly valued and influential in their field.

Society of Mexican American Engineers and Scientists

http://mymaes.org/

MAES aims to increase Mexican American and Hispanic professionals and researchers in the sciences. MAES strives to provide role models for, meet the needs of, and provide resources for professionals and students in the field.

Latino STEM Alliance

http://www.latinostem.org/

This is a nonprofit organization that aims to connect with students through partnerships with various schools, private industry, and community groups. LSA encourages students to consider STEM-related careers through community-based enrichment programs.

Cuban American Association of Civil Engineers

http://c-aace.org/

Helping Cuban professionals since 1960, this organization provides scholarships to engineering students as well as providing a networking platform for engineering professionals in the United States.

Great Minds in STEM—College Captains Program

http://www.greatmindsinstem.org/college/college-captains

College Captains are college students who share their experiences with and mentor pre-college students interested in pursuing STEM degrees.

FILM

Eva (2011)

A dystopian future where humans and self-aware machines coexist. In Santa Irene, a successful cybernetic engineer has returned to build a child robot.

La Ultima Muerte (2011)

Jaime, a researcher of experimental medicine, must save the life of a young boy near death in this futuristic story.

Plurality (2012)

A science fiction film from Chile that tells the story of a government that watches every move you make through your DNA.

Protocolo (2013)

Through his short film school senior project, Rodrigo Hernandez brings a sci-fi film about a malfunctioning cloning company machine.

Spare Parts (2015)

With little experience and few resources, four Latino high school students form a robotics club and take on the country's top robotics champion: MIT.

Stand and Deliver (1988)

Relive the story of Jaime Escalante, who inspired his California high school students to pass their AP calculus tests.

Viaje a Marte (2005)

When Grandpa asks if you want to go to Mars, of course the answer is yes! This story tells what happens when you return from your out-of-this-world journey and nobody believes you.

Waste Land (2010)

A documentary about collectivism, sustainability, and environmental protection in Brazil.

BOOKS

Antonia Novello, U.S. Surgeon General

The story of a young girl born in Puerto Rico with a chronic health condition who went on to become an important figure in health and U.S. Surgeon General for the Bush administration.

Ay, Mija!: Why Do You Want to Be an Engineer

Multiple stories to celebrate the accomplishments of Latina engineers who continue to strive in a male-dominated career.

Ellen Ochoa: The First Hispanic Woman in Space

A brief book for the reader interested in becoming an astronaut and following the accomplishments of Ellen Ochoa.

Ellen Ochoa: First Latina Astronaut

A short book that chronicles the journey of Ellen Ochoa's road to becoming an astronaut.

Hispanic-American Scientists

The story of 10 Hispanic Americans who have contributed to science as far back as World War II.

Hispanic Scientists: Ellen Ochoa, Carlos A. Ramírez, Eloy Rodriguez, Lydia Villa-Komaroff, Maria Elena Zavala

Discover the life work of these scientists, inventors, and aviators from a diverse array of backgrounds.

Jaime Escalante: Inspirational Math Teacher

Follow Jaime Escalante's journey from teaching math in Bolivia to inspiring high school students in California to pass the AP calculus exam.

Latinos in Science, Math, and Professions

An A-to-Z list of Latinos who influence and contribute to research in math, science, and other professions.

Mario Molina: Chemist and Nobel Prize Winner

As a Nobel Prize winner, Mario Molina dedicates his life to the pursuit of scientific knowledge and the betterment of humankind. This book chronicles his life, ambitions, and accomplishments.

Paths to Discovery: Autobiographies from Chicanas with Careers in Science, Mathematics, and Engineering

Discover how these brilliant women developed a passion and a talent for math and science and became leading researchers at major universities.

Space Rocks: The Story of Planetary Geologist Adriana Ocampo

Follow the inspiring story of this Buenos Aires-born planetary geologist. Discover how she landed a job with NASA as a teenager and solved a 65-million-year mystery.

INFORMATION FOR FAMILIES

National Center for Women and Information Technology

http://www.ncwit.org/latinas-information-technology

For families that are English language learners, the National Center for Women and Information Technology has profiles of Latinas in STEM, news articles, videos, and resources, all in Spanish.

GIRLS Inc.: Tips for Encouraging Girls in STEM

http://www.girlsinc.org/resources/tips-encouraging-girls-stem.html

This resource provides parents and educators with various steps to take for encouraging a child who expresses an interest in the STEM fields. Though it specifically addresses girls, it can be used to help any student pursue a course of action for their science-related interests.

MAES la familia blog

www.mymaes.org/blog/

A resource for Latino students and their families to help discover, explore, and familiarize themselves in the fields of science and engineering. This blog is a collection of stories, advice, and event announcements in the world of STEM.

REFERENCES

Cantú, N. E. (Ed.). (2008). *Paths to Discovery: Autobiographies from Chicanas with Careers in Science, Mathematics, and Engineering.* Los Angeles: UCLA Chicano Studies Research Center Press.

Gravenhorst, E. C. (2006). *Ay, Mija!: Why do you want to be an engineer?* Illustrated by S. Santos. St. Louis, MO: E. C. Gravenhorst.

Guzmán, L., & Guzmán, R. (2006). *Ellen Ochoa: First Latina astronaut.* Berkeley Heights, NJ:Enslow Publishing.

Hawxhurst, J. C. (1993). *Antonia Novello, U.S. Surgeon General.* Brookfield, CT: Millbrook Press.

Hernandez-Cruz, R. (Director/Producer). (2013), *Protocolo.* [Motion picture]. Mexico: Crento de capacitacion cinematografica.

Hopping, L. J. (2005). *Space rocks: The story of planetary geologist Adriana Ocampo.* New York: Franklin Watts.

Kent, D. (2004). *Mario Molina: Chemist and Nobel Prize winner.* Chanhassen, MN: Child's World.

Liu, D. (Director/Producer). (2012). *Plurality.* [Motion picture]. USA: Traffik Frameworks.

Maillo, K. (Director/Producer). (2011). *Eva.* [Motion picture]. Spain, France: Canal+Espana, Escandalo Films.

McNamara, S. (Director/Producer). (2015). *Spare Parts.* [Motion picture]. USA: Brookwell-McNamara Entertainment.

Menéndez, Ramón. (Director/Producer). (1988). *Stand and Deliver.* [Motion picture]. USA: American Playhouse, Olmos Productions.

Newton, D. E. (2007). *Latinos in science, math, and professions.* New York: Facts on File.

Oleksy, W. G. (1998). *Hispanic-American scientists.* New York: Facts on File.

Paige, J. (2004). *Ellen Ochoa: The first Hispanic woman in space.* New York: Rosen Publishing Group.

Ruiz, D. (Director/Producer). (2011). *La Ultima Muerte.* [Motion picture]. Mexico: Lemon Films.

Schraff, A. E. (2009). *Jaime Escalante: Inspirational math teacher.* Berkeley Heights, NJ: Enslow Publishers.

St. John, J. (1996). *Hispanic scientists: Ellen Ochoa, Carlos A. Ramírez, Eloy Rodriguez, Lydia Villa-Komaroff, Maria Elena Zavala.* Mankato, MN: Capstone Press.

Walker, L., Harley, K., & Joao, J. (Directors/Producers). (2010). *Waste Land.* [Motion picture] Brazil, UK: Almega Projects, O2 Filmes.

Zaramella, J. P. (Director/Producer). (2005). *Viaje a Marte.* [Motion picture]. Argentina: JPZtudio.

About the Editors
and Contributors

Vijay Kanagala (PhD, Iowa State University) is an assistant professor of higher education and student affairs administration in the department of leadership and developmental sciences at the University of Vermont. A former student affairs practitioner with extensive experience in multicultural student affairs, social justice education, and diversity programming and training, Kanagala's primary research engages with three critical areas of higher education. These include issues related to 1) college access and success of first-generation, low-income students, 2) collegiate experiences of underrepresented, underserved, and understudied students of color, and 3) employing spirituality and contemplative education/pedagogy in student affairs preparation programs. His teaching and learning pedagogy is not only about working with students to cultivate skills and knowledge to be competent student affairs professionals, but it is also about creating a transformative classroom experience that invites an ethic of care, compassion, and empathy while addressing social justice issues.

Laura I. Rendón (PhD, University of Michigan) is professor emerita of higher education at the University of Texas-San Antonio. Rendón is a research specialist on college preparation, persistence, and graduation of low-income, first-generation students. She is also recognized as a thought leader in the field of contemplative education. In 2013, the Texas Diversity Council recognized her among the most powerful and influential women in Texas. A native of Laredo, Texas, Rendón's passion is assisting students who, like her, grew up in poverty with hopes and dreams but not knowing how to realize them. Rendón is credited with developing the theory of validation, which colleges and researchers employ as a framework for working with and affirming low-income students. Rendón has designed and coordinated the yearly Latino/a Student Success Institute for the American Association of

Hispanics in Higher Education. She is the author of *Sentipensante (Sensing/ Thinking) Pedagogy: Educating for Wholeness, Social Justice and Liberation* and coeditor of *Educating a New Majority and Transforming the First Year of College for Students of Color*.

Rosa M. Banda (PhD, Texas A&M University) is assistant professor of educational leadership at Texas A&M University-Corpus Christi. Dr. Banda's primary research interests include high-achieving Latinas in engineering, gifted poor students of color, educational leadership, faculty diversity, and qualitative research.

Ripsimé Bledsoe (MEd, Concordia University) is a doctoral fellow in the department of educational leadership and policy studies at the University of Texas-San Antonio. Ripsimé has extensive experience in both faculty and student success positions at both two- and four-year institutions. Her emerging research explores academic readiness among diverse, low-income, first-generation students along with examining organizational structures and practices that best promote retention and persistence.

Vincent D. Carales (EdD, The University of Texas at San Antonio) is an assistant professor of higher education leadership and policy studies at University of Houston. His research interests include understanding the experiences and educational outcomes of first-generation, Latino, low-income community college students. He is also interested in examining federal, state, and institutional policies related to diversity, equity, and college affordability.

Sarah Maria Childs (MEd, The University of Vermont) is the assistant director of The Mosaic Center for Students of Color at The University of Vermont (UVM). Sarah seeks to support and empower the student of color community at UVM via programs, direct services, and collaborations with students and campus partners. Sarah is also a doctoral candidate in the educational leadership and policy studies program at UVM. Her research is centered around the experiences of Latinx undocumented college students.

Leslie A. Coward (PhD, The University of Texas at Austin) is project manager in the graduate school of biomedical science with Baylor College of Medicine, where she is the head of the office of postdoctoral affairs. She has nearly 20 years of experience in higher education developing and managing STEM retention and student academic success programs. Her research interests are in the areas of organizational behavior and leadership, diversity, and inclusion in higher education and minority male academic success.

Marcela Cuellar (PhD, University of California, Los Angeles) is an assistant professor in the school of education at the University of California, Davis. Her research focuses on postsecondary access and equity, Latina/o college students, and Hispanic-serving institutions (HSIs). She earned a BA from Stanford University and a MA from the University of San Diego. She was a first-generation college student and also worked in college outreach programs.

Alonzo M. Flowers III (PhD, Texas A&M University) is an assistant professor in the school of education at Drexel University and a senior research fellow with Boston University. Dr. Flowers specializes in educational issues, including academic identity development of students of color in STEM education. He has recently co-authored the book, *The African American Student's Guide to STEM Careers,* which focuses on practical educational tools for African American students to navigate the STEM pipeline.

Juan Carlos Garibay (PhD, University of California, Los Angeles) is an assistant professor of higher education at the University of Virginia. His publications include "STEM Students' Social Agency and Views on Working for Social Change" (*Journal of Research in Science Teaching*), "Racially Inclusive Climates within Degree Programs and Increasing Student of Color Enrollment: An Examination of Environmental/Sustainability Programs" (*Journal of Diversity in Higher Education*), and "Achieving Equity within and beyond STEM: Toward a New Generation of Scholarship in STEM Education."

Demeturie Toso-Lafaele Gogue (MEd, The University of Vermont) is the first-generation programs coordinator at the University of Redlands. He is a first-generation Pacific Islander American who is passionate about serving underrepresented and underserved students in higher education. His research interests include college access and completion of first-generation students as well as the racial and ethnic identity development of students of color.

Josephine J. Gonzalez (MEd, The University of Vermont) is a residence hall assistant director at New York University. She is passionate about college access, supporting first-generation college students and residential education. Josephine received her Bachelor of Arts in gender and women's studies from the State University of New York at Plattsburgh (SUNY Plattsburgh).

Dimitra Jackson Smith (PhD, Iowa State University) is a tenured associate professor of higher education at Texas A&M-Commerce. Her research includes distinct, interrelated strands that focuses on the education, preparation, and career exploration of students in science, technology, engineering, and mathematics (STEM) fields; community college leadership and transfer students; minority-serving institutions; and two-year and four-year institutional partnerships and collaborations. Dr. Smith's research has been published in peer reviewed journals such as the *Community College Review, Community College Journal of Research* *and Practice, Journal of Black Studies*, and the *Journal of Women and Minorities in Science and Engineering*, to name a few. Her research has led to a children's book series that focuses on introducing children to STEM-related activities.

Kimberly A. Koledoye (EdD, Sam Houston State University) is a professor and program coordinator of Student Success at Houston Community College. Her research interests include minorities in STEM fields, social justice issues in higher education, student success, developmental English, and first-year experience programs. In addition to authoring several instructional materials, her publications include *Differences in STEM Baccalaureate Attainment by Ethnicity* and *Differences in STEM Degree Attainment by Region, Ethnicity, and Degree Type*.

Frankie Santos Laanan (PhD, University of California, Los Angeles) is professor of higher education at The University of Alabama. His research focuses on the impact of colleges and universities on individuals and society. Specifically, his research investigates the role of community colleges as educational pathways for women and underrepresented students in STEM disciplines, transfer and articulation policies, career and technical education, and accountability. He has published articles in *Community College Review, Community College Journal of Research and Practice, Journal of Women and Minorities in Science and Engineering*, and *Journal of College Student Retention*.

Jose Adrian Leon (Joey) (MEd, The University of Vermont) is a residence director at DePaul University in Chicago, Illinois. He provides community development for students living on campus and helps connect them to campus resources. He currently serves on the Divisional Committee for Social Justice and Inclusion Competency to provide student affairs professionals at DePaul training and development on inclusion and diversity practices.

Amaury Nora (EdD, University of Houston) is professor and associate dean for research and co-director of the Center for Research and Policy in Education in the College of Education and Human Development at the University of Texas at San Antonio. Professor Nora's research focuses on Hispanic STEM student academic achievement, pre-college and collegiate psychosocial factors impacting adjustment to college and student persistence, access to higher education for diverse student populations across different types of institutions, academic and social experiences influencing cognitive as well as noncognitive student outcomes, and theory building and testing.

Sarah Price (MEd, The University of Texas at San Antonio) is the program manager for PIVOT's Roadrunner Transition Experience at The University of Texas at San Antonio. In this role, she primarily supervises peer mentors, and empowers and validates underserved, first-generation and transfer students. She also coordinates program planning and assessment efforts and delivers workshops on student success strategies. Her research interests include examining the experiences of LGBTQ students, political activism on college campuses, and heteronormativity in the workplace.

Stella L. Smith (PhD, The University of Texas at Austin) is the associate director for the Minority Achievement, Creativity and High-Ability (MACH-III) Center in the Whitlowe R. Green College of Education at Prairie View A&M University. Her research focuses on the experiences of faculty and administrators of color in higher education, African American females in leadership in higher education, and access and inclusion of underserved populations in higher education.

Karina I. Vielma (EdD, The University of Texas at San Antonio) is a research fellow in the college of engineering at The University of Texas at San Antonio where she specializes in education and community outreach initiatives. Her research interests center on issues of equity in science, technology, engineering, and mathematics (STEM) fields. As a first-generation college student and graduate of the Massachusetts Institute of Technology, her mission is to promote programs that motivate more women and underrepresented students to persist and excel in STEM careers.

Cynthia Diana Villarreal (MEd, The University of Texas at San Antonio) is a PhD student in urban education policy at the University of Southern California's Rossier School of Education and a graduate research assistant at the Center for Urban Education. Her scholarship uses organizational and sociocultural theory to understand and reduce inequities experienced by minoritized student populations in higher education.

Index